Penguin Books
A Guide to the Dordogne

Born in 1937, James Bentley has been Vicar of Oldham, Lancashire, Conduct and Senior Chaplain at Eton College, Windsor, and Maurice Reckitt Research Fellow in Christian Social Thought at the University of Sussex. He holds degrees in Modern History, Theology and European Studies.

A regular broadcaster (as well as a writer of television scripts for others), he has served on the Central Religious Advisory Committee of the B.B.C. and the Independent Broadcasting Authority. He particularly likes broadcasting on the World Service of the B.B.C. His books include *Ritualism and Politics in Victorian Britain* (1978), *Between Marx and Christ* (1982), a study of the dialogue between Christians and Marxists in German-speaking Europe, *A Children's Bible* (1982), a biography of *Pastor Martin Niemoller* (1984) and *Oberammergau and the Passion Play* (Penguin, 1984). He reviews for *Country Life* and the *New Statesman*. His work has been published in *Theology*, the *Journal of Ecclesiastical History*, the *Journal of Theological Studies*, the *Expository Times*, *The Times*, the *Guardian* and the *Listener*.

When not working in Britain, James Bentley lives with his wife and two daughters in a house in the Dordogne.

BY THE SAME AUTHOR

*Oberammergau
and the Passion Play*

A Guide
to the Dordogne

JAMES BENTLEY

PENGUIN BOOKS

Penguin Books Ltd, Harmondsworth, Middlesex, England
Viking Penguin Inc., 40 West 23rd Street, New York, New York 10010, U.S.A.
Penguin Books Australia Ltd, Ringwood, Victoria, Australia
Penguin Books Canada Ltd, 2801 John Street, Markham, Ontario, Canada L3R 1B4
Penguin Books (N.Z.) Ltd, 182–190 Wairau Road, Auckland 10, New Zealand

First published by Viking 1985
Published in Penguin Books 1986

Copyright © James Bentley, 1985
All rights reserved
Grateful acknowledgement is made to Cyril Connolly and Hamish Hamilton
for permission to reproduce the 'magic circle' on p. 16 from Cyril Connolly's
The Unquiet Grave, copyright © 1944 by Cyril Connolly; and to Faber and Faber
for permission to reproduce part of 'Montaigne' from Collected Poems
by W. H. Auden on p. 122.

Made and printed in Great Britain by
Richard Clay (The Chaucer Press) Ltd,
Bungay, Suffolk
Set in Monophoto Sabon

Aux Turnacois et leurs amis

Contents

LIST OF ILLUSTRATIONS
9

ACKNOWLEDGEMENTS
11

MAP OF THE DORDOGNE
12

1. THE COUNTRY OF ENCHANTMENT
15

2. THE PAST IN THE PRESENT
18

3. THE FOOD AND WINE OF THE DORDOGNE
40

4. THE DORDOGNE AND THE BRITISH
61

5. CHURCHES IN A LANDSCAPE
84

6. BEFORE THE DAWN OF HISTORY
100

7. THE CRADLE OF POETS
112

8. A GAZETTEER OF THE DORDOGNE
138

9. RECIPES FROM THE DORDOGNE
226

FURTHER READING
234

INDEX
237

List of Illustrations

1. Aerial view of the river Dordogne, with the Château Montfort and the village of Montfort.
2. Château and village of Hautefort.
3. Sixteenth-century Château de Losse, on the river Vézère.
4. Aerial view of Sarlat Cathedral – bottom right, the 'Lantern of the Dead'.
5. The village of Beynac-et-Cazenac, on the bank of the river Dordogne, nestling under its formidable château.
6. Tower of the Hôtel de Maleville, Sarlat.
7. Geese and a pigeon-loft, Sainte-Nathalène.
8. Market place at Monpazier.
9. Fortified twelfth-century abbey church, Saint-Amand-de-Coly.
10. Gaulish huts, Breuil, near Les Eyzies-de-Tayac.
11. The fortifications of a *bastide*, Porte des Tours, Domme.
12. Aerial view of Périgueux with the river Isle and Saint-Front Cathedral.
13. The twelfth-century apse of the abbey church of Cénac-et-Saint-Julien.

The author and publishers are grateful to the following for permission to reproduce photographs: Office Départemental du Tourisme de la Dordogne for nos. 1, 2, 5 and 12; Studio Tourny for nos. 3, 4, 6, 7, 8, 9, 10, 11 and 13.

Acknowledgements

Space simply will not allow me to thank by name all those who have toured the Dordogne with me, poking into nooks and crannies, looking for exquisite forgotten villages and out-of-the-way prehistoric shelters. But I must thank my wife, who reads maps wonderfully and also wrote out the traditional Dordogne recipes at the end of this book.

James Bentley

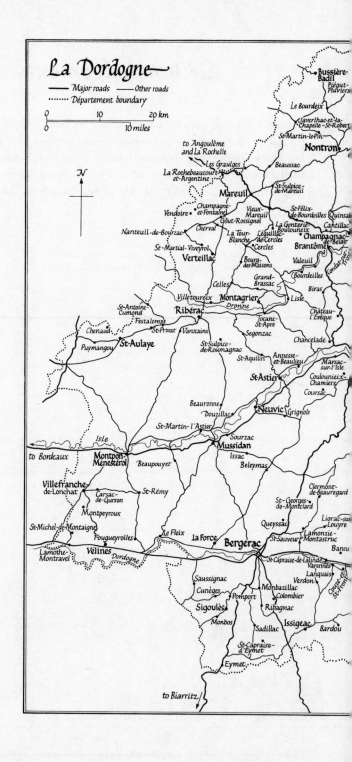

La Dordogne

— Major roads   — Other roads
········ Département boundary

0   10   20 km
0   10 miles

N

Bussière-Badil
Piégut-Pluviers
Le Bourdeix
Javerlhac-et-la-Chapelle-St-Robert
St-Martin-le-Pin
Nontron
to Angoulême and La Rochelle
Les Graulges
Beaussac
La Rochebeaucourt-et-Argentine
St-Sulpice-de-Mareuil
Mareuil
Champagne-et-Fontaine
Vieux-Mareuil
St-Félix-de-Bourdeilles
Quinsac
Vendoire
Gout-Rossignol
La Gonterie-Boulouneix
Cantillac
Nanteuil-de-Bourzac
Cherval
La Tour-Blanche
Céquillac-de-Cercles
Champagnac-de-Belair
St-Martial-Viveyrol
Cercles
Brantôme
Verteillac
Bourg-des-Maisons
Valeuil
Condat-sur-Trincou
Celles
Grand-Brassac
Bourdeilles
Villetoureix
Montagrier
Lisle
Biras
Ribérac
Dronne
Château-l'Évêque
St-Antoine-Cumond
Festalemps
Tocane-St-Apre
Chenaud
St-Privat
Vanxains
Segonzac
Chancelade
Puymangou
St-Aulaye
St-Sulpice-de-Roumagnac
St-Aquilin
Annesse-et-Beaulieu
Marsac-sur-l'Isle
St-Astier
Coulounieix-Chamiers
Coursac
Beauronne
Douzillac
Neuvic
Grignols
St-Martin-l'Astier
Sourzac
Isle
Mussidan
to Bordeaux
Montpon-Ménestérol
Beaupouyet
Issac
Beleymas
Villefranche-de-Lonchat
Clermont-de-Beauregard
Carsac-de-Gurson
St-Rémy
St-Georges-de-Montclard
Montpeyroux
Liorac-sur-Louyre
St-Michel-de-Montaigne
Queyssac
Lamonzie-Montastruc
Fougueyrolles
Le Fleix
St-Sauveur
Baneuil
Lamothe-Montravel
Vélines
La Force
Bergerac
Dordogne
St-Capraise-de-Lalinde
Varennes
Saussignac
Verdon
Lanquais
Cunèges
Monbazillac
Colombier
Sigoulès
Pomport
Ribagnac
Issigeac
Bardou
Monbos
Sadillac
St-Capraise-d'Eymet
Eymet
to Biarritz

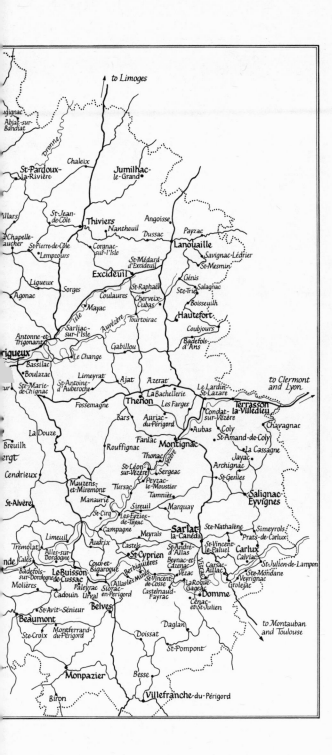

The Country of Enchantment

A few months before the outbreak of the Second World War, the writer Henry Miller decided to take a long holiday. He began with a tour of the Dordogne and later came to see this as a stroke of genius on his part. 'Just to glimpse the black, mysterious river at Domme from the beautiful bluff at the edge of the town is something to be grateful for all one's life.' It seemed to him that part of France was not French or even European, but rather 'the country of enchantment which the poets have staked out and which they alone may lay claim to'. He called it 'the nearest thing to Paradise this side of Greece'.

Towards the end of the same war Cyril Connolly wrote his most famous book, *The Unquiet Grave*, first published as by 'Palinurus'. Anxious, as always, about the depersonalization of modern life, Connolly included in his book a magic circle which he called 'a charm against Group Man' (see overleaf). At the top of this circle is the Dordogne. The first of what Cyril Connolly called his 'peace-aims' was to own a yellow manor farm inside this magic circle.

But long before the days of Henry Miller and Cyril Connolly men and women knew the romantic charm of the Dordogne (or Périgord as it used to be called). This was the land which Sir Lancelot, exiled for the love of Guinevere from the Round Table, divided among the knights who followed him. In the sixteenth century the most famous son of the perfectly preserved medieval town of Sarlat, Étienne de La Boétie, wrote that the rivers Garonne, the Rhône and all the rest shamelessly envied his own river Dordogne. And the legendary Cyrano de Bergerac, recreated by Edmond Rostand in 1898, sang of the valley of the Dordogne, 'green and peaceful on summer evenings'.

Even in the hell of the First World War the poet John Peale Bishop, on active service in the Dordogne, brooding on the death of his friends and fellow-soldiers, could not help contrasting the horror with the extreme beauty of the countryside in which they were suffering and dying:

> ... we descended
> and saw in a niche in the white wall
> a Virgin and child, serene
> who were stone: we saw sycamore:
> three aged mages
> scattering gifts of gold.
> But when the wind blew, there were autumn odours
> and the shadowed trees
> had the dappling of young fawns.
>
> And each day one died or another
> died: each week we sent out thousands
> that returned by hundreds
> wounded or gassed. And those that died

were buried close to the old wall
within a stone's throw of Périgord
under the tower of the troubadours.

John Peale Bishop hoped that the courage and waste of those young
men would avail something. Yet the only consolation at the end of his
most moving poem is the extraordinary charm of what is to my mind
the most beautiful region of the whole of France:

> . . . the leaves fell
> and were blown away: the young men rotted
> under the shadow of the tower
> in a land of small clear silent streams
> where the coming on of evening is
> the letting down of blue and azure veils
> over the clear and silent streams
> delicately bordered by poplars.

During the second savage war of the twentieth century Henry
Miller, too, drew hope from this great region of France, 'hope for the
future of the race, for the future of the earth itself'. He added: 'France
may one day exist no more, but the Dordogne will live on just as
dreams live on and nourish the souls of men.'

The Past in the Present

A paradise is not created by chance. That the Dordogne offers such a remarkable diversity of landscape, agriculture and architectural beauty is due to a blend of history, nature's blessings and human caprice. The rivers of the Dordogne have served as thoroughfares and barriers. Its castles were built both to make conspicuous display of the wealth of their owners and to defend this wealth. Some of its massive churches, too, were built for defence as well as for the glory of God. If Cyrano de Bergerac found the Dordogne peaceful as well as green, over the centuries many of its inhabitants led turbulent and sometimes calamitous lives; many of them were wretchedly poor. All this past remains visible in the present. If today the Dordogne offers the visitor a sweetness and an extraordinary variety of delights, this too derives from its sometimes unhappy past.

Once you begin to read the past in the present, you long for more history. Who, for instance, was the Marshal Bugeaud whose massive square lies west of the ancient cathedral of Périgueux? Who was the Jacques de Maleville now commemorated by a bust high on the bluff at Domme? Why is there a curious inscription over the door of the church of Monpazier, proclaiming the allegiance of Frenchmen to the worship of the Supreme Being? What ghosts inhabit these castles? And why are some of them ruined, even burned to the ground?

To ask what the people of the Dordogne thought of the English in the Middle Ages, what they later felt during the Wars of Religion, how they coped with the Revolution, with Napoleon Bonaparte and the traumas of the nineteenth century, is to begin to understand the genius of this region. To look at the humbler houses of the Dordogne as well as its massive castles and noble 'hôtels', to enquire about their origin and about those who long ago lived in them, is to take the place seriously. To try to find out what life is like today for a farmer in the Dordogne is to offer the proper courtesy that a tourist owes to his host, as well as to enrich one's own understanding of this earthly paradise.

The area is in fact older than its name. The present *département* of the Dordogne was created as late as 1790, during the era of the French Revolution, out of old Périgord with its fluctuating boundaries. When some objected that the *département* they were about to create was completely bisected by the river Dordogne, the redoubtable Mirabeau countered with the successful proposal that the whole region take the name of the river. But still today no Frenchman claims to live in the Dordogne, for only mermen and mermaids live in rivers. People here live in Périgord and call themselves Périgourdins.

The whole *département* covers an area of 3,500 square miles. It also excludes some places that, to the unwary, seem to be part of the Dordogne. Many of us, visiting Souillac, wrongly suppose we are in the Dordogne. To my regret this book can nowhere dwell on the splendid carvings and sculpture of the Church of Saint-Pierre at Beaulieu-sur-Dordogne, for the town is not in the Dordogne at all but in Corrèze.

Today far fewer Frenchmen and their families live in the *département* than when it was first created. Each year a thousand Dordogne farms disappear. From nearly 200,000 at the end of the nineteenth century, they number today fewer than 50,000. Part of the problem consists in the French laws of inheritance, which rigidly and fairly divide properties among children and thereby create farms that simply cannot support a family. In a region as diverse in its terrain as the Dordogne, mechanization of farming is difficult and life for the farmer is still hard.

As if to compensate for this depopulation, the Dordogne has become one of the most popular tourist regions of France. Splendid camp sites and hotels welcome the British, the Belgians, the Dutch, the Germans and the Americans. The national tourist board of France grades hotels with impeccable thoroughness. In this region standards rarely fall. Périgord is a gastronomic paradise, and splendid meals in restaurants and hotels appear to be astonishingly cheap. And the region specializes in *les gîtes de la France*. A *gîte* means, literally, a shelter or a resting place. *Gîtes* for tourists consist of privately owned self-contained cottages, usually attached to a farmhouse. Even here the high standards of the French prevail. *Gîtes* are listed by the government by means of a system giving them successive marks designated by ears of corn. In some a farmer and his wife serve the food and join their paying guests at table.

In response to the vast influx of tourists, the people of the Dordogne have displayed great resource and energy. The *département* now provides a remarkable feast of culture: Sarlat has its annual theatre festival at the height of the tourist season, when members of the Comédie Française forsake Paris to perform for a cosmopolitan summer audience; twelfth-century churches become excellent concert halls for organ and trumpet concertos; in 1983, in the small village of Grolejac (which, as its name implies, was once inhabited by the Gauls) I saw a performance of Jarry's *Ubu Roi*. And for those who want other entertainment, the Dordogne offers discothèques, circuses (with sometimes a single family occupying the paydesk, walking the tightrope and cajoling the performing goat), and gentle descents of its rivers by canoe and kayak.

Above all, the natives of the Dordogne offer a warm welcome. If in the Middle Ages the British and the French fought over castles such as Beynac and Castelnaud, all that is forgotten. Often a hand-painted sign outside a hotel proclaims not only its good food and wine, its comfortable rooms and facilities, but also *son accueil* – its welcome.

The rivers create part of the sweetness of life in the Dordogne. There are four great ones, as well as many smaller tributaries. To the north is the river Dronne (a Frenchman would say that the Dronne is not a *rivière* but a *fleuve*, since on the Dronne one can sail a boat against the current, and this is impossible on a *rivière*). In the middle is the river Isle. To the east is the river Vézère. And bisecting the region is the long and (in this part of France) leisurely Dordogne.

The river Dordogne rises far from the *département* which bears its name, in the Massif Central, 1,720 metres above sea level, at the foot of the Puy de Sancy. Here it tumbles swiftly down the mountainside, and 290 miles later, having been swollen by the Vézère and the Dronne, it reaches the plains of Bergerac and flows into the Atlantic, having itself become a tributary of the river Garonne.

Not surprisingly, the Romans named this area Aquitaine – a land of waters. Although the river Dordogne flows fast enough in places to provide hydro-electricity, it also flows gently and magnificently between limestone cliffs of a unique charm. In her classic book *Three Rivers of France* Freda White brilliantly summed up its quality.

Here is not a great river, but a wide and living stream. It is entirely natural, flowing along with varied current between banks that are usually tree-fringed, curving to meet cliffs or steep slopes from one side of its bed to the other. The river-plain looped by each link gives space and repose to the view. This is not Claude's Campagna, but there is an elegiac air to the Dordogne which often recalls the landscapes of Claude; the tree-framed water and atmosphere of diffused light may account for it.

Its sister rivers are quite different in character. The Vézère, which springs to the north of the region, at the foot of Mount Bessou in Limousin, journeys speedily for 120 miles until it joins the river Dordogne near Limeuil. The Isle rises just south of Limoges and travels even further – 150 miles – before joining the river Dordogne at Libourne, while the Dronne travels in the same direction, finally joining the Isle ten miles north of Libourne.

Each tributary of the river Dordogne flows through its own special areas and towns. On the Isle lies the capital of the whole region, Périgueux. (At the time of the Revolution *three* cities were deemed the capitals of the Dordogne: Périgueux, Sarlat and Bergerac. The plan was for each successively to serve as capital city for one year. Périgueux started the cycle; the plan was forgotten; and Périgueux remains the capital to this day.) The river Vézère must have been specially attractive to prehistoric man, who lived on its banks and decorated the caves on either side of the river.

The river Dronne flows through the ancient abbey town of Brantôme. If you hire a small plane and fly over Brantôme you see what must be the perfect arrangement of a tiny town protected to east and west by its river (for the Dronne here divides itself and flows round Brantôme) and on the north side by its abbey. Charlemagne gave to the abbey, which he himself founded, a corpse which he believed was the body of one of the children murdered by King Herod in his attempt to kill the infant Jesus. The abbey became famous and rich, but its monks and abbot never allowed their taste to run to vulgar display. From an aeroplane you can clearly see the exceptionally fine belltower, built in the eleventh century after the destruction of the old abbey buildings, as well as the seventeenth-century home of the monks. If, instead of flying, you drive through Brantôme, you can see these buildings romantically reflected in the river, as well as the little classical summer house built by a sixteenth-century abbot. Today the seventeenth-century building is the town hall of Brantôme, splendidly restored in the nineteenth century by the architect Paul Abadie – a man as unjustly reviled in France as once was the great Victorian Sir Gilbert Scott in Britain.

Yet of all these rivers Freda White clearly loved the Dordogne best, above all where it flows between castles. 'The cliffs that border the valley might have been created to please warriors who sought a high rock to build on and a wide view from their towers,' she wrote. She knew, of course, of the noted châteaux on the Loire. The castles on the Dordogne, she conceded, are not the palaces of the Loire, 'raised for princes to visit in the hunting season'. But, as she rightly observed, 'they are better situated, for the Dordogne is a lovelier river than the Loire'.

There are castles everywhere in the Dordogne, not just along the river. They number altogether well over a thousand. Legend has it that St Peter was charged to sow castles all over France. He gathered many in a sack, but as he was passing over Périgord the sack tore open, strewing the countryside beneath with keeps, battlements, turrets and towers.

The truth is less charming. The castles of the Dordogne were built during the Hundred Years War and afterwards quite simply to defend those who owned them, and the villages clustered around. Many were fought over, conquered, sometimes demolished and then rebuilt. Those who conquered them were often vicious. Château Montfort, on the great bend (or *cingle*) of the river Dordogne near Turnac, is one of the most romantic and instructive in this respect. Its name derives from Simon de Montfort (father of the Simon much revered by nineteenth-century British historians for his defence of the liberties of parliament against the monarchy), who captured it in 1214 and partly demolished it. In the Hundred Years War, and once more during the reign of Henri IV, it was again burned to the ground. Owned by the Turenne family, it had been besieged in 1404 and 1409 and abandoned in 1461. The family returned, and during the Wars of Religion became

Protestants, making Château Montfort a refuge for the Huguenots of Périgord. Today it stands high above the river, on a rock which rises vertically 90 metres high, its huge tower surviving from the fifteenth century, its graceful wings dating from the sixteenth century, the rest restored 300 years later, and all standing on twelfth-century foundations.

Building in Périgord in the seventeenth century was cheap. The region was packed with gentlemen and nobles. Castles were now built for visual pleasure as well as for defence. Parquet floors or tiles, sometimes arranged in ingenious geometric patterns, indicate the increasing wealth of the region.

A prelude to this flowering can be seen at Castle Losse at Thonac. Built in 1576 by Jehan Lemarre, master mason of Gourdon, for Jean de Beaulieu de Losse, a courtier of François I, captain of the Scottish guards, adviser to Henri IV, governor of Verdun and Lyon, it stands, like Montfort, on a rock high above a river (this time the Vézère). With its massive circular tower and machicolations, built of ochre stones which glow red in the autumn sunsets, Losse retains the aspect of a medieval castle in spite of its renaissance origin.

Freda White tells the famous story of how the owner of Castle Losse refused to lend money to the miserly owner of the neighbouring Castle Belcayre (Castle Losse is noted for its remarkable echo): 'Losse, a canny man, cried to the echo: "Is Monsieur de Belcayre a good payer?" "Mousseur de Belcayre ei teu buon pagaire?" "Gaire! Gaire!" "Watch out!" answered his echo, and poor Belcayre did not get his loan.'

In truth, this epoch of rich Périgourdins seems to have produced a fine quota of misers. The marquis who built the magnificent Château Hautefort is said to have been the model for Molière's *L'Avare*. At least one of his successors shared his meanness. On 6 October 1680 Mme de Sévigné recorded that M. de Hautefort had died, refusing to take his English medicine on the grounds that it was too expensive. His servants had said to him, 'Sir, we shall give you only a few of the pills.' 'Too many,' he replied, as he died. Nevertheless, he constructed a splendid castle, the flower of renaissance architecture in the Dordogne, built over twenty years beginning in 1640. His successors, with the help of the French government, have proved worthy custodians of Hautefort. On 1 September 1968 a fire destroyed a substantial part of the château, including its finely carved wooden chimneys and eighteenth-century doors. Fortunately the two great towers and the little manor house at the entrance were saved. Now the whole has been meticulously restored. The superb gardens, the round seventeenth-century towers, and the formal staircase inside, are all open to the twentieth-century visitor.

Much of the history of the Dordogne can be read out of the walls of many of its castles. Further north than Hautefort, scarcely inside the Dordogne, stands the castle of Jumilhac-le-Grand, on a rock dominating the valley of the river Isle. Jumilhac-le-Grand has the jolliest, most irregular roof in all France, with its dormer windows, corbels, weather vanes, mansards and turrets. The keep is so bizarrely constructed as to have earned the nickname 'the marquis's hat'. Adjoining the castle is its former chapel, with an eight-sided belltower. The whole was created over a period of four centuries, beginning in the thirteenth. The side wings date from the seventeenth, one of them possessing a magnificent Louis XIII chimneypiece and an even finer Louis XIV staircase.

The ownership of Jumilhac-le-Grand, as it comes down to us, is a blend of history and legend. History tells us that it first belonged to the Knights Templars, and that Henri IV gave it to a master forger who had provided him with a good many reliable cannons. In the eighteenth century the owners took the title 'marquis'. After the Revolution Jumilhac-le-Grand fell into disrepair, but in our own century – from 1927 onwards – Count Odet de Jumilhac restored it beautifully. As for legend, the visitor to Jumilhac-le-Grand is invariably shown the room of La Fileuse (the spinner). Unfaithful to her husband, one Châtelaine of Jumilhac-le-Grand was, it is said, condemned to spend the rest of her life confined to this room, decorating its walls with incompetently portrayed animals, trees and celestial beings and leaving her own portrait over the doorway.

The owner of a castle – even one among so many – can scarcely avoid the sin of arrogance. And the other side of arrogance is petulance. This, too, can be read out of the walls of the castles of the Dordogne. The Châtelaine of Mareuil, supposing that Queen Catherine de' Medici might visit her home, began to decorate a room in honour of the royal favour. But this was the time of the Wars of Religion and Hautefort was loyally Catholic: Catherine had no need to waste time visiting those whose allegiance was assured. The visit was cancelled: the châtelaine cancelled the new decorations. And to this day one can see at Mareuil a half-decorated salon.

Infinitely more touching is the history of the castle at Les Milandes, nine miles south-west of Sarlat. Les Milandes is close by the bleak, magnificent castle of Castelnaud, built in the twelfth century to dominate the valley of the river Dordogne and the river Céou. Castelnaud has been beautifully restored. In the sixteenth century it was still a harshly imposing and aggressive fortress. In 1488 the wife of its lord, oppressed with living in such a savage place, begged her husband to build her a more charming home. Les Milandes was the result.

François de Caumont, Lord of Castelnaud, and his young wife Claude de Cardaillac, built a huge renaissance house, with fine stone roofs, close by the river. In the next century the owners of Les Milandes were ennobled with the title 'marquis' and 'marquise'. The castle fell on bad times after the Revolution, but was restored in the nineteenth century.

In the early 1930s the cabaret artist Joséphine Baker, with her companion of those years, Pépé d'Albertine, drove to Sarlat in a borrowed Bugatti Royale, ate some pâté and judged the Dordogne to be 'civilized and wild by turn'. They drove on to Les Milandes and the castle entranced Joséphine.

Joséphine had been born among the poorest of the poor in east St Louis, Missouri, in 1906. As a child she slept in a cellar, sharing a box with a dog. Having suffered and been enlightened about race hatred in the savage St Louis riots of 1917, she left America at the age of nineteen as a member of a black dancing troupe. She reached Paris and within a year was the highest-paid entertainer in Europe. After her amazing performances at the Folies Bergères she was known as 'the Charleston Queen of Paris'. In the Dordogne she found peace. 'God did his work well here,' she exclaimed. On her first visit to Les Milandes she observed its ruinous state, its one bathroom, not realizing that she would return as a Resistance fighter (later to receive the Legion of Honour, plus Rosette, from General de Gaulle). In 1939 she came again. 'How peaceful it was, in its beautiful setting,' she said. It was, she observed, hard to believe that elsewhere people were fighting, suffering and dying. But here she hid enemies of the Nazis – a naval officer, a British Air Force captain, a Pole and her Belgian friends.

Joséphine bought Les Milandes and – still marked by the sufferings of her childhood – determined to make it a place for reconciling races, nations and creeds. Little by little, between her theatre engagements, she furnished and refurbished the castle. There in 1947 she married the agent Jo Bouillon, who did his best to put his financial expertise at her disposal. She worked and worked in the theatre to pay for the château and its upkeep, renovating rooms, shipping garden statuary there, planting trees in an attempt to make the 120 acres attached to Les Milandes into a pleasure garden. There she and Jo Bouillon opened a restaurant, called (in the local patois) *Lou Tornole* – 'Please come again'.

Then she met Pope Pius XII and told him of her plan to adopt at Les Milandes orphaned children of all colours and religions, in order to fight racism and to proclaim the unity of the human race. Joséphine almost succeeded. She called her adopted children 'the rainbow tribe'. They arrived at Sarlat in countless ways – by air, by the French consul's car, brought by her friends in the theatre. 'My children have proved that there are no more continents, no more obstacles, no more problems to prevent understanding and respect between human beings,' she asserted, 'no more excuses that colour and religious differences prevent unity.' At dinner, as she once wrote, the napkin rings of her 'tribe' read Akio (Korea), Jari (Finland), Jean-Claude (France), Jeannot (Japan), Luis (Colombia), Moïse (Israel), Brahim (Algiers), Mara (Venezuela), Koffi (the Ivory Coast), Marianne (France), and Noël (France). Possibly Joséphine over-indulged her adopted children. Some critics judged that they were totally undisciplined and too pampered. Certainly those hired to tutor them usually fled after about three weeks. Joséphine herself had few doubts. 'My ideal is universal brotherhood,' she said, 'a dream I have realized at Les Milandes.'

But her dream was costlier than even she could pay for. The village close to her castle now possessed a Place Joséphine, complete with a statue of the Virgin Mary whose face resembled Joséphine's. Once a decaying, deserted place, it now housed seventy persons, all supported by work at Les Milandes. But even Jo Bouillon's financial skills could not control Joséphine's impossible ambitions. To her, Les Milandes was 'like something in a scenario'; it was 'my' château, and she believed she could achieve anything there. She decided to make money by creating a gambling casino in the grounds. Her friends from Las

Vegas told her that everything about the project was perfect, 'except for one thing: no one would come'. By 1952 she was 27m French francs in debt. In 1953 the debt was 37m (old francs); in 1954 nearly 64m; in 1956 nearly 83m; in 1957 much more than 83m. In 1960 Jo Bouillon finally despaired, and he and Joséphine separated. 'My last ten years have been a constant struggle with businessmen, lawyers, financiers,' she wrote. Four years later Les Milandes was sold. As Jo Bouillon observed, it almost killed Joséphine. No more would she roll back the carpet in her château and do 'Bake that Chicken Pie' and other numbers which she had first performed at the Memphis Theatre long ago.

Yet such a story of the failure of great ideals should not depress one unduly in the Dordogne. The region is filled with ruins as well as flourishing and restored castles. And these ruins also have a charm of their own. One which combines both the grandeur of a great ruin and the promise of future restoration is the castle of Mareuil, built in the fifteenth century as the family home of one of the four barons of Périgord. The main buildings have been restored in the past quarter of a century. But of the moat only part remains, just as its once flamboyant gothic chapel is in ruins. Once the home of the troubadour Armand de Mareuil and of the Talleyrand-Périgord family, Castle Mareuil was abandoned in 1770. It fell an easy prey to the destructive elements of the French Revolution. And yet today, high up on its stone wall, it presents a romantic enough image.

And the visitor who tours its underground prison can readily imagine the cruelty with which the grandees of the past kept down the peasants of the Dordogne. Inspired by another such ruin, the castle of L'Herm, the greatest novelist of this region, Eugène Le Roy, wrote his finest work, *Jacquou le Croquant*. Set in the early nineteenth century, the novel tells of the rebellion of those 'poor Périgord peasants of former times, deliberately kept in ignorance, badly fed, badly clothed, always sunk in toil, counting for nothing, despised by the rich'. Jacquou leads the rebellion which, in Le Roy's novel, succeeds in burning to the ground the Castle of L'Herm.

Rendered famous by Eugène Le Roy, the castle already possessed a bizarre history. It was built in the heart of one of the Dordogne's deepest forests in 1512 by John de Calvimont, and here his granddaughter was murdered in a plot hatched by her husband François d'Aubisson and her mother Anne d'Abzac. The ruin is enormously impressive, with its gothic doorways still intact and its massive chimneys bearing the arms of the doomed Calvimont family.

Eugène Le Roy's novel is a timely reminder that the social structure symbolized by these castles involved exploitation of the poor. Le Roy set his story of Jacquou the *Croquant* in the first half of the nineteenth century, but the *Croquants* proper were a phenomenon of the late sixteenth and the seventeenth centuries. *Croquant* originally meant a person who grinds his teeth, and it came to stand for the ground-down poor who gathered in the forests of the Dordogne and neighbouring regions of France to riot against and attempt to destroy those who oppressed them. The programme of those who rioted in the Dordogne in 1594 has been described by the historian Emmanuel Le Roy Ladurie.

It embraced struggle against the nobility who treated rustics like slaves, doubling or tripling their rents; the motto 'liberty'; solidarity of the rustic third estate regarding loss of religion; refusal, if possible, to pay tithes, tailles, and rents; repression of Catholic League and royalist rogues who had 'stolen the oxen and raped the girls'; defence of the country folk against the urban bourgeoisie, who set high prices on their wares and demanded high rents for fields and farms purchased for a song; resistance to the tax agents who ransomed the country districts to line their own pockets; and, to conclude – a form of agitation peculiar to the working class – strikes and the posting of pickets in gentlemen's vineyards.

The revolts were put down with singular brutality. The leader of the rising of 1594 was broken on the wheel in the market place of Monpazier. That the poor continued to revolt throughout the next century indicates the depth of their degradation. The most serious *Croquant* rising occurred in Périgord in 1636. Royal officials, who lived in the towns but were often also landed proprietors, were lynched, and the rural peasants, subsisting as best they could on pathetically small plots of land, attacked the great estates. Oddly enough, they did not blame the monarch himself. '*Vive le Roi!* No salt tax!' was their paradoxical slogan. They were against '*ces messieurs de Paris*'. And once again they were brutally put down.

Despite repeated protests during the reign of Louis XIV, the poor remained poor. The Dordogne was still a poor region 200 years later.

Its farming was out of date. Worst off were those who were allowed by their masters to keep scarcely a third of what they produced. Farm labourers were only a little better off. For vast stretches only heather grew, and in the productive western parts of Périgord maize and wheat were cropped and cropped without the respite necessary to enable the land to recover its richness. In the forests peasants scratched livings as best they could – as charcoal-burners, wandering tinsmiths, grinders of knives and scissors, goatherds, old clothes merchants, and the like.

It was possible to make a slightly better living as a potter, basket-weaver or maker of wooden clogs. But most work was so poorly paid that the lower classes inevitably were led into petty crime simply to survive. Millers, weavers and tailors were considered especially prone to this. A Périgord proverb ran, 'Seven millers, seven weavers and seven tailors make twenty-one thieves.'

Life in the eighteenth century was even worse for the poor of the Dordogne. Until the introduction of the potato twenty years before the Revolution, their staple diet was the chestnut. Occasionally a peasant family tasted pig or game. Eggs were a rare treat. Maize flour was made into a ball, sometimes with a little added fat, to be boiled and eaten as (in the local patois) a *mique*. Although around Domme and Sarlat, as well as in the plain of Bergerac, wine was made, the ordinary peasant could rarely afford to drink it. No less than six harvest failures between 1709 and 1789 brought death and starvation to the lower orders in society.

Not surprisingly, by 1789 the poor of Périgord were ready for the Revolution. Anger against the nobility and governing classes reached a fury in 1789 when it was discovered that these oppressors had no intention of giving up their customary rents. Castles were attacked, records destroyed, manors pillaged.

The Church, too, suffered because of its association with the ruling classes. In the seventeenth century, would-be rebels had displayed a frustrated violence towards the State religion. In May 1652, for instance, the Frondeur Balthasar had pillaged the village of Saint-Astier. He burned down houses and stole their furniture. He sacked the abbey church, despoiling its sacred objects and removing the bones of Asterius, the sixth-century hermit who had given the village its name. When the Revolution started the process was carried further. The community of monks was dissolved and its members driven out. At the same time the Marquis of Puyferrat, who claimed suzerainty over Saint-Astier, was exiled and dispossessed of his lands.

Since the country clergy of Périgord were often as poor as the peasants, they benefited from the decision of the government to confiscate the Church lands and in recompense to pay the clergy a salary. The French Revolution was not an atheist affair. Over the portal of the ancient church of Monpazier was now inscribed: 'The people of France recognize the existence of the Supreme Being and the immortality of the soul.' The legend is still there.

Périgord even produced its own revolutionary mystic, the once-famous Suzette Labrousse. Born at Vanxains near Ribérac in 1747, a member of a local influential family, she was at first considered a hysterical idiot when she announced her divine mission to reform the clergy and put down the great ones of the earth. When her parents sought to have her married, she avoided this fate by adopting the dress of a nun and throwing quicklime over her beautiful face. In the small village church of Vanxains she was vouchsafed a vision instructing her to go about the world as a poor beggar, remedying evil in the Church and urging humility on the rich. Her parents put her in the convent of St Ursula in Périgueux, where she attracted the attention of Bishop Pontard by prophesying the Revolution. He took her to Paris. There she joined the Jacobin party and was befriended by the Duchesse de Bourbon. She boldly decided to visit the Pope in Rome. Pius VI did not approve of the Revolution, and Suzette believed that she now had a mission to persuade him not only to let the French Church accept the Civil Constitution of the Clergy but also to abandon his own secular powers. Unfortunately in Rome she was arrested and for a time disappeared. Not till 1798 did her Parisian friends discover that she had spent six years imprisoned in the castle of St Angelo. The experience seems to have broken her. She returned to France, but took no further part in politics, and died in 1821.

A more typical son of the Revolution – also a Périgourdin – is Jacques de Maleville, whose proud bust today dominates the bluff at Domme. De Maleville represented Domme in the councils of the Revolution. He was one of the editors of the new Civil Code. And he strikes me as an excellent, balanced man. In 1801, for instance, he published a pamphlet setting out his view on divorce and separation.

His arguments are surprisingly modern; his conclusions eminently sane. He was well aware that divorce and separation can be justified. 'When it comes to scandal, shouting matches, family quarrels and the hate occasioned when spouses are ill-matched,' he wrote, 'as well as the bad example set to the children, separation can completely prevent it all.'

But, Jacques de Maleville argued, these are not the only considerations. He asked whether the gain was so great as at first appears. How does it affect the population in general? Was not the family the basis of all social stability? 'The hero who defends the republic, the legislator who works only for its good, the artisan who gives it life by his daily work, the farmer who feeds it, all these are motivated by fraternal love and filial tenderness.' So, de Maleville concluded, in matters of divorce and separation, reconciliation of the warring spouses is by far the best.

Jacques de Maleville of Domme is also fascinating because he perfectly represents one of the chief aims of the French Revolution: to open careers to men of talent, however humble their birth. In 1798 he had been attacked by a local journalist, who called himself 'The Observer of the Dordogne'. De Maleville fought back with an open letter, in which he insisted that the Dordogne would not become a region like the Vendée, fighting for the return of the monarchy, the nobility and the old corrupt Church. Those who longed for that, said de Maleville, did not love France as he did. But, he declared, 'the threats of those with evil intentions will not keep the legislators or me from rigorously fulfilling our duties'. Then Jacques de Maleville added a cry from the heart that can still move us: 'I was born in mediocrity and have reached where I am today – in spite of having to bring up six children at home – by my own efforts and parsimony.'

Parsimony continued to be a necessary virtue in the Dordogne. The French Revolution did not solve the problems of the poor of Périgord. In so far as the Church had tried to run the old structures of charity, its destruction was a disaster for the poor. The revolutionary legislators talked about relieving poverty by State action, but actually did nothing. The Convention at one point prohibited not only begging but also private almsgiving. The people of the Dordogne for the most part remained poorly fed throughout the nineteenth century – though not as poorly fed as a century before, and now many of them were actually taking a glass of wine or so with their meals. The authorities even feared a revolt by the Sarladais against the tax on drink.

Like the rest of France, the region was deeply divided by the turbulent events of the early nineteenth century. Périgord provided valiant soldiers for Napoleon. The famous Daumesnil, born at Périgueux in 1776, fought in all Napoleon's campaigns and lost a leg at Wagram. The emperor made him Governor of Vincennes. When Blücher demanded he surrender, he replied, 'I shall give you Vincennes when you give me back my leg.' In 1873 his fellow-citizens proudly erected a statue to him in the Cours Michel Montaigne, Périgueux, prominently displaying his wooden leg.

Napoleon's greatest fighting cock was Fournier-Sarlovèze, who was born in Sarlat in 1773. He was so arrogant that for a long time Napoleon would not honour him. Fournier-Sarlovèze therefore plotted against the emperor, was found out and sent back to Sarlat from Paris. But he was such a great fighter that Napoleon forgave him and made him a Baron of the Empire. During the war in Spain he rode into Salamanca Cathedral on his charger, galloping as far as the choir. He broke into a barricaded convent and astonished the terrified inhabitants by singing the holy office in a voice like thunder. As a general in Napoleon's Russian campaign, he charged 5,000 cossacks with only 800 men, to cover the retreat of the Grand Army. He returned to Paris with frozen feet and gangrene.

Fournier-Sarlovèze made his peace with the restored monarchy. He was confirmed in his barony (and then took the addition 'Sarlovèze' – that is, 'son of Sarlat' – to his surname). Not everyone was able to make peace as he did. Roux-Fazillac, who was born in Excideuil in 1746 and had represented the Dordogne in Paris during the Revolution as a member of the Legislative Assembly and of the Convention, who had visited America in the company of Lafayette, and had voted for the execution of Louis XVI, was exiled in 1816. This man, who had once administered the new *département* of the Dordogne, was not allowed back until 1830. He died at Nanterre in 1833. Another exile of 1816 was Jacques Pinet, who had been born at Saint-Nexans in 1754, served in the Legislative Assembly and the Convention and been a district administrator and judge in Bergerac. He too was allowed to return to France only in 1830. He died at Bergerac fourteen years later.

Yet after the Revolution and the defeat of Napoleon, the principles of liberty, equality and fraternity lived on in the Dordogne, in spite of new rulers. In 1830 the citizens of Domme lit a huge bonfire and danced round it singing, 'Long live the king! Long live Louis-Philippe! Long live the poor! Down with the rich!' The wealthier citizens of nearby Sarlat disliked the last two slogans, debated whether to march on Domme, and prudently declined. On 18 November 1830 they were alarmed to learn that a group of Domme bandits had decided to march on Sarlat and were already halfway there, at Vitrac. Most of the would-be attackers decided to call the attempt off. Sixty of them did march into the town, ate a copious meal and withdrew without further incident. The Sarladais proclaimed that the people of Domme had been misled by agitators. Eventually, after a show of force by Sarlat, the citizens of Domme calmed down.

By and large the July monarchy was popular in the Dordogne. In Périgueux the new régime was greeted with jubilation and fireworks. General Bugeaud, who had been born at Excideuil, made his peace with the régime, became a Marshal of France and found new glory in pacifying Algeria. But another indication of the general poverty of the Dordogne is that many inhabitants departed to begin a new life in the country. When Louis-Philippe abdicated in 1848, the citizens of Périgueux celebrated with a public banquet and with fêtes, but the reaction of 1850 led to anger and public uprisings in the Dordogne. The authorities arrested the editor-in-chief of the *Républicain de la Dordogne*. The cult of Napoleon I was still strong in the countryside of Périgord and helped to swell a huge petition for the re-election of Louis-Napoleon as President of the Republic. But when he seized power by the *coup d'état* of 2 December 1851 there was an insurrection by democratic socialists in Bergerac which had to be put down by troops. Some men were imprisoned, others were exiled to the colonies.

Yet under whatever régime, nineteenth-century Périgord did not prosper, save in a few towns. Some industries even declined. For many years the peasants had worked in winter as iron-forgers. At the beginning of the nineteenth century a hundred or so forges were still producing huge quantities of forged iron and steel. Those who owned forges had been comparatively rich employers. But as the century wore on, only the protective import duties on iron and steel made abroad by better techniques kept the French industry alive. Napoleon III abolished that protection. Within twenty years only one forge survived in the whole of the Dordogne.

Once again the countryside was depopulated, as families sought work in the towns. And as the century progressed, a further disastrous blow devastated the economy of the Dordogne. Phylloxera destroyed its vines. A London gardener had discovered the phylloxera aphid in a Hammersmith greenhouse in 1853. One millimetre long, the insect feeds on the sap of vines, mostly attacking young roots, and kills them. In 1854 it reached the Midi and, by way of the Gironde, it came to the Dordogne.

Wine production in the region has never fully recovered from the phylloxera aphid, which destroyed vines in some areas that were just beginning to bring a little more wealth to those who owned them. In 1866 the *département* possessed 96,000 hectares of land supporting vines. By the end of the century these had been reduced to scarcely more than 31,000 hectares. Half a century later the number had increased, but only by another 5,000 hectares.

Yet paradoxically, the poverty of the past contributes to some of the charm of the Dordogne today. It produced the many cottages and peasant houses which dot the forests of the region, usually within shouting distance of each other, cluster in tiny villages and hamlets, or take shelter under the walls of a castle.

In the past such houses, low and dilapidated because their inhabitants could not repair them, were less attractive. In Eugène Le Roy's novel the boy Jacquou gloomily surveyed his own home:

It had but one room, and that not very large, serving as a kitchen and a living room – the usual arrangement in all the old farms around here. Since it possessed only one shuttered window, with no glass in it, in bad weather the light crept in a little over the door and down the low wide chimney. The unplastered walls were dirty, and the floor of the loft all blackened by smoke.

In one corner stood the roughly carpentered bed in which Jacquou, his father and his mother all slept. At the back of the house was a kneading-trough, with a lump of stale bread, a tart dish, and a sack of corn raised on a piece of board because the floor was damp. From the roof hung sheaves of maize and a few balls of string. Jacquou came to think it abominable 'that Christians, as we call them, should have to be lodged like beasts'.

Today, their floors properly paved, their lofts often converted into bedrooms, well-lit at night and cool during the day, such houses are highly prized. Many have been bought as secondary residences by the British, the Dutch and the Americans, as well as by the French themselves.

They are beautifully constructed, made originally with earth for mortar. As one travels towards the south of Périgord, the stones become more and more ochre and even almost white. In the distance some of them appear golden. Further north houses are tiled, but in the region of the long escarpment known as the Causse, stones – no doubt cheaper than tiles – provide the roofs as well as the walls. Piled steeply and regularly on top of each other, requiring strong oaken beams because of the weight, this way of roofing a peasant's home came to be prized by the rich as well. In Sarlat, for example, formidable town houses are roofed with *lauzes*, as they are called. To roof a house in this fashion today is extremely expensive. Many *lauzes* have been replaced with tiles. But often enough the tiler has left two or three rows of the stones as a reminder of the past.

In all these houses the chimney was a vital feature of the room. It was wide, so that people could sit on either side. Usually a huge beam serves as mantelpiece, supported on hewn stone pillars, some of which are carved in the style known as 'rustic Louis XIII'. Massive iron firedogs served as spits and a place to keep water boiling. A long chain hanging down the chimney supported the cooking pot. If today cooking is no longer done over the fire – though many an old man and his wife keep their coffee pot warm there – the firedogs and the old heavy chains, and sometimes a huge heavy ornate piece of metal to throw out the heat, are still prized. (To buy them second hand from the many *brocanteurs* of the Dordogne is a costly business.)

Equally delightful is the furniture of the Dordogne. In past days the skilled artisans could make fine furniture, but often could not afford to buy it themselves or even repair the few pieces they possessed. Le Roy's Jacquou possessed (apart from the bed) only a miserable cabinet, riddled with holes, lacking a drawer, with one of its rotten legs replaced by a flat stone. For meals he sat with his parents on benches at a wretched table. All this contrasted with the lavish furniture of the rich ones in the great château.

Today not only is good furniture taken for granted in the Dordogne. It is also still made, for the most part, in the well-tried old-fashioned way. As with chimneys, the golden age of Périgord furniture-making was that of Louis XIII in the early seventeenth century. The style is heavy, perhaps even solemn – certainly solid. Beds have powerful, curved wooden supports (even if they no longer need to bear a whole family). Twisted wooden pillars are a favoured decoration.

The eighteenth century did something to lighten traditional Dordogne furniture – but not much. The Louis XIII style remained the norm until the time of Louis Napoleon and today is entirely acceptable to many Périgourdins. Not much is made of oak. Fruit trees are favoured by the traditional furniture-makers: the wild cherry, the pear, and above all, walnut, with the poplar providing wood for drawers. Beech and elm are also used. Traditional Dordogne furniture uses little brass for ornament, preferring forged iron. Pride of a bedroom will be a huge wardrobe, heavily carved and decorated. Chests, coffers, desks, cabinets, hosiery holders and sideboards two stages high are all still made in the patterns of yesterday and (like the furniture of the fireplace) authentic secondhand examples can be bought at *brocanteurs* – at a price.

The remarkable number of different woods available for making furniture indicates the variety of crops produced by the soil of the Dordogne. Woodland still covers over a quarter of the *département*. The conquest of farmland from the forest was a slow and hard process. And the fruits of this farmland are as varied as the trees of Dordogne forests.

This is partly because the Dordogne is not, geographically, a unity. Périgourdins still acknowledge this by designating different regions by different colours. The area around Ribérac, comprising some of the most open regions of the Dordogne (though it also contains the deep Barade forest), has long been known as Périgord *Blanc*. More recently the area of the north, bordering on and in many respects resembling Limousin, has begun to be called Périgord *Vert*. And for centuries the area around Sarlat and to the south, the region most resembling the Midi, has been known by the name – slightly sinister to English ears – of Périgord *Noir*. No one is quite sure why. A society, 'the friends of

Sarlat and Périgord Noir', debates why and also debates the extent of the area of Périgord Noir. It is said that the darker leaves of oak and chestnut explain the colour *noir*, especially at dusk. Another explanation is the quantity of truffles (the so-called 'black diamond' of cooking) grown in Périgord Noir. A third reason offered by many is that this is the area through which flows the river Dordogne itself, bearing with it the dark secrets of its ancient cliffs and the castles that surmount them.

But another reason for the polyculture of the Dordogne lies in its conservative character – in spite of the fact that those who farm it are today determined to survive the vicissitudes of their way of life. Yet farmers still own parts of fields widely separated from each other, almost reminiscent of medieval strip farming.

This variety adds enormous charm to the Dordogne. The rich valley of the Dronne supports cereals, nuts, beef cattle and fat fowl. The fertile regions around Bergerac produce the best-known wines of the Dordogne. But there are many acres of poor land, which the farmers work incessantly to care for their maize and tobacco.

Tobacco is an excellent example of the industry of the Périgord farmer, especially where he is not blessed with the most fertile soil. He needs to choose exactly where he plants it, for the plant needs sunshine every day. He must work to cut off the bad leaves as well as the heads of the tobacco plant. Above all, he must find his best plots of land for tobacco-growing, and then he must enrich it further. Philip Oyler's classic book *The Generous Earth* notes that in the Dordogne the tobacco plant 'likes a deep rich soil and is therefore planted only in the valley, not on the adjoining slopes. In practice,' he adds, 'they apply more dung to this than to any other crop.'

In France the tobacco industry is a government monopoly. All that is grown, cropped and dried by the farmers of the Dordogne is bought by the government and turned in government-owned factories into cigars, cigarettes and snuff. Yet the Dordogne tobacco-farmer is proud of his work. Each year a 'tobacco road' programme (*la route du tabac*) is arranged for any tourist who wishes to watch the way tobacco is grown and processed. Growers open their doors to visitors. At the two greatest centres of the industry, Sarlat and Bergerac, conducted tours are arranged for those interested in this curious crop. Bergerac is especially worth a visit in this respect, for here is Europe's only museum of tobacco. Here five centuries of history, from that October in 1492 when Christopher Columbus first saw American Indians putting dried leaves into their pipes and lighting them, are on display. Drawings and paintings, pipes, advertisements, snuff-boxes, and all the rest of the paraphernalia with which smokers surround themselves today and have done for 500 years, are set out in Bergerac.

What the films, exhibitions and gardens of the experimental institute and museum of tobacco at Bergerac do not stress is that smoking cigarettes can ruin one's health. But as this fact slowly dawned on smokers, the consumption of tobacco declined. Schooled by the centuries of crises in their sources of income, the Périgourdins have responded, especially in the past twenty years, by replacing tobacco with strawberries, a crop hitherto thought to be the speciality of nearby Quercy.

Equally varied are the animals grazing in the valleys and on the slopes of the Dordogne. The area around Thiviers is the home of the goat, from which comes the deliciously soft *chèvre* cheese. It is perhaps depressing to the tourist to learn that many of the 175,000 sheep raised in the Dordogne will eventually end up as pet food, but the fact does not depress the farmer. Once the raising of pigs was a purely family affair. Now, with over 120,000 of them in the Dordogne, it has become one of the *département*'s important industries. The rearing of geese, above all for their excellent pâtés made from their swollen livers, has been supplemented recently by rearing ducks, which also supply an excellent, succulent pâté.

The Dordogne produces more walnuts annually than any other region of France. And here again, the diverse conditions that obtain in various parts of the *département* enable the farmers, by selecting different varieties, to supply the market from the beginning of the season till the end of December. The pleasure in all this for the visitor is that walnuts are readily available at the traditional fairs and markets throughout the Dordogne. Ribérac, for example, holds a walnut market every Wednesday from October to December. Montignac holds its nut market on the same days throughout October and November, selling chestnuts as well. Brantôme's walnut market is held every Friday in October and November. Villefranche-du-Périgord holds a chestnut market every Saturday in the last three months of each year.

The list is endless. These fairs and markets, which have existed for centuries, offer a delight to the tourist and originate in the peculiar history of this region of France. A University of California dissertation, published in 1979, alleged that the fairs – which are less frequent than the markets – are losing their importance in the culture of Périgord. The dissertation, called 'A Dying Culture', based itself on the sudy of one Dordogne peasant family between 1960 and 1970. My own experience, which is drawn simply from going to these fairs and markets, is that the dissertation's conclusion is far too pessimistic. The fairs of the Dordogne do not represent a dying culture. The annual fair at Périgueux, held on the first Wednesday in September, is a splendid affair. No one in the region of Le Bugue in the holiday season should miss one of its two annual fairs – the one held on 25 August. (The other is on 30 September.) The annual fair at Rouffignac is held on the 21 August. At Bergerac on the first and third Tuesday of every month is the kind of cattle fair at which city-dwellers can dream of their lost origins in the countryside. At Ribérac basket-weavers hold a fair every Wednesday from May to September.

These fairs and markets today serve those who live all the year round in the Dordogne and those who visit this *département* as tourists. Each Friday, before I get out of bed in the Dordogne village where I live, the farmer's wife at the end of the field is selecting fowl for the Saturday market, killing the birds and plucking them. Each Saturday at the market Périgourdins in berets carry such birds by their legs, sometimes along with a couple of live rabbits. And in summer the tourists photograph it all and – if they are wise – buy just such a rabbit to cook *à la périgourdine* when they get back to their own holiday homes.

❧ 3 ❧

The Food and Wine of the Dordogne

Writing of the Dordogne, Lot and Tarn in 1952, Freda White declared that, 'if you visit the river-country you will find yourself in a gastronomical paradise'. The French themselves have known this for a long time. 'In Périgord one does not simply eat well,' wrote André Maurois; 'one eats in style.' And when Horace Napoléon Raisson published one of the earliest books of *cordon bleu* cooking in 1834, he took as his pseudonym A. B. de Périgord.

French culinary literature is a unique genre, very highly regarded by a nation that adores its stomach. At the very end of his life Alexandre Dumas the Elder set his mind to writing a cookery book. Dumas had published 300 other works. He was worn out. 'My last work shall be a book about cooking,' he decided, 'created out of my memories and my imagination.' The celebrated author of *The Count of Monte Cristo*, *The Three Musketeers* and *The Man in the Iron Mask* delivered the manuscript of his *Grand Dictionnaire de cuisine* to the publisher in March 1870. He died in the same year, happy to have achieved his last ambition. The book appeared three years later.

I recommend anyone with an interest in food to try to get hold of a copy of the translation (see Further Reading) and read some of it (and indeed to do the same with the writings of the other masters of French culinary literature who will appear in this chapter). To do so is to be transported into a remarkable world. Many of these writers published under bizarre pseudonyms. Henri Babinski published his *Gastronomie pratique* of 1907 under the name Ali-Bab. Maurice Edmund Sailland, founder of the French Academy of Gastronomes and to my mind the greatest of these masters, published under the title Prince Curnonsky.

All of them depict the art of eating as one of the glories of civilization. As Dumas expressed it, 'the savage eats from need, the civilized man from desire'. And, as we shall see, all of them exalt the cooking and food of the Dordogne, of Périgord.

Not all that these writers recommend is to be taken totally seriously – even when they are writing of the dishes of the Dordogne. For instance, in Ali-Bab's cookery book, *lièvre à la royale* – one of the great Périgord dishes, now eaten throughout France – is given a recipe ten pages long. So many condiments, truffles, cognac and *foie gras* were added to the dish that, as Dr Theodore Zeldin observes, the taste of the hare virtually disappeared.

In fact, some of the greatest citizens of Périgord itself have been less than enthusiastic about its cooking. Michel de Montaigne contemptuously dubbed gastronomy '*la science du gueule*' (perhaps best translated as 'the science of the gullet'). The chef of Cardinal Caraffa tried to initiate Montaigne into the secrets of fine food. Montaigne observed, 'He spoke of this *science du gueule* with a gravity and magisterial countenance, as if he were talking to me of a deep point of theology.' Yet in spite of himself, Montaigne contributed to the spread of the reputation of Dordogne cooking. His friend Henri of Navarre was so taken by the food he had received from Montaigne that when he became Henri IV he appointed a man of Périgord, Briade de Saint-Cernin, as his chef. Today the *Guide Michelin* turns Montaigne's insult on its head by describing Périgord – this time in a compliment – as 'the kingdom of the gullet' (*le royaume du gueule*).

Montaigne is, however, an exception. Most citizens of Périgord would agree with André Maurois that to prepare a meal in the Dordogne 'is one of the fine arts'. Eugène Le Roy introduced one of his books with the epigraph, 'This book is purely Périgordian. Whoever does not love garlic, *chabrol** and walnut-oil, won't understand a bit of it.'

Such a blend of literature and taste is no doubt unfamiliar to many of us. None the less, those of us who are not French are able to distinguish between food as pleasure and simply eating to live. We know when cooking is a chore and not an art. Inspired by the French,

---

* The Dordogne habit of mingling wine with the dregs of one's soup.

the American Frank Cornishie agreed that 'the sense of taste falls properly into the realm of aesthetics'. Observing that painting, architecture, sculpture and music each use one of the five senses, Cornishie marvelled that eating requires four: sight, touch, taste and smell. For my part, simply to *hear* something sizzling in a pan adds to the joy of food, thus using up the fifth sense. But over a century and a half ago, in his famous *Physiology of Taste*, the Frenchman Jean Anthelme Brillat-Savarin felt obliged to invent a *sixth* sense, a sense intimately bound up with food, love – and Périgord.

Brillat-Savarin is a famous figure in French culinary literature. He is the philosopher of food. A lawyer, who survived the French Revolution and its aftermath (though not without difficulty), he died in his seventies. Twelve years after his death, in 1825, his *Physiology of Taste* was published. He gave it the subtitle, 'Meditations on Sublime Gastronomy'. Writing fifty years later, Alexandre Dumas recognized Brillat-Savarin as a dangerous rival and tried to diminish his reputation. He was, wrote Dumas, 'neither a gastronome nor a gourmand. He was just a big eater!' Dumas claimed to have seen Brillat-Savarin fall asleep at meals. He said his rival had been fat and looked like a parson. (This was a shrewd insult. Brillat-Savarin himself had described *abbés* – those younger sons of aristocrats who had taken holy orders and had 'money, no superiors, and nothing to do' – as 'short, thickset, plump, well-dressed, cajoling, very polite, inquisitive, gourmands, alert, insinuating, and, insofar as any of them still survive, corpulent and very pious'.)

The sixth sense invented by Brillat-Savarin was the 'genesic sense' (*le sens génésique*), the sense which he believed brought the sexes, male and female, together. Brillat-Savarin expounds the importance of other senses, too. 'Unless smell plays its part,' he wrote, 'there is no perfect taste.' Indeed, he suspected at times that smell and taste were ultimately the same sense. To him the mouth was 'the laboratory' and the nose 'the chimney'. But the influence of his notion of the genesic sense on later culinary writers is enough to disprove the dismissive remarks of Alexandre Dumas. What is more, as we shall see, in writing of the relationship between food and love, Brillat-Savarin laid particular importance on the food of the Dordogne.

'Those who know how to savour refined food,' he declared, 'know how to taste a sophisticated kiss.' Prince Curnonsky took up the

theme with gusto, in his *La Table et l'amour* (subtitled 'A New Treatise on Modern Love-potions'), written with André Saint-Georges 125
years later. Curnonsky quotes an attack on passionate love in a poem
by Alfred de Musset:

> *Amour! Fléau du Monde! Exécrable folie,*
> *Toi qu'un lien si frêle à la volupté lie,*
> *Quand par d'autres nœuds tu tiens à la douleur,*
> *Si jamais par les yeux d'une femme sans cœur*
> *Tu peux m'entrer au ventre et m'empoisoner l'âme,*
> *Je t'en arracherai quand je devrais mourir!!*

> [Love! Scourge of the world! Atrocious folly,
> You who are flimsily bound with sensual delight
> When by other coils you bind us to sorrow,
> If ever – by means of the eyes of a heartless woman –
> You manage to enter my stomach and poison my soul,
> I shall tear you from them when it is time to die!!]

But Curnonsky will have none of it. 'How those Romantics exaggerated!' is his comment. And he quotes Brillat-Savarin on food and
wine, to clinch his point: 'People who suffer from indigestion or get
drunk know neither how to drink nor how to eat.' The same is true of
lovers. If love makes one jealous or ill, it is no longer love but rage –
the equivalent of indigestion after eating badly.

What, then, is the food of love? Above all, in the eyes of both
Curnonsky and Brillat-Savarin, it is the truffle; and the truffle is
the glory of Périgord. 'The finest truffles of France,' wrote Brillat-
Savarin, 'come from Périgord and Upper Provence.' The truffle, said
Curnonsky, is 'the perfumed soul of Périgord'. For Brillat-Savarin, the
truffle kindled all the senses, not least the sense of taste and the
genesic sense. It is, he wrote, 'a great word whose sound engenders
gastronomic and erotic thoughts both in those who wear skirts and in
those who wear beards'. He told the story of an upright woman, a
friend of his, who forty years before had *almost* lost her virtue after
eating part of a truffle from Périgueux. 'I never eat them now,' she
said, 'without being a trifle more careful in the midst of my enjoy-
ment.'

Such speculations are, perhaps, beyond the reach of the staid British, who are more likely to rest content with Curnonsky's less extravagant claim that, 'The truffle is not a positive love-potion, but on occasion it can make a woman more loving and a man more lovable.' What we should accept without question is Curnonsky's authoritative description of this glory of Dordogne cooking.

Born at Angers in 1862, Curnonsky was brought up by his grandmother, since his mother died giving him birth and his father disappeared soon afterwards. In 1930 he had the good fortune to slip on a badly cleaned platform of the Paris Métro, which brought him compensation of 20,000 francs and a lifelong free railway pass. As a result he was able all the more easily to pursue his ambition of learning about and writing of the food of France. But even before then, his supremacy in the field had been acknowledged by his peers. In 1927 *Paris-Soir* had invited 5,000 gastronomes (restaurateurs and chefs) to elect a prince of gastronomy. They chose Curnonsky. He wrote and ate with gusto and skill until ten a.m. on 22 July 1956 when, at the age of eighty-four, he fell from a fourth-floor window in Laborde Square (near the Parisian Church of St Augustin), bounced off a veranda and expired on the pavement.

The truffle, Curnonsky asserted, is 'the *sacrum sacrorum* of the gastronome, a name never pronounced by a gastronome without touching his hat'. To write the history of the truffle, he declared, 'would be to undertake a history of civilization, in which truffles have played a more important role than the laws of Minos and the statutes of Solon'.

For many years men and women wondered what these black, ugly balls covered in pyramidical lumps really were. Pliny the Elder was certain that they were nothing more than balls of earth. (He said he knew of a patrician official in Spain who had eaten one and found a coin in it.) In fact they are a kind of mushroom, reproducing by spores like other mushrooms. They grow underground, attaching themselves to the roots of certain oak trees when the heat and humidity are right, and give out a spawn which lives in symbiosis with the trees. Those who have long cultivated them can spot, from the dead grass around the trees, that truffles are likely to be there. But the traditional way of discovering them was to bring up female pigs to like them. The fully grown sow, in her desire for the truffle, can smell its remarkable aroma when it has ripened in November, and digs it up. Then the farmer fights off the animal and keeps the truffle.

There are in fact thirty or forty sorts of truffle; but only the *Tuber melanosporum*, which Brillat-Savarin called 'the black diamond of cooking', is interesting. Brillat-Savarin asserted that truffles never gave anyone indigestion. (He added that if a man or woman suffered indigestion after a meal cooked with truffles, the malady came from greed, not from the truffles.) He had a medical friend, Dr Malouet, who 'used to swallow enough truffles to give indigestion to an elephant, and yet lived to the age of eighty-six'.

Today the people of the Dordogne have trained dogs as well as sows to smell out and dig up truffles. But even so, crops are falling. Whereas in 1900 the Dordogne produced 150 tonnes of truffles a year, today production amounts to no more than 10 tonnes a year. As Henri Deffarges, President of the Committee of Propaganda for Truffles, observed in 1954, 'Man fights all his life against the inertia and indifference of those who own truffle country.' One result, however, of the shortage of the truffle is that those who do grow them also grow rich. In 1981 I found that Dordogne truffles were selling at 900 francs a kilo.

Rare or not so rare, the black truffle is an essential ingredient of Dordogne cooking and greatly contributes to its renown and quality – so much so that *Larousse gastronomique* (followed by many others) suggests that the phrase 'à la périgourdine' always indicates that a dish has been garnished with truffles. This is not in fact true in practice – since truffles are so expensive – but it *ought* to be! A more serious error is the often-repeated statement that truffles were relatively unused and unsung until the eighteenth century at the earliest. Reay Tannahill's *Food in History* roundly declares, 'it was not until the nineteenth century that the French came to appreciate their true delicacy'. Patrick Turnbull's book on the Dordogne observes that the cultivated truffle dates from experiments at the Château de Bouquet at Sorges in the 1840s. But the truth is that the French adored the truffle long before this. The poet Eustache Deschamps sang its praises in the fifteenth century, as did Brantôme (whose real name was Pierre de Bourdeille) 100 years later and Lagrange-Chancel in the seventeenth century. Citizens of the Dordogne themselves were extremely proud of their prowess with the truffle in cooking. In 1789, at the outset of the French Revolution, some of them published a political squib called 'The Turkey Cooked with Truffles' (*La Dinde aux Truffes*), subtitled

'The Patriotic Gift of the People of Périgord to the National Assembly'. Its opening paragraph reads:

The reputation of our turkeys cooked with truffles is too well known to you, worthy Parisians, for us not to hope for a favourable reception to the present we are sending you. It is a patriotic gift, worthy to be offered to you, since it will ensure the good health of France. However, it isn't a turkey, nor one of our red partridges, nor one of our excellent pâtés. It is something even rarer, better suited to your taste. It is a word, a pure and simple word, that we are offering you.

To wrap up a piece of political advice under the guise of a traditional dish is a sign of a mentality which thinks and dreams first and foremost of food.

That is the mentality of the Dordogne. Coupling the Dordogne with nearby Quercy and the Rouerque (now known as the *département* of Aveyron), Prince Curnonsky observed, 'These three old regions of France, which have maintained their great traditions of cooking for centuries, can be grouped in a magnificent gastronomic province, one of the richest and most original that the fine gourmand could dream of: the ancient Guyenne.' Though well aware that the truffle was the most sublime of nature's gifts to the region, Curnonsky treasured Périgord for many other delights. 'It is,' he wrote, 'the paradise of truffles, of *cèpes* [another remarkable mushroom], of *confits* [which we shall speak of later], of *ballotines*, of *foie gras*, of the spicy delicatessen of the countryside, which is at once trusted, healthy and flavoured with a taste of the soil.' The poet Brantôme sums up and symbolizes the glory of the cooking of Périgord, just as Rabelais symbolizes Anjou, Touraine and Poitou, said Curnonsky.

It is worth pausing momentarily to speak of one of the dishes which so whetted the literary taste buds of Curnonsky: the *ballotine*. A *ballotine* is a rolled piece of spiced, boned meat. Probably the finest such preparation is *ballotine de lièvre à la périgourdine*, which consists of rabbit, stuffed with its own succulent meat along with truffles and *foie gras*.

One foreigner who perspicaciously spotted the astounding culinary riches of the Dordogne was the American Waverley Root. He described Périgord, 'where gastronomic greatness bursts forth', as 'a name synonymous throughout France with fine food'. Waverley Root, who began his career as a writer on cookery by surveying French restaurants, noted how highly the Parisians rated their two Périgordian establishments – the Rotisserie Périgourdine, just off the Place Saint-Michel, and the Restaurant A. Sousceyine, at 35, Rue Faidherbe. He also noted how expensive it was to eat there, whereas eating in the Dordogne itself is astonishingly cheap, even today.

Waverley Root even pointed to the area he believed to be the absolute acme of Dordogne cooking. 'The Sarladais,' he wrote, 'a little triangle of land between the Vézère and the Dordogne in the south-east corner of the Périgord, clustered about the town of Sarlat ... shares with Périgueux, capital of the Périgord, the honor of providing the best food in the territory.' I live in the Sarladais, and I agree with his judgement.

Even the potatoes in this region are cooked remarkably. Potatoes were introduced into the Dordogne only in the 1770s, at a time of great famine. They were so rare that leaflets explaining how to cook them were printed at the time. The Sarladais proceeded to make an extraordinary delicacy of them. To prepare *pommes [de terre] sarladaises*, peeled potatoes are sliced thinly. Layers of the potatoes are placed in melted goose fat in a large frying pan. Between the layers of potatoes are placed layers of thinly sliced truffles – not too many. They are fried gently for half an hour, garnished with salt and pepper, and then turned over for another fifteen minutes. Finally parsley is added. The result is enthralling, both to the sophisticated taste of adults and the palates of schoolchildren. To an English child, it is as if our ubiquitous chip had been somehow transformed by culinary magic.

The use of goose fat is vital. Elsewhere in France people cook in butter. It is a compliment to say to a chef or host, 'You don't stint the butter in your house.' In the Dordogne cooking is invariably done in fat – if not goose fat then fat from another animal or walnut-oil – never butter. This fact enabled Prince Curnonsky to make one of his most celebrated puns, on the famous motto *Sans peur et sans reproche* (without fear and without reproach). 'Périgord cooking,' he declared, 'is *sans beurre et sans reproche*' (without butter and without reproach).

The *whole* of the goose is in fact used in Dordogne cooking. This care to waste nothing is what helps to make eating so cheap in the region. Anyone who strolls, say, along the Rue de la République in Sarlat will see for sale in shop windows the formerly slender necks of geese transformed into swollen *cou farci*, succulently stuffed with chopped pork, truffles and a little *foie gras*. Curnonsky begins his list of characteristic Dordogne dishes with the sentence, 'It is the country of stuffed goose neck, of *sauce périgourdine* and of *sauce rouilleuse* (those two culinary miracles), the classic land of that rich and sumptuous cuisine which is no longer cooked in butter, as north of the river Loire, but in the succulent fat of poultry or pork.'

Of Curnonsky's two miraculous Dordogne sauces, *sauce périgourdine* (or *sauce périgueux*) is the better known. The many ways of making it vary only slightly. Alexandre Dumas (whose recipes were usually at least fifty years old when he wrote his cookery book) gives the following instructions:

Peel and dice two or three truffles. Put them to one side, covered. Put one-and-a-half glasses of brown sauce into a pot, along with a few table-spoonsful of good veal broth. Add some of the truffle peelings, and put the pot on to a lively fire. Stir and reduce by one third. Then slowly stir in one third of a glass of good Madeira, add the truffles, boil for two minutes, and remove from the fire.

Anyone who cares to make this sauce in the Dordogne can be spared the trouble of making good veal soup by buying it – ready-made – in a bottle from many butchers. (I buy mine from the excellent butcher in the main square in Domme.)

Sauce périgueux is delicious with beef dishes, and indeed with veal and eggs too. Curnonsky's second culinary miracle, *sauce rouilleuse*, is used to flavour a fricassée of fowl, especially chicken. I do not recommend anyone to try to make it, unless he or she is skilled at killing chickens and collecting their blood – for this gives the sauce its characteristic rusty colour. Curnonsky loved it with hare and rabbit, as well as with chicken. His recipe for *poulet sauce rouilleuse* was:

Cut the chicken into pieces and sauté with fat, little onions and flour. Add salt and pepper, and mix with some light stock. A few moments before serving, thin down the blood with a little sauce and replace on a low flame for several minutes, being careful not to boil.

Although the memory of a holiday can be renewed by eating at home the food of the region, it is not always easy to find the proper ingredients – especially if one lives far away from the Dordogne for most of the year. I am not one of those who believe that one ingredient can readily substitute for another in a classic dish. Shrimp, for example, is simply not crayfish, whatever some cookery books might assert! Even so, an appendix to this book contains a good number of Périgord recipes – for use both in that delectable region and also, where the necessary ingredients are obtainable, to provide gastronomic memories for those who cannot live there all the year round.

But most people in the Dordogne will wish to savour its culinary delights in the countless excellent and cheap restaurants of Périgord.

As in most French restaurants, in Périgord you are offered set menus at fixed prices – by far the best value for money. The cheapest restaurant may simply offer a *plat du jour*, which varies at the decision of the chef or restaurateur. All the set menus offer remarkable value and (apart from the one offering simply the *plat du jour*) a fair amount of choice.

For those who – like myself – often prefer to eat the *plat du jour*, all one needs to do is merely ask what it is. Here that excellent virtue, humility, comes into its own. The humble man or woman is not afraid to take along a pocket French–English/English–French dictionary. The waiter or waitress will always write down the name of the dish, if one's ears don't catch it, or if it is unfamiliar. In fact, a pocket dictionary is invaluable, both for examining the menus which are always displayed outside French restaurants and for sizing up the menu inside. I shall never forget once dining in the Hôtel-Restaurant Saint Albert in Sarlat and leaving my pocket dictionary in the car outside. No doubt most readers will know the meaning of the word *cailles* which appeared on the menu that evening. I didn't. Fortunately my car was parked close by, and I sped to it, retrieved the dictionary and discovered that we were being offered quails ('that most darling and lovable of game', as Alexandre Dumas described them). I had never eaten quails before. They were astounding – cooked that evening with *raisins* (which our pocket dictionary reminds us means grapes and not raisins).

It is also important, in the Dordogne as elsewhere in France, to arrive for meals at a restaurant in good time – certainly by 12.30 for lunch and around 7.30 for dinner. On Sundays and holidays it is wise, if you know which restaurant you plan to use, to reserve a table. Every Sunday when I'm in the Dordogne, after we've been to the little romanesque church in Grolejac, I and my family eat at one of the hotels in Vitrac. In the high season, were our table not permanently reserved, we would often have been turned away. Restaurants soon fill up.

At the Vitrac hotel I always choose the menu with *brochet* (pike), served cold in a parsley sauce – unless they are serving kidneys (*rognons*), in which case I forget about the pike. In French restaurants a meal takes a long time. There are usually at least four courses. None of them is too big. ('The glutton demands quantity,' declared Dumas, 'the gourmand quality.') Cumulatively, they leave one entirely satisfied.

One peculiarity of the Dordogne does add to the length of a meal. Elsewhere in France soup has virtually disappeared from the midday menu of restaurants. The meal begins with an *hors d'œuvre*. In the evening soup returns and the *hors d'œuvre* disappears. But in the Dordogne, restaurants still serve soup and *hors d'œuvre* at both meals. Here is a legacy of the peasant life of the past. For the poor, soup was practically the only available meal – it was sometimes very poor soup, too. Peasants ate soup not only during the day but also for breakfast. One way of thickening it was to pour the stock over bread – a habit known in the Dordogne as *'tremper la soupe'*. Today country restaurants in the Dordogne still serve excellent soup containing slices of bread, as well as the more usual clear or vegetable soups.

Périgord food often takes long to prepare – there are several courses, and eating is a leisurely, social activity – so any visitor to the region would do well to heed the advice of A. de Lacrousille (himself a great lover of the Dordogne): 'We do not recommend the tourists to present themselves unannounced at a fine inn, demanding instant chicken, ready to eat in a quarter of an hour.' Here, too, is the place for a sentence from Raymond Oliver's *Art and Magic of Cookery*: 'A restaurant is not a stand at a race-meeting, and the fact that such and such a dish is advertised as a "speciality" does not give those who choose it the right to be noisily disapproving if it does not please them.' Thirdly, we should rejoice at Alexandre Dumas's definition of eating as 'a major daily activity which can be accomplished properly only by the wise'.

Such wisdom in France has often been found among the humble as well as the great of this world. Although the development of much French cooking derives from the art of chefs working in royal and noble kitchens (whose skills spread elsewhere when the Revolution destroyed those kitchens), in the Dordogne, as the survival of 'soup with everything' indicates, the long-hoarded traditions of peasant cooking, handed on by word of mouth, have greatly contributed to what we enjoy today. But there is more to it than this. Waverley Root attributed the wonder of Dordogne food to a mixture of the sound, hearty peasant cooking of the Massif Central and the rich cuisine of the highly urbanized Bordeaux region. He added that people have been preparing food there for longer than anywhere else in France, for this is the country of prehistoric man!

For whatever reason, Périgord cooking is cooking fit for kings. The great diplomatist Talleyrand judiciously chose a chef from the region in order to astound the palates of the lordly delegates at the Congress of Vienna.

In Vienna, however, he could not draw on the natural resources of the Dordogne countryside, which also play their part in the richness of Dordogne cooking: the truffle and the twelve other important mushrooms (from the *cèpe* to the *girolle*); the eels, lampreys, pike, morels, barbel, salmon, trout and crayfish provided by the rivers of Périgord; the plentiful mussels and crab; the game which abounds in the forests (50,000 people annually buy a permit to shoot in the Dordogne). Everywhere waddle the great geese of Toulouse. And to give extra piquancy to dishes and cakes as well as providing oil, the walnut grows throughout the region, and especially around Sarlat.

The Dordogne grows more walnuts than any other *département* of France. One of its ancient legends concerns Aymery de Beynac, a knight whom duty had taken away on the Crusades. Far from home and from his lady, he decided on a pact with the devil. 'If you will take me back to my fief in Beynac,' he promised, 'I will invite you to my table and offer you as dessert a fruit which grows in Périgord and gives strength, light and heat. If you guess what it is before I give it you, then I shall be yours.' The devil agreed, put Aymery in his haversack, and sped with him to his father's castle. There Aymery had a great sack of walnuts brought to the table. 'See these fruits,' he cried. 'They possess a divine savour. Their golden oil lights our torches. We give their liqueur, the *eau de vie* from these nuts, to those who are weak. And if you need a fire, throw their shells on to a light and you will have an unequalled flame, brighter than that which burns in Hell.' At this Satan sheepishly picked up the sack, made a hole in the château wall and took to his heels. People said this was the first time he had ever lost such a contest.

Yet none of these ingredients would have been of much value had not the people of Périgord developed their remarkable culinary skills. The specialities in particular reveal these skills: their *confits* and their *pâté de foie gras*.

A *confit* basically consists of large pieces of goose or duck preserved in its own fat. Cloves, garlic, rosemary and bay leaf are used to give different flavours to the *confit*. The technique is found elsewhere in France (notably in the Languedoc). But in the Dordogne the addition of truffles, as well as the many local variations in the basic recipe, makes *confit* uniquely delicious and frequently a gastronomic surprise.

Foie gras is similarly a dish known throughout France and enhanced in the Dordogne by the remarkable truffle. 'The *foie gras*,' wrote Curnonsky, 'appears to gastronomy as a pure marvel of the culinary art and one of the masterpieces which has assured the glory of our country.' For over fifty years he shouted from the rooftops that 'the *foie gras* is the king of *hors d'œuvres*'. Many eat it at the end of a meal – in his view, foolishly. For him it merited a place apart. It should be loved for itself alone. 'All who know how to eat,' he pronounced, 'must acknowledge and salute its pre-eminent worth.' It should be eaten by itself, first.

In the Dordogne it isn't eaten first because, as we have seen, *hors d'œuvres* are invariably preceded by soup. It isn't always eaten alone, since often *foie gras* is served along with *jambon de pays*. But its worth, especially when flavoured with the truffle, is universally acknowledged.

Much nonsense is written about the supposed cruelty involved in preparing the livers of living geese in order to create *pâté de foie gras*. When Alexandre Dumas wrote on this subject, his imagination got the better of him – and of the truth. 'The animals are subjected to untold tortures,' he wrote, 'worse than those suffered by the early

Christians.' Their feet, he alleged, were nailed to the floor to stop them moving around and running off their fat. Their eyes were put out, so that nothing they could see might distract them. They were stuffed with nuts and given not a drop to drink.

All this is untrue. To swell their livers, geese (and ducks) are merely force-fed three times a day on boiled maize. A skilled feeder can deal with eighty or so geese an hour. This happens in late October or November. (Some country activities are determined by nature, some by mankind. So pigs are killed in the Dordogne in January and February, when nothing can be done in the fields, so as to provide *char-cuterie* and *confits* for the rest of the year.) After a month of this extra feeding, the birds are killed. Their swollen livers, with the addition of truffles and sometimes either cognac or the sweet white Périgord wine from Monbazillac, produce one of the most delicious tastes known to mankind.

The people of Périgord devote much care to creating *pâté de foie gras*. The colour of the liver taken from the goose is specially import-ant. It must be uniformly ochre-yellow – otherwise the liver is rejected. Even when very cold, the liver must be supple to the touch, to ensure that it is not *too* fat. Usually the very large livers are of poorer quality than the smaller ones. Finally, the liver must bear its characteristic smell, but not too much.

In view of these gastronomic delights, it is difficult in the Dordogne to agree with Alexandre Dumas's dictum that 'meat is merely the material part of a meal: the spiritual part is wine'. Even so, no Dor-dogne meal is complete without a glass or two of wine. And it is gratifying to find Dumas actually praising the British in this connec-tion, through one of our greatest queens. Describing the statue of Queen Anne in front of St Paul's Cathedral, Dumas observed that 'she commits the impropriety – which might be said to characterize her whole reign – of turning her back on St Paul's, reserving her regal smile for the great wine merchant whose emporium stood on the opposite corner of the road'.

I do not personally share Alexandre Dumas's high estimation of our devotion to wine. Some lingering puritanism mars our character in this respect. As late as 1920 the great George Saintsbury was still striving to remedy this. Postmaster of Merton, journalist, literary critic, historian, Oxford professor of English and wine-bibber, George

Saintsbury completed his last long book, *A History of the French Novel*, and was free to relax and write his *Notes on a Cellar-Book*. The envoy to this book is an attack on 'prohibitionists'. As a devout high-churchman, Saintsbury was well-equipped to demolish those who attacked wine on supposedly religious grounds. He observed that 'few theologians will disagree with me when I say that thanklessness towards God and malice towards men constitute about as awkward a "soul *diathesis*" as can be imagined'. On this basis Saintsbury proceeded to a magnificent denunciation of 'prohibitionists' which should be read by all Englishmen and women as they cross the Channel towards France.

When the doctors and the Reverends (self-dubbed and others) and the occasional magistrates who cackle about the mischiefs of alcohol, condescend to face facts, there may be something more to say to them. But no more at present, except to urge the most strenuous opposition to the subdulous and impertinent foreign interference [i.e. the diastrous U.S. example of prohibition]; and to express regret that Archbishops and Bishops, if they do not definitely set themselves against the advice of St Paul and the practice of Christ, should join movements, the clear effect and in some cases the hardly disguised object, of which is to make the adoption of that advice and the imitation of that practice impossible.

The wisdom of George Saintsbury (of which more shortly) is well complemented by the writings of that son of Périgord, Michel de Montaigne. Montaigne found drunkenness a gross and brutish vice, for he held that 'the worst condition of a person arises when he loses knowledge and control of himself'. Yet he found himself forced to concede that his distaste derived more from sensitivity than reason, for he recognized that drunkenness was less malicious or harmful to others than most other vices. (He wrote, of course, before the twentieth-century scandal of the drunken driver – a person against whom French laws are, rightly, very strict indeed.) He argued that in the days when people drank less, there was more lechery. Good wine he perceived to be one of the few comforts of old age: 'drinking is almost the last pleasure that the years steal from us'. Even when he told stories illustrating the evil consequences of too much drink, Montaigne usually drew their sting at the last moment. He recounted the tale of a chaste widow who lived in Castres. After becoming drugged with too much drink, she found that she had been made pregnant without even knowing the man responsible. Yet Montaigne's tale has a happy ending. The widow went to church, announced what had happened and promised to pardon the culprit if he would admit his sin. The man turned out to be one of her young farmhands. The two fell in love. 'They are still alive,' observed Montaigne, 'and married to each other.'

So this great Périgord philosopher perceived both the vice of brutish drunkenness and the blessings of wine. He went so far as to disagree with those who would take a glass of wine only at a meal. 'Like shop apprentices and workmen we should refuse no chance to drink,' he wrote, 'and keep this desire always in our mind.' His own disposition was to drink best *after* eating. 'For that reason,' he explained, 'my last drink is almost always my largest.' I myself have independently reached this conclusion.

Without naming names I should like to suggest that some of those who presume to criticize or diminish the wines of the Dordogne should first read George Saintsbury and Michel de Montaigne. One otherwise fine book on the wines of France includes those from Bergerac and Monbazillac among 'The Lesser Wines from Mountain and Plain', adding that 'Bergerac is probably more famous for Cyrano, who came from there, than for its heady red and white wines'. George Saintsbury would have rebuked such discourtesy. Oddly enough, he himself disliked the wine known as Saint Émilion, made from grapes grown just outside Périgord on the north side of the river Dordogne, named after an ancient hermit who once lived there, and generally praised by connoisseurs. But Saintsbury was far too wise to mock a wine simply because he himself disliked it. 'I have said nothing about the wines of Saint Émilion – even the noted "Cheval Blanc" – because I have never cared much for them,' he wrote in *Notes on a Cellar-Book*. 'But I certainly do not wish to say anything against them.' He knew that a wine that no one would class as great could none the less give great pleasure. 'To mention all the good non-classed wines, Médoc or not, that I have drunk and enjoyed would be endless,' he said.

This was precisely the view of Montaigne. 'If you make your pleasure depend on drinking only good wine,' he warned, 'you condemn yourself to the pain of sometimes drinking bad wine. We must have a less exacting and freer taste. To be a good drinker, one must not have too delicate a palate.' To my mind, the visitor to Dordogne hotels is extremely well served by asking for the *'réserve du patron'* (or *'cuvée de la maison'*) when ordering the wine for a meal. He will certainly be served the cheapest bottle on the wine list, filled with an excellent unpretentious wine chosen by the restaurateur for his customers.

I must add my view that the wines of Périgord have also long been underestimated, overshadowed by the more famous (and more expensive) wines of Bordeaux. Of the 36,000 hectares of vine-growing land in the Dordogne, 20,000 lie on either side of the river in the region of Bergerac. Most of these vineyards are owned by families (the average plot is around only five hectares in size), though something like a half of the families have joined together in *caves coopératives*. White wines grown in the region are, beginning with the dryest, *sec*, *liquoreux* and *moelleux*. As its name implies, *liquoreux* wine, which tastes sweet and luscious, also contains some liqueur, because of the small amount of unfermented grape sugar added during fermentation. The grapes which make the white wine of the Dordogne are mostly the species Semillion, Sauvignon and Muscadelle.

Red and rosé wines in the Dordogne derive mostly from the Cabernet-Sauvignon, Cabernet-Franc and Merlot grapes. A committee of tasters, drawn from ninety-three Périgord communes, decides which wines may be given the coveted title *'Appellation d'Origine Contrôlée'*. Unique to the Dordogne among the *départements* of France is the fact that this distinction is given to both red and white wines, in roughly equal proportions, making about 50 million bottles a year altogether.

There are two excellent methods whereby the visitor to Périgord can become familiar with the different wines of the region. One way is to visit one of the *caves coopératives*. The best known and biggest is at Monbazillac, a few kilometres south of Bergerac on the way to Eymet, and situated near the splendid sixteenth-century Château Monbazillac, with its jolly pointed roofs and four chubby turrets. Since Monbazillac became a Huguenot town during the Wars of Religion, Château Monbazillac now houses a Protestant museum. As if to drive a final nail into the coffin of English puritan objections to good wine, it is this Protestant château that today houses the wine-tasting centre of the Dordogne's largest *cave coopérative*.

Château Monbazillac welcomes visitors every day of the week all the year round, taking parties in groups for a small fee and even providing English guides in July and August. Visitors to other *caves coopératives* are welcome if they first telephone and make an appointment. But the second and equally delightful method of tasting and learning about the wines of the Dordogne is to find one of the wine-fairs, such as the one held on a couple of days each August in the village of Cénac. Here not only the large *caves coopératives* but also the small family wine-makers set up little booths and invite the visitor to taste their produce entirely free of charge and without obligation. The walls of the tents are festooned with pictures of Cyrano de Bergerac, with his legendary long nose, sniffing a glass and pronouncing himself satisfied with its bouquet (*'Un vin qui a du nez . . .'*). As well as tasting the wines at the various stalls – and almost certainly eventually coming away from the fair with a case of a dozen bottles or so – the visitor can arm himself with shoals of literature, with maps and guides and booklets of recipes for cooking in Périgord wine. Often beginning, in the manner of George Saintsbury, with an invocation of Holy Scripture (such as Ecclesiasticus 21.27), the leaflets not only extol the virtues of the wines one has just tasted but also explain how they were created and offer advice to those who might want to lay them down for drinking in coming years.

What then are these wines? The best known is Monbazillac itself, created from grapes grown on 2,700 hectares of land south of the river Dordogne around Château Monbazillac. The soil is chalky clay. In this part of Périgord the climate is almost that of the Midi. The grapes become exceptionally mature because the situation of the vineyards causes morning mists followed by extreme heat as the sun dissipates them. The vine-growers leave the grapes of Monbazillac on the vines until very late in the autumn, waiting for what is known as the 'noble rot' (*la pourriture noble*). This is caused by a mould or fungus known as *botrytis cinerea*, which attacks the skin of the grapes. Water escapes, the berries shrivel up, and then, very carefully, they are handpicked, cut from the vines with special scissors.

These grapes produce a remarkable, very sweet, golden-yellow wine, with a superb aroma. The finest Monbazillacs (such as those named 'Grande Réserve', 'Château Monbazillac' and 'Château Septy') deserve keeping, for they age beautifully when properly stored in slightly humid conditions at a constant temperature of 15 degrees.

They should be drunk very cold, at around 5 degrees. They are a splendid apéritif, beautifully accompany *pâté de foie gras* and are strong enough to be drunk alongside an ice-cream or sorbet.

Périgourdins also cook with the less great vintages. A ripe melon, cut in half, is enhanced by the addition (to each half) of a glass of Monbazillac, a trace of Angostura bitters and a few slices of walnut. In Périgueux bars a cocktail is served made of eight tenths Monbazillac, one tenth Grand Marnier, one tenth Campari and a slice of orange.

Whereas Monbazillac is always white, those Périgord wines carrying the name Bergerac can be red, white or rosé. Vineyards producing Bergerac wine provide 250,000 hectolitres of white wine and 150,000 hectolitres of red wine each year. The Monbazillac region covers no more than five communes of Périgord; the whole Bergerac wine-producing area embraces no fewer than ninety-three.

And Bergerac wines have been drunk for far longer than Monbazillac wine, which dates only from the sixteenth century, when the monks of the Abbey of Saint-Martin replaced the forests south of the river with vines. For centuries before that Bergerac wines had been so much relished as to threaten the wine-trade of Bordeaux. A document of 1254 describes the enmity between the wine-makers of the two regions. The people of Bordeaux tried to resist the right of the wine-makers of Bergerac to sell wines outside their own region until 1520, when a decree of François I insisted on freedom of trade.

Today it is possible to drink Bergerac rouge, Bergerac rosé, Bergerac blanc sec and Bergerac blanc moelleux. The people of the *arrondissement* are modest about their wines, describing them as possessing 'neither arrogance nor vanity'. Even so, Bergerac wines are exceptionally pleasant to drink. Bergerac rouge is a fine shimmering red, fruity, and quite powerful when drunk young. It can age well (any dealer will tell his customers whether or not to lay a particular bottle down), and Périgourdins often drink it slightly chilled.

They drink Bergerac rosé as a summer refreshment and regard it as the finest wine to accompany spicy southern food. Bergerac blanc sec is splendidly thirst-quenching – the kind of wine that Montaigne would have drunk at any time of the day – and, served chilled (though not quite so chilled as Monbazillac), complements the fine *hors d'œuvre* and seafoods served in Périgord. Finally, Bergerac blanc moelleux, with its fine bouquet, can be drunk from its earliest years as a companion of *foie gras*, of melons and of all kinds of desserts, its flavour differing markedly from Monbazillac – not only because the latter is made from the noble rot, but also because the clay on which the wines of Bergerac blanc moelleux grow is siliceous rather than chalky.

A great Dordogne wine which could be forgiven for arrogance is Pécharmant. The Pécharmant vineyards are situated north of the river a few kilometres west of Bergerac, and cover some 170 hectares. 'Pech' is a Périgord word meaning hill. This 'charming hill' is built up of a soil deriving ultimately from the granite substructure washed down long ago from the Massif Central and now topped with clay containing traces of iron. The producers of Pécharmant carefully limit the amount they will sell, so as not to devalue the quality of their wine. It derives its chief characteristics – its body and its bouquet – from the Cabernet-Sauvignon grape. Cabernet-Franc brings it more delicacy. Because the makers of Pécharmant hold that the Cabernet grapes lack the subtlety they desire, the Merlot grape is added. Finally the long-grown red cot grape known as Malbec adds its own particular velvety smoothness to create in Pécharmant a magnificent full-bodied red wine which needs to wait three or even four years before it should be drunk and reaches its best only after five to seven years laying down in a good cellar. (Some wine-lovers wait even ten years before drinking a treasured vintage.)

In the Dordogne Pécharmant is drunk with game, with red meats and with cheese. It is vigorous enough to be drunk with a *contre-filet* cooked with roquefort cheese, but gentle enough not to spoil the taste of snails done in pastry with *cèpes*.

These are not the only wines that will have been tasted by those who visit the *caves coopératives* or the Dordogne wine-fairs. Just west of the Pécharmant vineyards are those vineyards from which comes the sweet white Rosette, its pale straw colour distinguishing it from another fine sweet white wine, that of Saussignac, whose vines grow south of the river. And it would be foolish not to sample the Montravel wines, created from vines grown over fourteen communes at the very western edge of the Dordogne, if only because the great Michel de Montaigne was born and lived here. Montravel, Côtes de Montravel and Haut Montravel indicate white wines which the Périgourdins describe as lively and fruity. All of them, sec, demi-sec or moelleux, possess fine bouquets. All have at least twelve degrees of alcohol content.

And, in addition, Dordogne produces that sparkling (or '*pétillant*') wine which its inhabitants like to drink chilled at parties, as well as an amazing number of different kinds of eau-de-vie. Eau-de-vie is made from plums, from walnuts, from apricots, from pears, from raspberries, from cherries, from bilberries and from much else. It is expensive and highly charged with alcohol. Wandering round a Dordogne winefair, the visitor is wise not to try too much.

Eau-de-vie, especially made from Dordogne walnuts, is a warming drink. It makes an excellent nightcap as well as a most satisfying end to any meal, adding its own richness to the gastronomic joys of Périgord.

In *Le Notaire du Havre* Georges Duhamel describes Laurent's first day at school. Chapter 5 begins with Laurent's mother getting the boy ready. She loved what she was doing, Laurent recalls. She 'held me very tightly, plaiting my hair in tiny bits, and purring lightly, as gourmets do when they are eating something exquisite' (*faisait entendre un léger ronron, comme les gourmets quand ils mangent quelque chose de fin*). On any day in the Dordogne, in any one of a thousand restaurants and hotels, towards the end of a meal one can hear the contented *ronrons* of countless satisfied guests.

❖ 4 ❖

The Dordogne and the British

'It is said that nothing is rarer in Paris than the finest wines of Bordeaux from a good year,' wrote Alexandre Dumas the Elder in his *Grand Dictionnaire de cuisine*, 'since the British, who adore them have carried them all off.' The British, like Dumas, have also for centuries adored the wines of Bergerac, of Domme, Saint-Cyprien, Montignac and Monpazier. These were in the past brought down the great river and shipped to England. So highly have the British regarded the wines of Bordeaux that we have invented the word 'claret', unknown to the French, to dignify them.

And for many centuries the British have been found in Périgord, today as tourists, in the past as invaders. Some of our greatest heroes and villains lived in Périgord for most of their adult lives. The brutal Simon de Montfort, justified by his total allegiance to the Papacy, pillaged and devastated the area. Richard Cœur de Lion was killed here. The region was ravaged during the Hundred Years War by the proud and ultimately tragic Black Prince. This same savage period created the remarkable *bastides* – fortified towns built by Englishmen or Frenchmen who hated and feared each other.

The English lost the Hundred Years War, but the mistrust it caused was finally forgotten only in the twentieth century, when Charles de Gaulle sought refuge in London to rally his country against Hitler. Then, many in the Dordogne preferred to side with the British rather than collaborate with the Nazis. It was during this time that Cyril Connolly longed for a yellow Périgord cottage. After the war the courageous, sad Nancy Cunard bought one.

The most romantic name in the whole story is that of Eleanor of Aquitaine. For fifteen years she was the wife of King Louis VII of

France, who had married her in 1137 when she was only fifteen. It was a marriage of convenience. Eleanor's dowry, inherited from her father, was Aquitaine. Louis was, in her view, ridiculously pious: 'I have married a monk,' she complained, 'not a king.' Nevertheless, she bore him two daughters.

They spent two and a half years away from France on a crusade. On this holy mission the ill-matched pair finally realized that they could no longer stand each other; they began to live apart. On their return it was conveniently discovered that they had married within the prohibited degrees of relationship as laid down by the Church. Their marriage was annulled.

Eleanor was still young and extremely beautiful. Moreover she was rich, able to confer the Duchy of Aquitaine on anyone she cared to marry. She loved gaiety, patronized the arts and was enchanted by the troubadours of Périgord. Two lords immediately sought her hand in marriage. Eleanor evaded them (one was the younger brother of her former husband). She sent urgent messages to Henry Plantagenet, Duke of Normandy and future King of England, and on Whitsunday 1152, only eight weeks after the annulment of Eleanor's first marriage, they were married in the cathedral at Poitiers. They commemorated the match by giving a stained-glass portrait of themselves for the foot of the east window of the cathedral.

Henry Plantagenet was now Duke of Aquitaine, but Louis VII refused to recognize his title. Henry spent the autumn of 1153 in Aquitaine, trying to enforce his and his wife's authority. One year later he became King of England. He and Eleanor were crowned in Westminster Abbey on 19 December 1154.

Thus began the involvement of England in the affairs of France, although the truth is that the early English medieval kings were as much French as they were English. As the historian Jules Michelet put it in his *Tableau de la France*, 'the sons of Eleanor – Henry, Richard Cœur de Lion and John – never knew whether they were Poitevins or English, Angevins or Normans'. King Henry II Plantagenet always dressed in the French fashion, wearing the short Angevin cloak, so that he was nicknamed 'court-mantel'. Eleanor grew estranged from him, partly because she disliked his habit of having children by other women such as fair Rosamund (daughter of Walter de Clifford), who bore him William Longespee, the Earl of Salisbury. The queen herself bore Henry five sons and three daughters. Some of his sons took French wives and even joined forces with the King of France against their father.

The son who remained faithful to Henry II and his claims on France was Richard Cœur de Lion. Richard, who succeeded Henry as king in 1189, met his death ten years later in Périgord. Like his mother, Eleanor of Aquitaine, he loved and supported the troubadours. The greatest of the troubadours, Bertran de Born, who lived in Château Hautefort, had fought against Henry Plantagenet, but Henry forgave him and he and Richard became devoted friends. Bertrand de Born called Richard Cœur de Lion 'Oc e No' (Périgord patois: Richard 'Yea and Nay'), but not because he vacillated or could not be trusted. On the contrary, Bertran was referring to the instructions of Christ that one need not swear on anything in heaven or earth so long as one's 'yea' meant 'yea' and one's 'nay' meant 'nay'. Richard Cœur de Lion was a man whose word could be entirely trusted.

The counts of Périgord had long recognized the dukes of Aquitaine as their overlords when Eleanor delivered the duchy to Henry Plantagenet. From time to time, however, they rebelled. Richard Cœur de Lion energetically asserted his father's rights over the duchy. On 11 April 1182 he launched a surprise attack on Count Élie of Périgord's fortress of Puy-Saint-Front. The fortress contained the bones of St Front himself, the apostle of Périgord. Its inhabitants threw in their lot with the kings of France, under the inspiration of Count Élie. They reckoned without Richard Cœur de Lion, who took the fortress with ease and then pressed on to take the eleventh-century castle of Excideuil, before marching north into Limousin. Richard did not try to hold on to the castles he had taken until he was joined by his father and his eldest brother. The three of them returned with their troops to force Élie, along with Aimar, Viscount of Limousin, to sue for peace. Aimar's first and third sons were taken hostage. Puy-Saint-Front surrendered and its walls were demolished.

Usually Richard Cœur de Lion was magnanimous in victory. When he captured the formidable castle of Beynac, he did not destroy it but replaced its lord with one of his own allies. He was generous to the monks of Cadouin, where he prayed before the alleged winding sheet of Christ, brought to Périgord from Antioch in 1117.

In 1199 he met his death. The château he was besieging, at Châlus, is no longer in Périgord but lies in the *département* of Haute-Vienne. The keep from which an archer fired the fatal shot still stands there. The lords of Gourdon rejoiced at the fall of their mortal enemy. Richard took three days to die, during which he forgave the man who killed him. But the archer was later flayed to death. The lords of Gourdon, whose vassal he was, were unable to save him. Richard's mother, Eleanor of Aquitaine, outlived him by five years; she died in 1204 aged eighty-two years.

No peace came to Périgord. As if the dynastic and feudal rivalries of these early medieval kings had not brought enough havoc to Périgord, the Church now decided to proclaim a crusade against heresy. Spreading into the region were the beliefs of the Cathars, who in France had come to be called Albigensians. These were Christians who genuinely hoped for perfection not in some remote heaven but in this life. They drew their inspiration from the mystics of the Levant (for the heresy – as the Church dubbed it – was strongest in those parts of Languedoc where textile merchants traded with Levantines). No doubt they were also attempting to come to terms with poverty, plague, famine, early death. In twelfth- and thirteenth-century France, the miseries of life outweighed its sweetness for most people. For such men and women, a doctrine which taught that the flesh and the material things of this life had been created by the devil, that these fleshly elements imprisoned the pure and happy soul, and that a man or woman could in this world escape the bonds of the flesh, was exceedingly seductive.

But these beliefs were also subversive of the structure of the Catholic Church, for its rites – baptism, the eucharist, holy unction – all implicitly assumed that material things could convey a spiritual blessing. In addition, the wretched standards of many contemporary clergy made it easier for Albigensians to reject the spiritual authority of the Church. As Pope Innocent III himself observed, the clergy were for the most part 'dumb dogs who cannot bark, who absolve the rich and condemn the poor, who accumulate benefices and give bishoprics to unworthy priests'. He added that in the diocese of Narbonne were parsons who 'abandoned their cloth, took women and lived as money-changers, lawyers, jugglers and doctors'.

For a time the 'heresy' and Catholicism lived together in peaceful

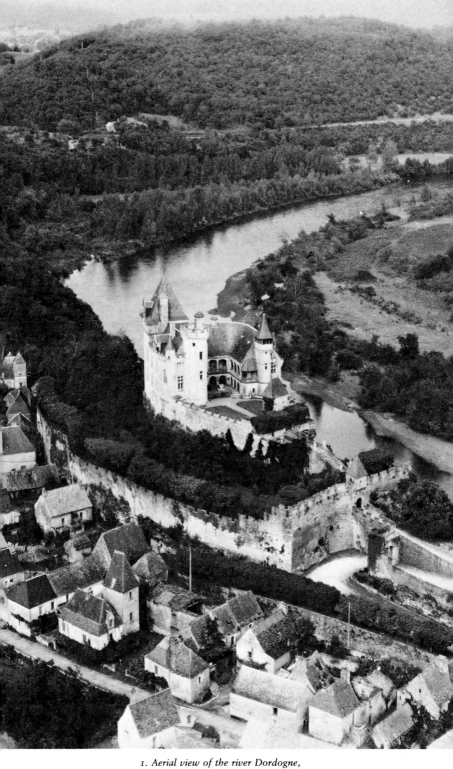

1. *Aerial view of the river Dordogne,*
with the Château de Montfort and the village of Montfort.

2. *Château and village of Hautefort.*

3. Sixteenth-century Château de Losse, on the river Vézère.

4. *Aerial view of Sarlat Cathedral – bottom right,
the 'Lantern of the Dead'.*

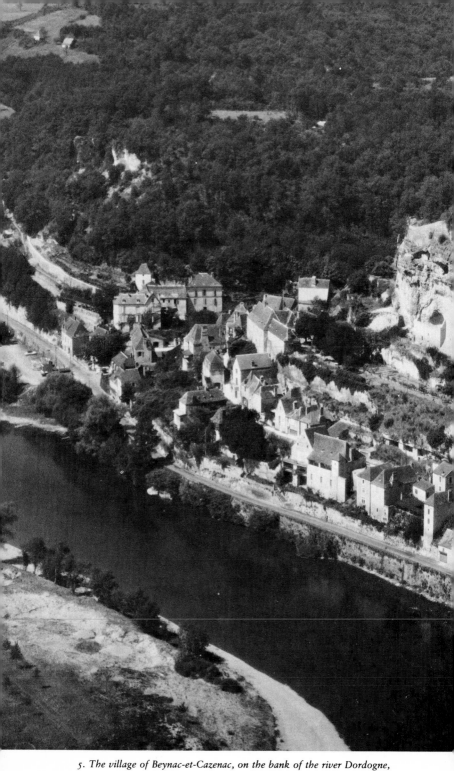

5. *The village of Beynac-et-Cazenac, on the bank of the river Dordogne, nestling under its formidable château.*

6. Tower of the Hôtel de Maleville, Sarlat.

coexistence. The Church, above all in the person of St Bernard, strenuously worked to reform the manners of the clergy and to convert the heretics. In 1147 the Abbot of Sarlat had invited St Bernard to preach against the Albigensians. He arrived in August as the town was suffering a terrible plague, cured many and attempted to convert others. He had little success in his second aim.

By the end of the century the Church was less tolerant. In 1208 Innocent III decided that the heretics should be destroyed, and the Albigensian crusade was led by the formidable Anglo-Norman, Simon de Montfort.

Contemporaries described him as gentle and chivalrous. In fact he was implacable, ambitious and brutal. Richard Cœur de Lion spared Château Beynac when he captured it; Simon de Montfort razed it to the ground. He was already Viscount of Béziers and of Carcassonne, but was determined to become Count of Toulouse. The Albigensian crusade gave him his opportunity to achieve all that his ambition desired. He offered his services without reservation to the Pope. Already he was rich. As Lord of Montfort and Évreux, he naturally took part in the quarrels between the kings of England and France, since he held lands under both combatants. The historian and Anglican Bishop Mandell Creighton observed that he 'seems to have used his position between them as a means of getting all possible advantage from both'. He shrewdly married Amiccia de Beaumont, sister and co-heiress of Robert, Earl of Leicester. Robert died, leaving de Montfort in possession of the earldom. Mandell Creighton wrote: 'He was a strange mixture of an adventurer, a statesman, a fanatic, a man whose character it is difficult to understand and sympathize with. He threw himself entirely on the side of the Pope, and strove, by making himself a zealous instrument of Papal vengeance, to secure his own aggrandisement.'

Happily for Périgord, Simon de Montfort's depredations mostly occurred further south. Even so, he destroyed a good deal in the region. The year 1214 saw Simon de Montfort seize Domme, Beynac and Castelnaud, and burn to the ground the château that today bears his name. He had only four more years to live. On 25 June 1218 he besieged Toulouse. Before the battle he attended mass, observing, 'Let us now go and die, if that is necessary for Him who was content to die for us.' During the siege his brother Guy was wounded. Simon de

Montfort rushed to his side. A stonemason of Toulouse heard the moans of de Montfort's brother and threw at the feared Simon a huge boulder which smashed his helmet, his skull, his teeth and his jaw. The scourge of the heretics fell dead.

The death of de Montfort did not bring peace to Périgord. England and France remained enemies until 1259. In that year the Treaty of Paris gave England the southern part of Périgord. The King of France took the northern part, including Périgueux, which had resolutely remained French throughout the struggles.

It was an unstable arrangement and suited neither side, but France remained relatively peaceful until the line of Capetian kings died out in 1328 and Philip I V assumed the throne. Philip was of the house of Valois. So was the King of England, Edward I I I – a Frenchman, though today he lies splendidly entombed in Canterbury Cathedral. In 1337 Philip decided to deprive Edward of the Duchy of Guyenne. Edward retaliated three years later by declaring himself King of France.

Thus began what nineteenth-century historians called the Hundred Years War, though it lasted over a hundred years and was more an interminable series of raids, battles and skirmishes than a continuous war. Anxious that its valuable wine-trade with England might be altogether destroyed, Bordeaux appealed for help to Edward III. Edward seized the opportunity to invade the entire region. His legendary son, the Black Prince, made his first devastating entry into Périgord.

These were the years when English archers won the famous victories of Crécy and Poitiers. In 1348 the chronicler Walsingham, noting the booty brought back by English soldiers, observed that 'few English-women did not possess something from Caen, Calais, or another town over the seas, such as clothing, furs or cushions'. But the course of the war in Périgord reveals that the notion that the King of England could for ever hold on to this part of France was ultimately absurd. Towns and castles were simply taken and then retaken. Bergerac, for instance, was captured by the English in 1345. The Earl of Derby became its lord. But the French took it back in 1377.

The carnage was great. From 1348 Pope Clement V I and his succes-sor, Innocent V I, sought, from their palace at Avignon, to bring about a permanent peace. The Black Prince, however, was determined to recapture those parts of Périgord that the French had taken from the English king. In 1355, in his twenty-fifth year, he landed at Bordeaux, and proceeded to ravage the countryside, using his new, brilliant and vicious tactic: the *'chevauchée'*. Knights on horseback made swift, devastating raids, pillaging and laying waste the French towns. Derby pushed inwards from Bergerac, reaching Domme, where some of the inhabitants went over to the English (only to be hanged in the main square of the town when the French took it back ten years later).

The capture of the French king at Poitiers in 1356 persuaded many Périgourdins that the English were the winning side. In 1359 two Sarladais merchants, Bernard and Sicard Donadéi, plotted with Gilbert of Domme to deliver Sarlat to the invader. The plot was discovered and the two merchants were arrested: Bernard died in prison; Sicard was sewn into a sack and drowned in the river Cuze. Gilbert of Domme took his revenge, burning down the outlying districts of Sarlat and savaging the countryside. The Sarladais sued for peace and were forced to pay Gilbert 500 gold florins.

The following year Sarlat was in any case obliged to swear fealty to the English king. The humiliating Treaty of Brétigny forced the imprisoned King of France to cede Périgord once again to the British, though Edward III renounced his claim to the throne of France.

For ten years there was relative peace. Then the French fought back, led by the famous chevalier, Bertrand Du Guesclin. The army of the Black Prince had been partly destroyed by disease and dysentery fighting in Castile. John of Gaunt, Duke of Lancaster, encountered similar problems in 1373, when he left London with 30,000 men to march to the Dordogne and join his ally John de Montfort, Duke of Brittany. On its way south Gaunt's army destroyed towns and villages, but was continually harassed by lightning raids of guerrillas. He could not solve the problems of feeding such a huge force. By the time he reached the Dordogne hunger and disease had reduced the number of his soldiers to 6,000. In these circumstances John de Montfort, faced with Du Guesclin's well-fed force (which was based on Montignac) prudently gave up the fight and withdrew.

Compared with France, England was a tiny country with (in those days) a tiny population. The English kings who hoped to hold on to their Aquitaine inheritance could only do so by hiring mercenaries and making alliances with local lords. Troops could not pillage for ever. Food needed to be paid for, unless the English were to keep down their duchy by terror alone. The money available to Edward III was running out. To make matters much worse for his ambitions, the French were in alliance with Castile, whose navy in 1372 had managed to sink an English convoy carrying not only men and horses but also £20,000 for the defence of Aquitaine.

Not surprisingly, the duchy was in French hands again by the end of the decade. But in the next century Henry V revived the English claim not only to Périgord but to the French throne as well. After the English victory at Agincourt in 1415 and Henry's betrothal to Catherine de Valois, the Treaty of Troyes formally acknowledged Henry as heir to the French king, who was now mad. The French were rallied by Joan of Arc. The English burnt her as a witch. But the war was nearing its end.

It ended on the banks of the river Dordogne itself, near a town which symbolizes the vain hope of England to own part of France. Libourne was built by, and named after, Roger de Leyburn, on the orders of Edward I. Situated at the confluence of the Dordogne and the Isle, it was designed as part of the defences of Périgord. Yet scarcely ten years after its completion Libourne was in the hands of the French.

Six miles or so up the river Dordogne from Libourne lies the town of Castillon. Today it is called Castillon-la-Bataille, since the final battle of the Hundred Years War took place here. In 1453 it was held by the forces of Henry VI of England. King Charles VII of France decided to besiege it.

John Talbot, Earl of Shrewsbury and Waterford, now aged seventy-five and the last survivor of Henry V's great generals, marched from Bordeaux in an attempt to relieve Castillon. In the ensuing battle the English troops decided to fight with their backs to the river, thus cutting off the possibility of retreating. Talbot's horse was brought down, the earl himself was trapped beneath it, and a French archer named Michel Perunin killed him with an axe. Many of his troops perished as they attempted to run away. The English held on to Bordeaux for another few months, but although Henry VI and Charles VII never concluded a formal peace treaty, the Hundred Years War was over.

For Périgord it had been a disastrous era. In addition to the depredations of war and the lawlessness it occasioned, plague and disease (including the Black Death) ravaged its population. Whole villages were abandoned and fell into ruin; others were viciously destroyed. Although the upper orders in society tried to insist on their rights when taken prisoner, the poor and humble were routinely slaughtered.

In *A Distant Mirror*, Barbara W. Tuchman's classic account of the calamitous fourteenth century, the story is told of Petrarch's mission to congratulate the French king on behalf of Galeazzo Visconti, after the king had been liberated from the English. The year was 1361. Petrarch was horrified with what he saw. 'Everywhere was solitude, desolation and misery,' he wrote; 'fields are deserted, houses ruined and empty except in the walled towns; everywhere you see the fatal footprints of the English and the hateful scars still bleeding from their swords.'

Petrarch's reference to the walled towns is fascinating to anyone who visits the Dordogne, for here are some of the most beautiful in France. Known as '*bastides*', they evolved as a measure of protection against the violence of the wars between England and France (all were built in the century preceding Petrarch's visit). Not all the *bastides* that survive in south-west France now lie in the *département* of the Dordogne, but three of the finest do – Beaumont, Domme and Monpazier. Today their peace and extreme beauty seem to belie their origins in one of the most vicious eras in the history of Périgord.

The *bastides* were completely new towns, built with the main eye on defence: defensive positions were chosen; massive walls were built around them, pierced by formidable gates; and within their walls the *bastides* reveal a pattern of houses and streets not seen in France since the Roman towns decayed. Usually three straight roads run the length of a *bastide*, with narrower ones forming a grid pattern by running the other way. Clearly the inhabitants felt the need to man any part of the town's defences with the maximum speed.

In one sense, the English can be said to have invented the *bastides* of south-west France. Certainly the first two of them, Lalinde and Villefranche-du-Périgord, were built in the 1260s on the instructions of King Henry III. But, as we have seen, Henry III was French as much as he was English. Alphonse de Poitiers, who built Villefranche-du-Périgord on Henry's behalf, was actually the brother of Louis VII, Eleanor of Aquitaine's former husband.

If, in this paradoxical sense, the English first created *bastides*, the

French enthusiastically took up the idea. French kings and English kings saw the same advantage in building these new towns. A *bastide* enabled a far-away monarch to lay claim to part of Périgord and set up there a group of citizens to support that claim.

Such hopes were not always fulfilled, for *bastides* were not in fact impregnable. Villefranche-du-Périgord, for example, changed hands more than once during the wars, was frequently destroyed and rebuilt, and now contains only vestiges of the thirteenth century – notably its massive towers and its market hall. Other *bastides* were seen to be too valuable to be destroyed; though taken and retaken, they survived intact.

Because the founders of *bastides* needed to persuade people to live in them, these towns were often granted charters conferring remarkable freedom on their citizens. Agents and seneschals, appointed by the kings, saw to the building of *bastides*, but did not remain there as overlords. They had other work to do. Captal de Buch, who founded Monpazier on behalf of Edward I, was one of the most remarkable soldiers ever to fight for England. His life was one of crusades and battles sometimes far away from his native France. The English king could not afford to leave so great a soldier in charge of a *bastide* in Aquitaine, nor would Captal de Buch have wished to stay there. The French so feared him that when Charles V finally captured de Buch, the French king scandalized even his own followers by refusing all offers to ransom his enemy.

Since *bastides* owed no allegiance to any local lord, none of them contains a castle. But castles had in the past given at least the illusion of security to those who lived near their walls. The citizens of *bastides* were content to be free from overlords, but they were less happy to do without the security of a castle, in spite of their huge surrounding walls and fine defensive sites. For this reason they frequently built not a castle but a powerful fortified church inside the *bastide*. The church at Beaumont, for instance (unusual in the Dordogne for its gothic style), is massive. If the thick double walls (which can still be seen there) failed to keep out invaders, the inhabitants could seek safety in the house of God; the solid buttresses and four powerful, crenellated towers were clearly designed for defence rather than worship.

One of the ways in which Philip the Bold persuaded Périgourdins to move into Domme was to build it high over the Dordogne on a virtually impregnable rock. Another was to give them jurisdiction

over all the small villages surrounding the *bastide*. Other *bastides*
were given similar privileges. As a result, the areas around *bastides*
became some of the few relatively prosperous and well-run parts of
Périgord in the turbulent fourteenth century.

And every *bastide* was granted the right to its own market, to be
used by the peasants and farmers of the surrounding land. This privi-
lege was incorporated in the architecture of the *bastide*: the market
was accommodated in a spacious market hall in the centre of the
town. At Beaumont this still survives, looking much as it must have
done when Lucas de Thaney built the town on behalf of Edward I in
1272. That at Monpazier seems perhaps even more delightful since the
whole *bastide* is still virtually intact. Captal de Buch founded it on
land which the English king had obtained from Pierre de Gontaut,
whose castle at Biron is only three kilometres away. Monpazier,
founded in 1284, took longer to complete than Edward I liked, for the
citizens he had designated as its future inhabitants were reluctant to
empty their purses on behalf of the English king. Today its walls, grid
plan, gates and market square are almost completely unspoilt: the
market square has a gothic arcade and the market hall retains its old
grain measures. Only the fortified church has changed, rebuilt in the
mid sixteenth century and given a renaissance doorway.

Monpazier survived, in spite of changing hands many times during
the Hundred Years War. So did Domme, the finest example of a
bastide built not by the English but by the French. High on its rock
overlooking the river, Domme was built with the customary grid
pattern of the other *bastides* – though the lie of the land makes this
sometimes go astray. The town was built with two churches, and in
the centre is the market square and market hall. Of the three great
gateways set in the massive walls surrounding Domme the Porte des
Tours is magnificent; the Porte del Bos only slightly less so. Philip the
Bold strictly laid down how the *bastide* was to be governed, with
consuls who changed every year and rigorously punished malefactors.
Philip spelled out the obligations as well as the rights of the inhabitants. You can still see the building where he established a royal mint,
said to be the oldest house in the *bastide*, bearing the inscription:

Maison du Batteur de Monnaie du Roy Philippe III le Hardi

+ 1282 +

Though Domme appears impregnable, the English took it in 1347 and again in 1417. Once taken, Domme was not easily retaken. In both centuries the English held on to this French *bastide* for over two decades.

After the English had been driven out of Aquitaine in 1453 Périgord did not find peace for long. Domme survived more or less intact the Hundred Years War, but during the Wars of Religion the Huguenot Captain Geoffroi de Vivans took the *bastide* and burned down one of its churches. Both sides committed atrocities for the sake of their version of the Christian faith. At least in these and the later sufferings of Périgord the English played no part, but the memory of two centuries of vicious struggles between England and France soured relationships between the two countries for centuries to come. Barbara W. Tuchman went so far as to judge that 'Between England and France the war left a legacy of mutal antagonism that was to last until necessity required alliance on the eve of 1914.'

Although in the First World War the Dordogne was the scene of no great battle, the *département* lost over 40,000 of its sons, fighting alongside the British. The lists of those who did not return are inscribed in village churches and by roadsides. I counted twenty-seven names amateurishly carved on the memorial at Ladouze, a hamlet comprising scarcely twenty-seven homes.

Mutual suffering brought the two countries together. Two writers in particular sought to interpret the British and the French to each other after the First World War, and both responded especially to the Dordogne. They were the Englishman Rudyard Kipling and the Frenchman André Maurois.

Kipling had liked the French since a childhood holiday in Paris with his father, and he had often toured the country before the Great War. When war broke out, he had a son ready to fight. John Kipling had been educated at Wellington, in those days the English public school with the most pronounced military traditions. He then crammed at a private school for entry to the Royal Military Academy at Sandhurst. In August 1914, not yet seventeen years old, he applied for a commission in the British Army and was turned down because of his poor eyesight. His father used his influence with Lord Roberts to get John a commission in the Irish Guards.

By the time John was sent to France in August the following year,

Rudyard Kipling was also there, visiting the battle areas. The father wrote to his son: 'Don't forget the beauty of rabbit netting overhead against hand-grenades. Even tennis netting is better than nothing.' The advice was pathetically useless. The following month, at the battle of Loos, John Kipling was shot through the head while attacking a position deep in the enemy defences.

Rudyard Kipling tried to take the loss stoically: 'he had his heart's desire and he didn't have a long time in the trenches . . .' he wrote: 'It was a short life. I'm sorry that all the years' work ended in that one afternoon – but lots of people are in our position – and it's something to have bred a man. The wife is standing it wonderfully tho' she, of course, clings to the bare hope of his being a prisoner. I've seen what shells can do, and I don't.'

But two lines of verse in Kipling's *Epitaphs of the War* show that inside his heart there was more bitterness:

My son was killed while laughing at some jest. I would
  I knew
What it was, and it might serve me in a time when jests
  are few.

As Kipling's biographer Charles Carrington observed, 'every visit to France after the war had the character of a pilgrimage'. On their first such visit the Kiplings turned aside to explore the desolated battlefield of Loos. Chiefly to honour his son's memory, Kipling became one of the Imperial War Graves commissioners.

Each year he would tour France in a motor-car. He absorbed the lore of the country, such as never to talk to a dog on duty or pulling a cart. He came across a fair in a town by a great river where the citizens (as today in Périgord) attached electric power wires casually to the tree trunks 'with no more protection than an occasional warning that if you touch them you will perish'. (In Britain, he added, 'a pensioned Civil Servant will guard every one'.) He discovered the kindness of the French. With one trivial exception, he declared, 'I have in twenty-five years of road-travel met nothing but kindness and prompt help from everyone – even from my ancient friends, the gendarmes.' He mused on the difference between the French and the English, deciding that the Frenchman's character was formed by his thrift, 'the acceptance of hard living which fortifies the moral interior as a small pebble assists the digestion of fowls'. This, averred Kipling, 'allows its practitioner to be as extravagant as he pleases in speech and oratory', whereas 'The Englishman's inveterate habit of waste explains his inveterate habit of understatement.'

And marvelling at the 'black diamond' of Périgord, Kipling wrote one of his remarkable animal stories about a dog that hunted truffles.

'*Teem*' – *Treasure-Hunter* is told in the first person by the dog himself. Teem has inherited his father's nose for truffles and his mother's practical philosophy. Though all three of them hunt truffles, the father is the true professional. 'Nothing could prevent my adored Mother from demanding at once the piece of sugar which was her just reward for any Truffle she found,' says Teem. 'My revered Father, on the other hand, contented himself with the strict practice of his Art. So soon as that Pierre, our Master, stooped to dig at the spot indicated, my Father moved on to fresh triumphs.'

Teem's marvellously sensitive nose can tell him at once not only that someone is pleasant but also whether he is kind, gentle and equable in temperament. His head is filled with wise saws, such as 'An honest heart outweighs many disadvantages of ignorance and low birth.' He finds a new master – a charcoal-burner. He falls into bad (human) company. But all comes out well in the end, and Teem learns the way to contentment through the old rule, 'Outside his Art an Artist must never dream.'

Through a dog Kipling introduced Englishmen to the delights of the Dordogne truffle. Through his stories of the Raj he taught André Maurois the qualities of the British imperialist: 'a good technician, devoted body and soul to his task . . . loyal to his friends and severe with the rebels', as Maurois put it. Maurois came to love the British when he was a liaison officer with the British Army in the Great War. (His first taste of battle was at Loos, where John Kipling died.) He came to marvel at an Englishman's reticence, sharing a tent and a bath-tub for six months with a British officer who never once asked was he married, what he did in peacetime or what he happened to be reading! In 1917 he conceived the idea for his first book: *The Silences of Colonel Bramble*. Colonel Bramble of the Highland Brigade, encamped outside Poperinghe in the First World War with his gramophone and box of records (containing 'The Bing Boys', 'Destiny Waltz', 'Caruso' and Mrs Finzi-

Magrini in 'La Tosca'), was, said Maurois, 'made up from ten colonels and generals compounded and kneaded together'. The taciturn Bramble hates arguments and murmurs, 'Pass the port' whenever Major Parker, the padre or Dr O'Grady try to draw him into one. When the French interpreter Aurelle provocatively cries that the French Revolution was carried out for the sake of the English, Bramble replies, 'Bravo messiou (*sic*). Stick up for your country. And please pass the port. I'm going to play you "The Mikado".' Whenever an enemy shell scatters gravel over Bramble, he humorously quotes from a padre's letter published in *The Times*: 'The life of the soldier is one of great hardship; not infrequently mingled with moments of great danger.'

André Maurois corrected the proofs of this, his first book, in March 1918 as the Germans were advancing on Amiens. The novel delighted both the French and the British. Within months of publication it sold 50,000 copies. At a dinner given for Maurois in 1921 at the Athenaeum, Lord Byng of Vimy said, 'We are all Brambles here.'

After the war and the death of his first wife Janine, Maurois, who was an Alsatian, sought solace with some friends in Périgord, in the little Château of Essendiéras between Périgueux and Limoges. He was entranced. 'At Essendiéras I fell in love simultaneously with the landscape of Périgord and with the woman who showed it to me,' Simone de Caillavet, daughter of the château. They married, and Maurois made Essendiéras the centre of his literary life. From here poured a stream of books interpreting the British not only to the French but also, in translation, to themselves: lives of Victoria, Disraeli, Shelley, Byron, Mrs Siddons, Mr and Mrs Bulwer Lytton, Cecil Rhodes, Sir Alexander Fleming, as well as a complete history of England and of the life and times of Edward VII, poured from his gifted pen.

In 1937 he gave three lectures in Paris on the English. 'When the English have adopted you,' he told his hearers, 'they will be your most faithful friends.' Wittily he explained to Frenchmen how to cope with the British character and British food. In conversation, he advised, 'If you are a world tennis-champion, say, "Yes, I don't play too badly." If you have crossed the Atlantic alone in a small boat, say, "I do a little sailing." ' He informed a Frenchman about to cross the Channel that 'In England there are two excellent meals: breakfast and tea. Keep your appetite for them. Introduce yourself to new pleasures in porridge, haddock, marmalade.'

The British, said Maurois, also 'like fighting with their backs to the wall'. Soon both Britons and Frenchmen would be once again in that position.

From his Dordogne home Maurois saw the approach of war. 'The vales of Périgord, lined with poplars and willows, were more beautiful and peaceful than ever in that month of July 1939. The purple roofs of the tenant farm of Brouillac in the evening sunlight stood in soft contrast to the green of the fields . . . But this enchanted silence seemed to be charged with mysterious menace,' he recalled.

When war broke out the Adjutant-General of the British army asked André Maurois to draw up ten commandments, to be distributed to every British soldier fighting in France. Maurois's tenth commandment read: 'The Alliance of France and England has been a political and military necessity. It must become a human reality. These two countries which need each other must hold each other in unreserved esteem. It is within your power to make ten, twenty, one hundred Frenchmen, regard England as an ally worthy of trust and affection.'

With these words Winston Churchill heartily agreed. In the First World War Churchill had come to admire the French soldier above all others. And in that war Charles de Gaulle had fought as an infantryman, was wounded three times and decorated with the Legion of Honour. These two giants were now to come together in the struggle of Britain and France against Hitler.

While de Gaulle was inspiring the French Resistance from his exile in London, the Dordogne played its part in that Resistance. The fate of one English *bastide*, Lalinde, is a grim reminder of the common cause of Britain and Périgord in that war. Lalinde today consists only of a few vestiges of its ramparts, along with the gate known as Porte Romane. Built in the thirteenth century by the Seneschal of Gascony on behalf of Henry III, this *bastide*, whose privileges, charter and design served as model for many others, was destroyed on the orders of the retreating Nazis in 1944, as a reprisal against the activities of the French Resistance in Périgord.

The Second World War brought Churchill and de Gaulle together, transformed the fortunes of both and in a curious way made its mark on the Dordogne too. Until 1938 Churchill had never heard of de Gaulle, who was still only a colonel and had written an ill-received book criticizing French defences. In that year, too, Churchill was himself an outsider in British politics. By 1940, after the withdrawal of 340,000 British troops from Dunkirk, Churchill was Prime Minister and de Gaulle (promoted to the rank of Brigadier-General) was in London begging him to authorize another British assault across the Channel and send more air squadrons to France.

By mid 1940 Marshal Pétain, the hero of Verdun, had formed a new French government and sued for peace. De Gaulle flew to London to set up a rival government-in-exile and to inspire from abroad the French Resistance. In a chapter which has for the most part described how the English and French have brutally slaughtered each other in Périgord it is good to be able now to give some account of how in the twentieth century they cooperated in the fight against Nazi tyranny.

The Dordogne first began to suffer from the war with the huge influx of refugees from Belgium and other parts of France who were fleeing the advancing German troops. By the middle of 1940 220,000 of these refugees had reached the *département*, to be accommodated in barns and outhouses and fed on rapidly dwindling supplies of food. After the armistice, the Dordogne remained part of the unoccupied zone of France, under the collaborationist government at Vichy, led by the eighty-four-year-old Marshal Pétain. There is little doubt that initially most Périgourdins were happy that the war was over. They looked forward to the return of captured French soldiers. But immediately several courageous opponents of collaboration made their views known. In Périgueux in one shop window was displayed a chamber-pot containing busts of Hitler and Mussolini. In the same city the Abbé Jean Sigala, professor of philosophy at the leading Catholic institute, resumed his duties after a short time as a prisoner of war and repeatedly denounced Pétain's policy.

Others, openly or in secret, set about gathering like-minded opponents of Vichy and the Nazis and tried to get in touch with de Gaulle in London. One such group was based on the small village of Saint-Antoine-de-Breuilh, nine miles from the spot where Talbot perished in 1453 and close by the ancient *bastide* of Sainte-Foy-la-Grande. Its leader was a Catholic, the son of a Protestant mother, and came of a family that had farmed at Saint-Antoine-de-Breuilh for 600 years. After hearing one of de Gaulle's first broadcasts from London, he and his friends set about gathering details of German troop and naval operations in and around the area and sending them to the government-in-exile by way of the British embassy in Geneva. When repeated messages elicited no reply, the group sent an elderly priest to London by way of Spain and Portugal. He took photographs of German and Italian ships and submarines in Bordeaux harbour, to convince the government-in-exile that the information was genuine. By November, de Gaulle's envoy had reached the Dordogne. He found a group of resisters thirty-strong, who took the code-name C.N.D., Confrères of Notre Dame.

Louis de la Bardonnie, the leader and founder of this group, himself observed that in 1940 resistance in France was the work of a very small minority. He remembered that at Sainte-Foy-la-Grande the parish priest, far from denouncing Pétain, put a huge portrait of the Marshal behind his altar on the grounds that he had saved France twice – once at Verdun in the First World War and now by suing for an armistice with Hitler. On the other hand, de la Bardonnie also knew friendly priests who would lend him a cassock if he needed a disguise. The Vichy authorities picked him up as a suspected resister in 1941 but could prove nothing against him and so released him after a few months. He and his friends saved many Jews from deportation and death during the Resistance and in general aimed at doing everything they could to harm the Vichy régime.

The ranks of such men were swollen suddenly when Hitler invaded Russia in June 1941 and every French Communist automatically became a resister. A further source of recruitment lay in exiles from the provinces annexed by Germany, for the Dordogne was one of the départements specially chosen to receive them. In 1942 two inspectors of police from Strasbourg were forced to leave their homes and live in Périgord. They immediately set about forming a group of resisters from other exiles from Alsace-Lorraine, code-named 'Bir-Hakeim'.

When the Allies invaded Normandy on 6 June 1944 the Resistance set about sabotaging the German retreat. De Gaulle had announced that members of the Resistance were soldiers, not civilians, and therefore if captured ought to be treated according to the proper conventions of warfare. This was special pleading. Technically the resisters were citizens of a country whose government had sued for peace and been granted an armistice. The German army treated them as traitors and, in its desperate attempt to conduct an orderly retreat, responded with punitive fury. Following a battle with the 'Bir-Hakeim' its survivors were publicly shot. After the war, when passions were still high, Freda White was told that the retreating Germans had taken twenty-eight women into the church at Saint-Vincent-le-Paluel near Sarlat, poured petrol over them and burned them to death. Either Freda White got her facts wrong, or she was being told one of the many false atrocity stories that circulated at the end of the war. At Saint-Vincent-le-Paluel I could find no monument to any murdered women, either inside or outside its romanesque church, though the vengeful Nazis certainly sacked its château in 1944, and outside the church is one polished, lonely plaque:

PERUSIN Mario

fusillé par les Nazis

le 28 Juin 1944

Elsewhere in the Dordogne, at the crossroads or village squares where they were executed, are similar monuments to the people of the Resistance, with the date they died. The sacked Château of Saint-Vincent-le-Paluel, with its lovely renaissance windows and delightful Rapunzel tower, is now being restored, rightly I believe. There is a time to forget. But it also seems to me good that in many parts of the Dordogne former members of the R.A.F. still meet annually to reminisce with their surviving *maquisard* friends and to pay tribute to their dead comrades beside the plaques marking where they were executed.

Freda White described these plaques as 'the last visible layer in this beautiful tragic land'. Thirty years later another layer has been added, directly connected with de Gaulle and the Resistance in the Dordogne and south-west France. De Gaulle's experiences in exile in London transformed the soldier into the politician and statesman. The Resistance brought him into contact with the remarkable man of letters André Malraux.

Just before the outbreak of the Second World War Malraux and his companion Josette Clotis had bought a house in the Dordogne, where he planned to write about the psychology of art. As soon as war was declared he offered his services to the French army. Imprisoned by the Germans, he escaped and fled with Josette Clotis to the Mediterranean village of Roquebrune in Free France.

In the autumn of 1942 he returned to the Dordogne and joined the Resistance. He tried to make contact with de Gaulle and with other Resistance movements throughout the whole of south-west France. By 1944, under the pseudonym 'Colonel Berger', Malraux was in charge of the Resistance group code-named F.F.I., which operated throughout the Dordogne, the Lot and Corrèze. With 1,500 men he fought to hamper the work of the German division formed specially to take reprisals on members of the Resistance and their families. He recounted how he was wounded, captured, imprisoned in Toulouse and threatened with execution. When the Germans fled the town Malraux claimed to have taken over the prison.

Many critics have observed that Malraux's account of his exploits always reads more like one of his novels than the unvarnished truth. None the less, de Gaulle was sufficiently impressed to appoint him minister of propaganda in his government after the liberation of France in 1944.

Malraux served as de Gaulle's minister for cultural affairs from 1958 to 1968. His house in the Dordogne and his experiences in the Resistance movement had deepened his love for and appreciation of the heritage of his country. Malraux's chef de cabinet for 1962, André Holleaux, recalled how the minister would speak of the rivers, the vineyards and the churches of south-west France 'with an incomparable eloquence'. Malraux was especially sensitive to the patterns and grouping of ancient buildings in the cities and towns of France. He was therefore proud to allow his name to be attached to the law of 4 August 1962, which provided not simply for the listing of buildings of historic or architectural importance but for the creation of 'protected sectors' of similar importance in the towns of his country.

Today the visitor to Périgueux or Sarlat can readily see the beneficial effects of this law. The splendidly restored cluster of buildings in Sarlat reached through the Passage Henry de Secogne has on one wall the tribute:

André Malraux

1901   1975

au résistant,

au ministre, auteur

de la loi sur la restauration
des villes historiques

The relationship between Winston Churchill and Charles de Gaulle during the war years was often one of passionate disagreement. But thirteen years after the war had ended de Gaulle, as Premier of the Fourth Republic, decorated Churchill with the Cross of Liberation, and in 1960, addressing both Houses of Parliament in London, he paid tribute to Churchill as 'the leader and the inspiration' of the struggle against Fascism.

The reconciliation between these two men symbolizes the end to the centuries of mistrust between the English and the French. De Gaulle kept Britain out of the European Economic Community for as long as he could, but he could not keep the British out for ever. Increasingly they discovered the Dordogne and many found an unexpected sweetness and welcome there. So many have bought holiday homes there that the French ruefully say that having lost Aquitaine in the Hundred Years War the British are trying to buy it back.

One rather sad but moving figure can represent those British who have found solace and peace in the Dordogne in the years after 1945. The English socialite, rebel, friend of jazz musicians, hater of racialists, and writer, Nancy Cunard, was first introduced to the Dordogne by Ezra Pound – 'old goofy Ezra' as she affectionately called him. In 1947, at the age of fifty-one, she fell in love with a twenty-four-year-old American named William le Page Finley. The following year she decided to bring him with her to live in the Dordogne. She found an old house, scarcely more than a barn, on a hillside just outside the hamlet of La Mothe Fénelon. 'I have now a HOUSE,' she wrote, 'a nutshell building complete for every dis-comfort and in-convenience, and a veritable network of fissures, but I adore it.'

Into it she put Manet's *Étude pour le linge*, inherited from the Irish author George Moore through her mother. She put in little else by way of furniture, save a desk for her dilapidated typewriter. In 1950, she told a friend, her Dordogne home had 'no lavatory, no water', but 'superb electric light and divine neighbours who load me with gifts, eatable gifts'.

Nancy Cunard planned to travel during the winter and spend late spring, summer and early autumn writing in her Dordogne home.

There she translated into French *Fountains in the Sand* by her friend Norman Douglas, and after his death in 1952 wrote a biography of him. The first book was not published, but *Grand Man* appeared in 1954. Two years later appeared Nancy Cunard's finest book, her memoir of George Moore, which she also wrote near La Mothe Fénelon.

But things did not go entirely well for Nancy Cunard. William le Page Finley could not stand their quarrels and her dirtiness and possessiveness. Their liaison broke up. Nancy began to drink far too much; even the peacefulness of the Dordogne failed to restore her. Visitors to La Mothe Fénelon in August 1964 saw in her home masses of books, some pictures, African wood sculptures, but few signatures in her visitor's book. Increasingly she suffered from emphysema, and had to be treated for it in hospital at Gourdon not far from her home.

Even in hospital she could be cheerful, noting that: 'There are hours here which I actually enjoy: those at this terrible typewriter.' But still she drank too much. On a visit to Franco's Spain she made so much trouble that she was imprisoned for several days and temporarily lost her reason. She returned to France, increasingly fragile and impoverished, her once-loved house musty, mildewed, neglected and sad.

Finally she was obliged to move to a hotel in Gourdon. Late in the summer of 1963 the American professor Charles Burkhardt visited her. She was, he recalled,

staying at the ugliest hotel in the Dordogne or perhaps in the world: raw, white, and new: downstairs a salon/café of pinball machines, local youth, a nervous young proprietor: upstairs tiny rooms, furnished and panelled in raw orange pine, so new it oozed under the thick varnish. When Nancy was able to leave her raw orange cubicle (where she had an old suitcase or two, as she always did, full of manuscripts or correspondence or ivory, and a bottle of rum, her favourite drink, on the bedside table), she descended and sat in a corner of the pinball salon, writing her letters, drinking rough red, which she would occasionally ask one of the boys to share a glass of, catching her breath between the Gauloises.

There she ended her days, fighting against Franco, Fascism and the world, dazed and bemused with the drugs they gave her at the hospital. The once-golden Nancy Cunard died alone in March 1965 in an oxygen tent, in the public ward of a Paris hospital.

I would rather not identify the Gourdon hotel so much maligned by Professor Burkhardt, since I frequently visit that town. But I must correct a mistake in his account: Gourdon is not in the Dordogne, but in the Lot.

❧ 5 ❧

Churches in a Landscape

A century of peace and prosperity blesses those who come after as well as those who have the good fortune to live through it. Such an era occurred in Périgord in the hundred or so years before the quarrels between England and France began to create poverty and wretchedness. It has left us a legacy of remarkable romanesque architecture. As this was an age of faith, the legacy chiefly consists of something like four hundred beautiful, though sometimes sadly neglected, churches.

Périgord had been converted to Christianity long before the twelfth century. The converts were descended from four Gaulish tribes, whom Julius Caesar had found living in confederation on the south bank of the river Isle in 52 B.C. Known as the Petrocorii (from which the word Périgord derives), these Gauls had built a town named Vesuna on the site of modern Périgueux. According to Caesar they sent around 6,000 men to fight alongside the ill-fated Vercingetorix when he rebelled against the Romans, but for the most part the Petrocorii contentedly accepted Roman rule, worshipping their own gods (including the goddess Vesuna).

To the British, spoiled as we are with our huge, mysterious Stonehenge, our Rollright stones and our Avebury ring, the vestiges of Gallo-Roman and Celtic art and architecture in the Dordogne may seem slight. There is, in fact, much to see. At Périgueux itself an impressively substantial part remains of the Tour de Vésone, a temple dedicated to the goddess of the Petrocorii, standing over 25 metres high and nearly 29 metres in circumference. There, too, is the Roman villa Pompeia. The museum at Périgueux displays a remarkable altar, carved with a pre-Christian bull-motif. And within the modern city is the Roman amphitheatre, now tamed and made into a peaceful garden and children's park.

Elsewhere in the Dordogne dolmens and tumuli testify to the lives of the inhabitants before the coming of Christianity to Périgord. Montcaret, on the very western edge of the Dordogne, is especially fascinating. Excavations have revealed a fine Roman thermal bath and remarkable Roman mosaics, with fish designs in rectangular fields. The villagers of Montcaret took care to waste nothing, even re-using Gallo-Roman sculptures to decorate some of the capitals in the apse of their church.

Today you walk out of the church directly into the newly excavated Roman remains, stepping back a further ten centuries into the past. At Montcaret there are in fact two layers of Gallo-Roman remains, the first destroyed by the Barbarians who invaded Périgord in A.D. 275, the second built in the fourth century A.D.

The Barbarians swept on to destroy much else in Périgord, including the old walls of Périgueux. But Christianity was spreading none the less. The process is shrouded in miracle and legend. The first missionary of the Dordogne was St Front, to whom the Cathedral of Périgueux is dedicated, though his body lies entombed beside the old wall of the city. A diocese was founded around Périgueux and the first bishop, Paternus, was consecrated in A.D. 365. From this moment dates most of the embroidering of the legend of St Front. To give apostolic authority to the see of Périgueux, the saint was said to have been born of the tribe of Judah in Lycaonia, converted by one of Christ's miracles, baptized by St Peter himself and chosen as one of the seventy-two apostles commissioned by Jesus according to the Gospels.

Earlier chronicles are more likely to tell the truth. Their witness is that St Front was a Périgourdin, born at Lanquais. Today Lanquais boasts a fine fifteenth-century château, well worth visiting for its furniture and its fine fireplaces as well as its interesting mixture of feudal and renaissance architecture. But the visitor should note near by the tiny hamlet of Couze-et-Saint-Front, whose name commemorates the first saint of the Dordogne.

The legendary St Front was both a mighty miracle-worker and a brave man. In Rome he threw a demon out of the daughter of a senator. In Périgord his zeal so annoyed the proconsul, Squirinus, that

St Front was banished. He went to Egypt, to live as a hermit. There he and his companions would have died of hunger had not Squirinus, overcome with remorse, arranged for seventy camels to bring them food. St Front, along with his companions, is said to have ridden back on the camels to Périgord, where he baptized the proconsul, his one-time enemy.

Certainly, by whatever means, many Périgourdins became Christians. In the sixth century Bishop Chronop built a little church over the tomb of St Front at Périgueux, to honour the man who began this conversion. But Christianity remained vulnerable to heathen invaders. Visigoths controlled the whole of Périgord until the Merovingian king, Clovis, defeated them at the battle of Vouillé near Poitiers in 507. Clovis was himself a convert from paganism. Such Christian monarchs were essential to the preservation of the faith. Soon Arabs were threatening Christians in the Dordogne, swooping northwards from Spain, destroying (for example) the Christian settlement of Calviac above Domme. The Carolingian king, Charles Martel, defeated them at Poitiers in 732.

Above all others, the grandson of Charles Martel, Charlemagne, was instrumental in fostering Christianity in Périgord, not simply by defeating its enemies but also by supporting the new monastic foundations of the Benedictines. His father, Pepin the Short, helped to found an abbey at Sarlat. Charlemagne gave to this abbey not only the bones of St Sacerdos, a bishop of Limoges who had been born near Sarlat in Calviac, but also a piece of the Cross on which Jesus was crucified and one of the thorns that had encircled the Saviour's head. He showed similar generosity to the diocese of Périgueux, giving to the see the vest worn by the infant Jesus. He himself founded the Benedictine abbey at Brantôme in 786, endowing it with the whole corpse of a Holy Innocent (known as St Sicaire).

Equally valuable for the defence of the faith was Charlemagne's decision to create vassals who would rule and protect Périgord. Between the thirteenth and early fifteenth century the descendants of these men, the counts of Périgord, were often at odds with the bishop and canons of Périgueux. Earlier, however, one of them, who took the name *Taillefer* ('sword of iron'), led the Périgourdins to defeat the marauding Vikings and founded the famous Dordogne family, the Talleyrands.

The religious orders began to flourish. The Benedictines built not only at Sarlat and Brantôme but also at Belvès, at Périgueux, at Saint-Privat-des-Prés, at Trémolat and elsewhere. The Dominicans also had a priory at Belvès, as well as at Saint-Pardoux-la-Rivière. The Cistercians built an abbey at Boschaud, at Cadouin, Le Dalon and Peyrouse. The Knights Templars established themselves at Sergeac. Augustinian canons founded houses at Saint-Cyprien, Chancelade, Saint-Amand-de-Coly, Saint-Avit-Sénieur and Saint-Jean-de-Côle.

They have left us a legacy of magnificent buildings. Even where the vicissitudes of Périgord life have destroyed the first buildings, the determination of monks and canons was often enough for them to rebuild, paying due respect to the earlier styles of architecture and utilizing the new. At Cadouin, for example, a free congregation of devout persons decided to found an abbey in 1115. Two years later they began to build a church, and then affiliated themselves to the Cistercians. Their church was completed and consecrated in 1145. Much was destroyed and rebuilt during the Hundred Years War. The abbey was desecrated during the Wars of Religion. The monks were expelled at the time of the Revolution. Then, in 1839, the *département* of the Dordogne bought the whole beautiful site and brilliantly restored the buildings.

Today Cadouin is magnificent. The interior of the church remains much as it was in 1145. A central aisle is flanked by two apses (unusual in Dordogne churches of the twelfth century). Each transept is topped by a dome, as is the crossing itself. These domes are a remarkable feature of Dordogne church architecture. They are found on the twelfth-century churches in Saint-Jean-de-Côle, Le Dorat, Carsac, Agonac, and others, and above all – though completely restored – on the Cathedral of Saint-Front at Périgueux. Their obvious affinities with Byzantine architecture have persuaded historians that pilgrims to the East brought back with them the idea of building in this fashion. The domes on Dordogne churches are cousins to those on St Mark's, in Venice.

Most twelfth-century churches in the Dordogne have an austerity that seems to have precluded too much decoration. At Cadouin much that was decorated has been despoiled, though its quality can be guessed at by the carved capitals that remain. Here, Cistercian austerity is best expressed by its buttressed western façade. In the centre is a round-arched doorway, with two 'blind' or blocked in archways to the north. Above are three narrow, round-arched windows, and above that a third row of nine blind arches, devout and stern.

This austerity starkly contrasts with the wildly exuberant cloister the monks of Cadouin built for themselves, in the architectural style known (not surprisingly) as flamboyant gothic. Ogive vaulting, delicate and variedly patterned tracery, betray its late medieval date. It was completed only in the sixteenth century, so that you can detect even renaissance elements. Today Cadouin forms a beautifully satisfying whole, the cool grey slates of the tower, the round red tiles elsewhere and the ochre stones of its walls a perfect complement to the green of the cloister garden.

The monks built their flamboyant cloister after their old one was destroyed in the Hundred Years War. The turbulence of medieval Périgord explains the existence of another group of churches before which the visitor pauses in awe. These are the immense fortified village or abbey churches – the equivalent of the massive churches of the *bastides*. *Bastide* churches were a second line of defence, the first being the town walls. Twelfth-century village and abbey churches were the *sole* defence of those living around them. As a result they are even more like castles than the churches in *bastides*.

Because today they lie virtually deserted, some of them seem to us bizarre. Saint-Amand-de-Coly once housed around 200 Augustinian canons. Today it is a tiny village. Only the ramparts of the former monastery exist, along with its immense church. The west tower of the church is fearful, even monstrous, with a great wide arch in which you expect to find not a door but a portcullis. It is as much a keep as a church tower. Inside the church, seeking refuge from their enemies, monks and villagers climbed to successive levels to defend themselves. Hidden staircases and hollow pillars all testify to the fear of sudden attack and destruction that daily obsessed them.

At the same time this was the place where they worshipped. Those who built it managed to combine a fortress with a house of God. The barrel vault soars to heaven. Three narrow windows light the altar, surmounted by a round open window, and a splendid dome covers the crossing.

Saint-Amand-de-Coly is an unusually powerful example of a fortified church, but it is by no means the only one of its kind in the

Dordogne. The Benedictine church at Trémolat was large enough to hold the whole village if need be. Its belltower is more like a keep. Charlemagne had built a church here, the birthplace of St Cybard who after his death in the sixth century worked many miracles. In the twelfth century part of this church was incorporated in the new one, so that the first of the four bays includes the old building and is two and a half metres thick. The other three bays are all topped by domes.

Some of these once-great churches are now ruins. Ferns and trees grow out of the despoiled remains of the church of the abbey at Le Dalon, built at the beginning of the thirteenth century and once one of the greatest in the whole of Périgord. The church was bought by a bourgeois revolutionary in 1790 and, thirty or so years later, deliberately destroyed and used as building material. Its sister abbey of Boschaud is today also a ruin, romantic and slightly frightening with half a dome impossibly suspended high above the nave.

Ruins have a charm that can make the visitor forget that once they were the centre of a lively faith and a busy life. Splendidly restored Cadouin preserves in its sculptures this faith and this busy life, depicting scenes from the Old and New Testaments, from the daily work of the monks and of their intellectual lives too – by showing tales from Virgil and the ancients. A fresco depicts the Annunciation. In the thirteenth century a visitor from Antioch brought to the monastery what purported to be the shroud in which Jesus was laid in the tomb. As a result the monastery of Cadouin was visited by pilgrims seeking to venerate this shroud until as late as 1932, when the cloth was proved to have been woven in the eleventh century.

The monasteries, offering hospitality as well as spirituality, made Périgord part of the medieval pilgrim way to Santiago de Compostela in Spain, where the shrine of St James the Great lies. From Limoges pilgrims would pass through Solignac in Haute-Vienne, where a monastery had stood since the seventh century. Thence the route branched. Pilgrim caravans would journey either through Sarlat and south to Agen (now the chief city of the Lot), where Christianity had been established since 346, or they would take the westerly pilgrim route by way of Périgueux and Bergerac. The routes joined together south of Mont-de-Marson, before taking the pass of Roncesvalles through the Pyrenees.

The religious vitality and inner stability of Aquitaine in this short period produced not only the great monastic churches but also an astonishing profusion of romanesque village churches. These churches, usually in the centre of small villages and hamlets, vary enormously, not only in style, but in colour. Those who built them used local stone, so that in north Dordogne they are made of granite, around Hautefort and Terrasson they take on a rosier hue, and elsewhere their huge stones are almost white.

In the Dordogne each romanesque church needs to be savoured for its own quiddity. In some hamlets the nave of the church stands alone, humble, without aisles. In others it is high, barrel-vaulted, aisled and ornamented. Occasionally, later worshippers set about transforming romanesque churches into quasi-gothic ones; but gothic makes only a timid appearance in the Dordogne. Sometimes the simplest pointed arch bemused Dordogne stonemasons. At Cherval they built a fortified church in the twelfth and thirteenth centuries and dedicated it to the soldier-saint, St Martin. They successfully built two domes, but the pointed arches of the nave wobble comically.

I am never ashamed by my frequent inability to work out exactly when a church in the Dordogne was built or embellished. Périgourdins continued to work in the romanesque style long after others had abandoned it. Moreover, the romanesque churches of the Dordogne, though recognizably of one great family, are inexhaustibly varied. The architectural historian Jean Secret is wise about this:

> If one has the impression of knowing all about romanesque Burgundy after visiting Autun, Tournus, Saulieu, Vézelay and Paray-le-Monial, and of knowing all about romanesque Auvergne after seeing Saint-Nectare, Orcival and Notre-Dame-du-Port, no one can claim to know all about romanesque Périgord on coming out of Saint-Front and Saint-Stephen in Périgueux, of Cadouin, of Saint-Avit-Sénieur or of Bussière-Badil.

The astonishing variety of Dordogne romanesque churches adds to the richness of the landscape and townscape of the *département*. It also enriches anyone who takes the time to look at them. You can stand in the village of Saint-Privat-des-Prés awed by the power of its cavernous doorway, or else quail before the overbearing, cruel bell-tower of Saint-Avit-Sénieur. You can try to read the meaning of the sculptures on the portail of Saint-Martin-le-Pin near Nontron, where a man carries a sheaf of corn on his back, pursued by a beast as big as him and the sheaf put together. You can ask what is the relationship between the cluster of towers, side aisles, blind arches, tiled roofs and roofs made of *lauzes* in one church, or why another possesses only a long straight nave. Conscious of the lack of documentation which makes even experts helpless, you can ask the possibly unanswerable question why the church at Faye, just outside Ribérac, presents on its west side not two blind arches but two blind *half*-arches. Or you can simply admire over its portal the tympanum (a rare phenomenon in Dordogne churches) depicting Christ ascending in glory and being censed by angels.

I sometimes think I should spend a month studying simply the belltowers of Dordogne churches, for they continually refresh by their variety. At Les Eyzies-de-Tayac and Prats-de-Périgord, for instance, they rise solid and forbidding, pierced with not a single opening till the very top. By contrast, the belltower of Issigeac church is a jolly octagonal affair with a little pointed cap. Sometimes a belltower is no more than an extension upwards of the west wall, pierced to take a couple of bells. Elsewhere, as at Agonac, it sits complacently athwart the crossing. Monks liked fine belltowers. At Chancelade the Abbey Church of Notre Dame has a splendid elaborate belltower three storeys high, the first storey decorated with blind arcades, the second with arched windows and the third simply pillars holding up the roof. In the same village the charming romanesque Parish Church of St Jean has no belltower at all.

Sculpture is rare enough in the romanesque churches of the Dordogne to bear travelling a fair number of kilometres to see. Thiviers is a small town in Périgord Vert, thirty-seven kilometres north of Périgueux. The church there was first built in the twelfth century, but much of it dates from considerably later. The belltower is a nineteenth-century addition. Between 1511 and 1515 the two domes of the church were gothicized, but the beautifully preserved romanesque carvings on the capitals inside the church are untouched.

Taken together as a group, these romanesque sculptures at Thiviers seem to represent the dark fears and the high hopes of medieval Christians. Man's need of salvation is depicted in a series of startling images. A man plucking grapes is attacked by a bird. Monsters swallow human beings, who cling desperately to coiled branches. Other men try to ride on the back of monsters or flee from them. Salvation from the evil powers of this world is represented by Samson conquering the lion. On another extremely beautiful capital stands Jesus, flanked by the Apostle Peter and St Mary Magdalene. To Peter he gives the keys to the kingdom of heaven, while the Magdalen, her long hair braided, gives a greeting with her right hand and carries in her left the jar of precious ointment with which she anointed the Saviour's head.

There are fine sculpted portals on Dordogne romanesque churches – at Saint-Sulpice-de-Mareuil, at Saint-Martin-le-Pin, at Saint-Martial-de-Valette and at the former Benedictine priory of Bussière-Badil, for instance. There are finely carved capitals at Vanxains and at Segonzac, formalized and scarcely representational, in contrast to the astonishing carvings both inside and outside the Church of Saint-Julien just outside Cénac, which rival in skill and allegorical content those at Thiviers.

The sculptors who adorned romanesque churches rarely carved a human being or animal simply for ornament or delight, though they clearly loved to create patterns of leaves, dog-tooth arches and stylized fruits and trees. At Cénac, the man carved on the exterior of the apse who presents his private parts and backside to the viewer is not there merely for bawdy fun. Just as fortified churches were designed to keep out the enemies of this world, so churches also were built to repel spiritual enemies. This grotesque man was put there to repel evil spirits by means of vulgarity. His activity is reinforced by the couple carved further round the apse, who embrace lewdly. Inside the church the romanesque sculptor expresses his faith and hope that the dangerous outside world may be tamed. Outside the church pigs are depicted reversing the order of nature by eating human beings; inside, a monkey performs for his trainer who scratches the head of another. The sculptor was not simply portraying a scene from medieval life but expressing the conquest of earthly disorder by the Lord of all creation.

Yet one romanesque church in Périgord clearly contradicts the dictum that because medieval man thought symbolically, medieval artists always worked in symbols. Ten kilometres west of Hautefort, at Tourtoirac, Abbot Richard of Uzerche established a Benedictine community in the eleventh century. The romanesque church attached to the abbey was later gothicized and today is much ruined, though the dome of the crossing is intact. The abbot's lodging, dating from the seventeenth century, is still there, beautifully situated on the river Auvézère. Most delightful of all are the carvings on the capitals of what remains from the old chapter house. I cannot believe that the sculpted monks, dancing round two by two and pulling each others' beards, were carved there for any reason but to make one laugh out loud.

The skills of the Dordogne sculptors were not entirely lost during the savage wars that succeeded this golden age of the church. Forty-five kilometres west of Brantôme is the fortified church of Grand-Brassac. Its two towers resemble keeps and its bare thick walls support three domes. The west façade is the setting for a remarkable group of sculptures, carved in different eras, brought together in a harmonious whole. Central to this group is the romanesque portal, with its stylized leaves and beasts, carved as an archway. Within this arch sit the Virgin and Child, carved with great delicacy in the sixteenth century. Above the arch are five larger statues, earlier in date and style, yet perfectly cohering with the rest. A bishop (or abbot) and St Paul stand to left and right. Above them Ss Peter and John kneel in prayer to Christ, who sits in majesty above them all. Four centuries of skilled, anonymous craftsmanship created this virtually unknown master-piece.

In spite of their frequently poverty-stricken lives, the Christians of the Dordogne continued to embellish the interiors of some of their churches after they had built them. In the Church of Saint-Amand-de-Coly is an inscription both extolling the virtues of Abbot William and begging the visitor to pray for him:

+ DISCAT Q(U)I NESCIT VIR NOBIL(IS) HIC REQ(U)IESCIT

Q(U)I RACHEL Q(U)E LIA Q(U)I MARTA F(U)IT ATQ(UE)

MARIA PSAL(M)OS CANTATE FR(ATRES) CHR(ISTU)M

Q(UE) ROGATE SALVET UT ABATEM W(ILHELMUM)

P(ER) PIETATEM

(You who did not know this, learn that here lies a noble man who was both Rachel and Leah, both Martha and Mary. Sing psalms, brethren, and pray that because of his piety Christ will save Abbot William.)

The Latin rhyme is as charming as the request.

At Brantôme in the thirteenth century a monk sculptured in bas-relief the massacre of the infants by the soldiers of Herod (for, of course, the monastery possessed the body of one of the children, given by Charlemagne). In the following century another monk sculpted a far happier scene, the Baptism of Jesus, in which both the Christ and the Baptist are laughing with delight. The fifteenth-century frescoes at Cadouin are matched by one in the chapel of Château Beynac depicting the Last Supper. In the Church of Saint-Pardoux-la-Rivière is a fine sixteenth-century statue of the Virgin carrying the Christ Child whose shirt is open to the waist. And the Church of Saint-Blaise at Annesse contains two striking seventeenth-century wood-carvings: the crucified Christ, with St John and the Virgin, over the altar; and a Virgin and Child in which Jesus puts his arm behind his mother's neck and she clings to his chubby stomach, her eyes already filled with apprehension for her baby.

To come across such works of religious art in the setting of a romanesque church is exhilarating; but similar legacies from our Christian heritage are not confined to Périgord. Special to this region of France are the strange, stiff, stylized romanesque carvings themselves, which can speak to us over the centuries if we will let them. If I had to choose between that wonderful, terrifying Virgin and Child at Annesse and the romanesque carvings at Causse-de-Clérans, I should choose Causse-de-Clérans, a virtually unknown hamlet near Baneuil, fifteen kilometres east of Bergerac. The twelfth-century castle here is almost totally destroyed. Only the keep stands beside the church, with its dome and its carved capitals. The tiny palm trees, oxen, birds and leaves sculpted by an unknown twelfth-century hand seem at first remote. What is the significance of the gestures of a fully dressed man and woman who stand next to an absurdly naked man? I do not know. But no one could mistake the meaning of the bishop, who stands stiffly holding his crozier in his left arm, blessing a kneeling man, while wild beasts horribly snap and bite at them. All the piety and terror of the twelfth century reaches out to us from this one carved capital in a remote, little-known romanesque church. Life is vicious; on every side mortal dangers threaten us; who shall deliver us from the body of this death?

And all this is a kind of bonus, for it is the churches themselves, not the carvings and capitals and frescoes and tombs inside them, that enrich the landscape of the Dordogne. They dominate villages, they stand alone, far apart from modern civilization. Often they are locked, but on those occasions when it is possible to go inside it is equally possible to work out which bits are romanesque, which bits are modern (from the machine-cut stones), which bits are gothicized and which bits would enormously benefit from having the hideous plaster scraped off their walls.

Why, then, are so many of these masterpieces in ruins or so sadly neglected? Many of them survived the Hundred Years War or were rebuilt later, only to be vandalized during the Wars of Religion. At this sad time the Cathedral of Périgueux was not Saint-Front, but the Church of St Stephen (Saint-Etienne-de-la-Cité), which the tourist often passes heedless on his relentless drive south through the city. Till 1575, when the Huguenots captured Périgueux by disguising themselves as peasants coming to market and then turning to attack the Catholics, the Church of St Stephen possessed four magnificent domes. The Huguenots destroyed two of them. They also set fire to part of the Church of Saint-Front, not daring to burn it down altogether for fear of setting fire to the whole city. The corpse of the saint was taken away and thrown into the Dordogne. His exquisitely sculptured tomb was demolished.

Bishop François de la Béraudière wished to restore his Cathedral of St Stephen in the next century, but lacked the wealth to do so. Both the cathedral and the Church of Saint-Front were spared further depredations by the Frondeurs only by the timely arrival of royalist troops, who entered the city to find the belltower of Saint-Front already piled high with tarred faggots, ready for lighting.

Such savagery, though on a far greater scale than anything that happened in Britain, is not unfamiliar to the student of our own religious history. The despoiling of relics and altars at the Reformation, the demolition of churches and of supposedly superstitious images and stained-glass windows at the time of the Great Rebellion is something everyone knows. What is unfamiliar to us is the hostility towards religion displayed at the time of the French Revolution. It left its mark on the churches of the Dordogne.

Priests were among the few classes of people who grew richer during the eighteenth century in France. When the Revolution started they suffered for it, and for their close association with the monarchy. Of the eighty persons guillotined in Périgueux, no fewer than seventy were priests. An era that supposed the millenium might arrive when the last king was strangled with the entrails of the last priest was equally likely to condemn all things priestly as superstition, unworthy of the Enlightenment.

The Church of Saint-Jean-de-Côle, seven kilometres west of Thiviers, contains what we today would regard as the most charming sculptures, depicting the great myths of our forefathers which some of us still live by. God the Father moulds the head of Adam, Noah falls down drunk, and an angel visits the Virgin Mary. The passions evoked by the French Revolution made it almost impossible for some of its heirs to take such an indulgent attitude to these old beliefs.

Thus there is a cold fierceness in Eugène Le Roy's *Jacquou le Croquant* towards the most charming manifestations of the old religion. On Christmas Eve 1815, Jacquou and his mother go to Midnight Mass and marvel at the manger in the castle church. 'The people knelt and prayed to the infant Jesus, lying in the manger on golden straw, between a thoughtful ox and a hairy ass who was eating hay from a small rack.' Eugène Le Roy describes the scene with tender skill: 'the holy Virgin in a blue gown, seated by her new-born babe, with St Joseph standing nearby, dressed in green, gently watching over them; at a distance the kneeling shepherds with their crooks shaped like crosses, adoring the holy infant; and in the further distance the magi, bearing gifts, guided by a star suspended from the branches above'.

Then Le Roy begins to undermine the charm of it all, skilfully allying the old religion with the hated nobility. 'At all these pretty things,' Jacquou observes, 'I and the others who were there stared greedily, eyes wide open with amazement. But soon we were forced to leave the choir, for it was reserved for the gentle-folk.' Finally the scene is transformed into one of meretricious trickery and stupid superstition. The peasants kneel before the little red-cheeked, flaxen-haired Jesus, 'when suddenly, all at once he opened his arms, moved his eyes from side to side, turned his head, and we heard the faint cries of a new-born babe. Then this crowd of superstitious peasants gasped with astonishment and admiration.' Some of them waited vainly for the miracle to occur again.

The Revolution led to the suppression of monasteries and nunneries. The law of 2 November 1789 put the wealth of the Church into the hands of the State, which undertook to supply the needs of the clergy and provide for worship and the needs of the poor. But the times were not favourable for religion. Once-great churches, such as St Stephen itself in Périgueux, were redundant and deconsecrated. Profiteers made their appearance on the revolutionary scene, to the detriment of the Church and its fine buildings. The man who bought and later destroyed the Abbey of Chancelade got it for as little as 1,050 francs.

It is in this context that the nineteenth-century restoration of the Cathedral of Saint-Front in Périgueux seems to me a remarkable achievement rather than the architectural disaster of conventional opinion. At the time of the Revolution Saint-Front was dedicated to the cult of the Supreme Being and denuded of its furniture. Even before 1789 it was in a sorry state, its broken-down domes protected by a covering of grey slates.

In 1841 the cathedral was classified as an historical monument. Ten years later the architect Paul Abadie was put in charge of its restoration. He decided to rebuild virtually everything. To him belongs credit for the magnificent views of the cathedral across the river and from the town, for he took down dwelling houses and other buildings which had been erected against two of its sides. Then he proceeded to demolish bit by bit the old and now dangerous structures, before rebuilding them with meticulous care in what he held to be true romanesque. Since the north transept had almost entirely disappeared in the sixteenth century, Abadie had to design one of his own. The restoration took almost half a century. Abadie gave up the work in 1882, two years before his death, and was succeeded as architect by de Bruyère. Finally, from 1891, the restoration of the cloister and famous clock-tower was completed under the supervision of Boeswillwald.

Much abuse has been poured over these three great nineteenth-century architects. Boeswillwald managed to escape some of it, because most of the clock-tower needed only renovation, the top alone being demolished entirely before rebuilding. Undeniably it is hard to defend Abadie's decision to replace what remained of the romanesque decoration with nineteenth-century versions, though perhaps he realized that the remaining original carvings (which are now in the Périgueux museum) would stand out absurdly among his new ones. Indefensible is the total disappearance, as a result of this restoration, of a more or less intact romanesque refectory close by the cloister. It is today hard to judge whether or not Abadie's decision to introduce geometric discipline into Saint-Front destroyed the irregular charm of the old building. It is certain that his machine-cut white blocks of stone lack the mellowness of the hand-shaped stones that one can see today in, say, St Stephen's Church at Périgueux.

But the restoration did save Saint-Front. The building today has great power. Study one of the overhead photographs of its five splendid domes and twelve pepperpot towers and it is impossible not to be impressed. Abadie's feeling for space and for the effect of shadows and beams of light make the interior as awe-inspiring as the exterior. The great chandeliers which he himself designed are magnificent. It has often been said that, in curing Saint-Front of its ills, Abadie and his successors regrettably used surgery instead of medicine. But maybe the centuries of neglect and destruction had made it too late for medicine.

It is undeniable that elsewhere in the Dordogne are fine churches now beyond repair and others almost so – in spite of the fact that the State now takes responsibility for their upkeep. Does secularization and the current decline of Christian belief in this part of the world mean that we must allow our Christian architectural heritage to disappear? At the end of the village where I live is a tiny chapel. Apart from carrying on its door the postbox, it was last used to baptize the only boy living in the village, and he is now twelve years old. Once it contained a fine seventeenth-century carved wooden retable, which was gradually crumbling into dust. Today this retable lies in pieces, alongside similar treasures from other forgotten churches, unknown religious prisoners hidden behind bars in a side chapel of the church at Domme.

Perhaps the solution is for people to take on the responsibility themselves, recognizing that the resources of the State will never be endless. A splendid example lies to hand in the Dordogne, in the church of Carsac-de-Carlux not far from Sarlat. Carsac church, dedicated to St Caprais, began life in the twelfth century as the chapel of a small priory. The great west door of this small chapel has five delicately proportioned arches. A dome was built just before the romanesque apse. Inside the capitals were sculpted. Then, in the sixteenth century, the nave and aisles were transformed by means of ogival vaulting and renaissance bas-reliefs. The whole was roofed in *lauzes*.

By the time of the Vichy régime Carsac church was in tatters. M. le

Curé, whose name was Roger Deltreil, set about restoring it, with the aid of the chief architect of the historical monuments of the *département*, M. Yves Froidevaux. Little could be done about the carvings over the arched doorway, but the Curé and his helpers chipped away the plaster that covered and protected the carvings inside the Church of Saint-Caprais. Today it is a gem, set in a picnic area, embellished with fine modern stained-glass and some moving, modernistic Stations of the Cross designed by Léon Zack. For those who do not believe, as well as for believers, the humble Church of Saint-Caprais at Carsac is an especially fine example of how Christian architecture has enriched the landscape of the Dordogne.

❖ 6 ❖

Before the Dawn of History

'If one were to compile a list of wonders for the Prehistoric World, on the model of the seven wonders of the Ancient World, it would have to include Palaeolithic Art,' wrote Ann Sieveking in her book on *The Cave Artists*. 'If a single example of this were chosen,' she added, 'it might be the Hall of Bulls at Lascaux in Dordogne.'

This wonder of the Prehistoric World was rediscovered only in 1940 by four boys from Montignac – Marcel Ravidat (then aged eighteen), Jacques Marsal and Simon Coencas (aged fifteen) and Georges Agnel (aged sixteen). A number of myths have grown up around their astonishing discovery. It is said, for instance, that Marcel's little dog fell into a hole near Montignac, that Marcel followed to rescue the animal and fell into the great Hall of Bulls. In fact, an old lady had told the boys that if they climbed into a hole near a tree root it would lead them down the side of the hill to the little château near Lascaux. The boys took a lamp, dropped pebbles into the hole, widened it, and then Ravidat fell down into it. He found himself in an amazing cavern, painted with four huge white bulls outlined in black. Around the legs of these beasts, horses, stags, oxen and deer ran amok, painted in black, purple, yellow and red. Marcel Ravidat ran to tell his schoolmaster about it all, and the schoolmaster was wise enough to inform the greatest living expert on Palaeolithic art, the Abbé Henri Édouard Prosper Breuil. Within a week the Abbé Breuil had reached Lascaux.

The discovery stunned even the experts. 'One of the most exciting experiences of my life was to be confronted by the fantastic paintings on the walls of Lascaux cave in south-west France,' wrote Richard E. Leakey. 'The vivid forms of horses, stags and oxen seem to leap out from the glistening crystalline surface on which they were painted some 14,000 years ago. These are not careful portraits of quiescent animals. They are bold images filled with action, movement and life.'

The Lascaux cave in the Dordogne comprises the most remarkable collection of prehistoric art known to mankind. The exuberance is overwhelming. Animals are superimposed on each other as if the unknown artists simply could not wait to find a different spot to start another painting. Sometimes they seem to stand alone; at other times they confront each other. The great bulls are examples of *Bos primogenius*, a species which died out three centuries ago but must have roamed this part of Europe for fifteen millennia at least. Chinese horses must also have wandered about prehistoric Dordogne, for there they are at Lascaux, complete with their tufted manes. A frieze of little horses runs along in its preoccupied way; shaggy, powerful bison stand grazing, their cloven hoofs delicately indicated by the artist; five stags, depicted only by their heads, antlers and necks, appear to be swimming across a river; and a cow leaps wildly, her rear legs high in the air.

The prehistorians were delighted to find that the great Hall of Bulls forms only part of this rich cave. The cavern narrows and then opens out to the left into a corridor leading to two more smaller recesses. And all this the artists 14,000 years ago took as their vast canvas. Not content with painting, they engraved animals on the walls. One of their most subtle tricks was to use a bulge or protuberance in the Lascaux cave to indicate part of an animal's body, painting the rest around it.

As well as depicting the vigorous animals that surrounded them, the cave artists reveal to us something of their own lives. Unique to Lascaux are abstract designs, chequerboard or 'tectiform' patterns. Were these tribal insignia, or do they represent the skins of animals, sewn together and used for shelter or clothing? Even more mysterious are long rows of dots, deliberately applied to the cave walls, indicating some long-forgotten but once-important calculations or numbering of days.

The cave artists at Lascaux also depicted their own interaction with the animal world. Mares might be domesticated, and the pregnant ones in Lascaux part of the economy of our earliest ancestors, but other beasts were dangerous. In one of the two recesses at Lascaux an artist depicted six lions, one of them, it seems, pierced by twelve arrows. Elsewhere similar arrows protrude from a stallion and a bison. It is scarcely possible to say whether these arrows (which some pre-historians declare to be harmless plants) were superimposed on the animals' bodies by later artists. But one grim composition at Lascaux reminds us that for prehistoric man life could be vicious and short.

A man, spindly drawn, almost a matchstick man, is falling back-wards, dead, between two wounded beasts. One of them, a rhinoceros, is limping away. Facing the man, having apparently just killed him, is a bristling, angry bison. But the bison itself has not escaped unscathed, for the dead hunter has disembowelled it with his spear. Lying useless on the ground beside the man is his decoy, a long stick topped by a bird.

The discovery of the cave of Lascaux brought thousands to nearby Montignac, on the way to visiting this wonder of prehistoric art. One main Montignac hotel changed its name to 'Hôtel de la Grotte' (Cave Hotel). But the cave is small and therefore inevitably ill-ventilated – the main hall itself is merely 30 metres long and 10 metres wide. The vast throng of visitors altered the delicate balance of humidity and temperature in the cave and the paintings which had been preserved for 14,000 years began to deteriorate. It was decided to close Lascaux cave to the general public and to restrict even the visits of pre-historians.

Yet Lascaux has continued to make its impact, through photographs and copies of its marvellous paintings and through the accounts of those who have been permitted to enter the cave. It has brought new prominence to those other lesser (though still astounding) examples of prehistoric art in the other *grottes* of the Dordogne.

Just as Michel de Montaigne warns that a person who will drink only great wines misses the pleasures of lesser wines, so inability to visit the cave at Lascaux should certainly not lead one to neglect the many other fascinating Dordogne caves that have now been opened to visitors. The first painted cave to be discovered in France, the Grotte de la Mouthe at Les Eyzies, though in no way so astounding as Lascaux, still amazes me. And it reveals to the modern world its own special secret: the only contemporary drawing of a Palaeolithic dwell-ing, a little hut, done in red and black.

Scarcely three kilometres from the Grotte de la Mouthe is the Grotte des Combarelles, which the Abbé Breuil and his colleagues discovered in 1901 and regarded as the finest in the Dordogne until they saw Lascaux. Close by is the cave known, rather terrifyingly, as the Gorge d'Enfer – again a cave whose revelations offer far less than Lascaux but none the less include their own quiddity – this time a rare carving of a salmon, no less than a yard long ('the one that got away' or a prehistoric fisherman's dream). As if to compensate for not offering you a plethora of painted animals inside the cave, the path to the Gorge d'Enfer runs through a collection of animals descended from those that roamed here in prehistoric times: emus, Préjalski horses, European bison and suchlike creatures, wandering about in the open air.

The early years of this century were fertile ones for prehistorians in the Dordogne. In the same year as the discovery of the Grotte de la Mouthe, another of the great French prehistorians, Denis Peyrony, spotted a fine frieze of coloured animals in the cave of Font-de-Gaume, close by the Grotte des Combarelles. Scholars have counted over a hundred and fifty beasts drawn in this one cave by our prehistoric ancestors. Two years later, in 1903, Peyrony was at Teyjat in Périgord Vert, where the Grotte de la Mairie had been discovered in 1889. There the prehistorian deciphered over fifty animals which prehistoric men and women had lightly engraved throughout the cave. Visiting the Grotte de la Mairie at Teyjat today, you marvel at Peyrony's acute eye, for the shapes of many of these carved animals become apparent to the layman only after the guide has traced them out with his stick.

The discovery of Lascaux provoked a fresh surge of research into the caves of prehistoric man, especially fruitful in the 1950s. At Le Bugue in 1951 a decorated cavern was discovered and given the bizarre name of Bara-Bahau (patois for the debris caused by falling rocks, for the end of the vast hall of Bara-Bahau is blocked by the remains of a gigantic underground landslide).

Five years later the prehistorians discovered that a cave at Rouffignac known for centuries contained hitherto unobserved rich prehistoric decorations. To understand how over two hundred and fifty carved and painted prehistoric animals could have remained unseen for so long, in spite of clear evidence that the Grotte de Rouffignac was not only well known but also much visited since the sixteenth century at least, you must visit the cave yourself.

Usually a cave visit requires a stout pair of legs as well as an equally stout pair of shoes. Since you must walk deep into the earth, where the sun never penetrates, you also need a woolly pullover. But at Rouffignac you can dispense with the stout shoes and legs, for visitors are taken through the cave on an underground electric railway. Whenever the guide stops the train, the unpractised eye sees nothing unusual about the cave walls, until he traces out, say, the claw marks made by a white bear during the Ice Age or the form of an ibex engraved by prehistoric man. I'm proud to say that I myself did spot the carving of a mammoth before the guide pointed it out – but since the Grotte de Rouffignac contains a hundred or so such mammoths, their fearsome tusks, huge heads and woolly skins brilliantly engraved, the achievement was perhaps not so remarkable. Finally, deep inside the cave, the train stops in a wide hall with a fairly low, flat roof, on which about 40,000 years ago our ancestors painted in brown and black outline a profusion of horses, galloping, grazing, standing startled. There seems to be no pattern to this prehistoric equivalent of Michelangelo's Sistine Chapel ceiling. The animals are superimposed on each other, run away from or into each other, as if the sheer exuberance of the artists simply made it impossible for them to stop drawing horses once they had started. And a sad indication of the blindness of some modern people compared with our primitive ancestors is that part of this masterpiece has been disfigured with later graffiti.

The impetus given to prehistoric exploration by the discovery of Lascaux led also to the opening up of caves that contain not drawings and carvings but extremely beautiful stalagmites and stalactites. Some of these today bear suitably romantic names – such as the Devil's Abyss (Gouffre du Diable) at Brantôme. Some have been known a long time. The one in the middle of Domme, for instance, was used as a hiding-place by the citizens when the *bastide* was captured by its enemies. Others are recent discoveries.

Sometimes a small, relatively unknown cave seems to sum up in miniature the whole of the mysterious prehistory of the Dordogne. Such is the Grotte de Villars, situated four kilometres outside the village of that name, near the Château of Puyguilhem.

The Grotte de Villars was discovered in 1953 by the Pot-holing Club of Périgueux. Its remarkably varied stalagmites and stalactites would have been considered excessive were they invented for Disney-

land; since they are real, they are marvellous. In many places a stalag-
mite and a stalactite have put a finger out to each other and joined.
Over the centuries some of these joints have thickened, and occasionally, when the earth has slightly shifted, they have cracked – neatly, if
slightly alarmingly. Elsewhere, long ago, a whole section of the ceiling,
perhaps a metre or so square, has fallen, leaving behind a flat surface
on which the fistulas of new stalagmites are forming. Bizarrely shaped
crystallizations twist their way up into narrow shafts above your
head. The colours are white, ochre and even red. The formations are
translucent. In places the glistening white snowy deposit reminds one
of the retreating ice that helped to create this cave. Narrow passages
open up into delicate fairy grottoes. And deep down is the course of
the river that once rushed through this underground cavern and now
only reveals itself as a shallow pool for a couple of weeks in spring, or
as a little stream in an unusually rainy month.

Caves are for the most part privately owned, and some owners have
attempted to increase their attractions by bathing the stalactites
and stalagmites in multi-coloured light, reminding me of Norman
Douglas's celebrated strictures on the grottoes of Capri:

> The foreigners liked colour in caves. The foreigners brought money. Colour
> in caves is cheap. Let them have it! Therefore, in a twinkling, the two-
> mouthed Grotto del Turco became the Green Grotto; the venerable Grotto
> Ruofolo put on a roseate hue sufficient to justify the poetic title of Red
> Grotto, and the Grotto Monacone . . . was discovered to be white – actually
> quite white!

Fortunately the Grotte de Villars is simply, excellently lit to display its
crystallizations. Under the light bulbs you can see already fungus
growing – a minor version of the problem that led to the closing of
Lascaux.

Five years after the discovery of the cave at Villars, black marks
were noticed on the wall of one gallery. Closer examination revealed
that these had been made with manganese oxide, mixed with animal
grease. The Abbé Breuil, then in his eightieth year, was called in, and
identified the marks as the work of prehistoric man. Near by was a
small hole, leading to a hitherto scarcely explored gallery. On the roof
of this gallery were paintings, in the same pigment, of a horse's head,
another galloping horse and a mountain goat.

The sharp eyes of professional prehistorians soon disclosed more secrets in the Grotte de Villars. They discerned where bears had clawed the walls of the cave. A bear's tooth was discovered. Then they traced out an engraving of the kind of bear we now find only in polar regions. They also found a bulge in the side of the cave which a cave artist long ago used as the bas-relief of a horse's flank; he then completed the horse in black paint. Near the entrance to the cave, *under* the stalactites, they excavated the ancient hearth where prehistoric men and women lit their fires. Near this hearth they found a painting of a man dancing wildly in front of a bison.

Prehistoric artists sometimes worked entirely in relief. One of the most impressive murals in the whole of Périgord is found in the shelter known as Cap-Blanc, just outside Les Eyzies. Cap-Blanc is formed by a massive outcrop of rock on the side of a wooded hill. In 1909 prehistorians removed piles of earth and stones which had filled the shelter, and found the skeleton of a Cro-Magnon woman, buried there, lying in the foetal position. The skeleton at Cap-Blanc today is a replica. Behind it, on the wall of the shelter, is the finest set of prehistoric bas-relief carvings I have seen: a couple of bison and a frieze of horses, one a mare in foal, another a perfectly recognizable Préjalski type such as today roam only in Poland. Some of the horses' heads are carved with extreme delicacy, their eyes and ears finely delineated.

The mural at Cap-Blanc is high-relief, not bas-relief. One horse is two metres long, and the whole frieze of horses stretches in a line fifteen metres long. Although it is one of the very earliest surviving works of art, the unknown sculptor knew already about composition and the grouping of figures. He has created not simply a series of animals but the portrait of a herd. Near the bottom right-hand side has been carved a hand. In this way, I like to think, the prehistoric artist signed his work.

Near this peaceful work of art – thousands of years old – is a brooding symbol of man's destructiveness: as you climb back up the hillside path from Cap-Blanc you can turn round for a magnificent view of the massive ruins of Château Commarque, built in the thirteenth century and destroyed by the English within a hundred years.

Prehistoric caves are found in other parts of the world – particularly in northern Spain – but more have been discovered in this part of

France than anywhere else. The National Museum of Prehistory at Les Eyzies, founded by Denis Peyrony, has brought together a vast collection of the tools and carvings of our prehistoric ancestors, including those bulbous figures strangely called 'Venuses'. In spite of the scholarly minds that have brooded over the meaning of these images, they are still shrouded in mystery. The curious 'Venus' from Monpazier, five centimetres high, has grossly exaggerated buttocks and vulva. Why? Why were the highly abstract images of women, carved in limestone in the cave of La Roche near Lalinde, crossed out and re-carved again and again? Why does the 'Venus' from Laussel carry in her right hand a bison's horn? Why are these figures so unrealistic (like almost every prehistoric depiction of human beings)? A woolly rhinoceros, which was discovered in a completely preserved state in Romania, confirms that the cave artists managed to engrave and paint such a beast with unerring accuracy.

The Abbé Breuil concluded that the paintings in the Grotte de Villars were made 30,000 years ago, though later scholars date them 2,000 or 3,000 years later than he did. Instinctively we tend to believe that life 30,000 years ago must have been nasty, brutish and short. Henry Miller had the imagination not to go along with this supposition. The Dordogne, he decided, 'must have been a paradise for many thousands of years'. To Miller, it seemed reasonable to conclude that men and women living in such a paradise could not have been without aesthetic and religious sensibility. If the Dordogne seems a paradise to us, he wrote,

> I believe it must have been so for the Cro-Magnon man, despite the fossilized evidence of the great caves which point to a condition of life rather bewildering and terrifying. I believe that Cro-Magnon man settled here because he was extremely intelligent and had a highly developed sense of beauty. I believe that in him the religious sense was already highly developed and that it flourished here even if he lived like an animal in the depths of the caves.

Cro-Magnon man is so named after the site in the Dordogne where five skeletons were discovered in 1868. He first appeared in Europe about thirty-five centuries before Christ. Today one of the leading hotels in Les Eyzies is named after him. The village also insults his memory by depicting him in a huge statue looking like an ape. In fact he stood tall, 1.77 m high, and the woman was only slightly smaller.

His face was broad. He was stocky and strong. The famous *Guide bleu* to Périgord and Quercy observes that you can still see people like that in Aquitaine, and I am inclined to agree. He was not *Homo sapiens* but a wiser species, now known to scholars as *Homo sapiens sapiens*. In short, he was like ourselves. If he was rather more inclined than we are to 'exit pursued by a bear', he was himself no savage. He lived in caves and also in the overhanging rocks of the Dordogne, where he was sheltered from storms and where excavations have revealed that (as at La Madeleine near Tursac) generations of men and women lived for many centuries. They adorned themselves with necklaces made of shells and sometimes bone pendants, as is the necklace found in the cave of Cro-Magnon. They could die peacefully. The skull of the old man found at Cro-Magnon has a curious depression in his forehead, the result of the disease which probably killed him.

Near Tursac, on the banks of the Vézère, are the two caves of Le Moustier, where *Homo sapiens*, known also as Neanderthal man, lived, died and was rediscovered in skeletal form in the nineteenth century. It is possibly irksome to modern man to learn that the brain capacity of *Homo sapiens* was larger than ours (though his frontal lobes were not so well developed). He made flint tools and reverently buried his dead – to be dug up centuries later by prehistorians. His brothers and sisters lived throughout Europe and as far afield as the Middle East.

Cro-Magnon man replaced him, and it is Cro-Magnon man who today communicates with us through his paintings and cave art. The Dordogne has revealed that the Cro-Magnons were also a varied race, for in 1909 at Combe-Capelle near Saint-Avit-Sénieur a smaller version was dug up; and even earlier, in 1888, archaeologists had excavated at Chancelade (in the Grotte de Raymonden) an even tinier skeleton, of a man no more than 1.55 m tall. He had a fine, high forehead, and the archaeologists christened him Cro-Magnon-Grimaldi.

The Cro-Magnons lived as nomads from about 30,000 B.C. for perhaps 20,000 years or more. They endured the Ice Age – in south-west France temperatures even then reached about 15 degrees centigrade on summer days. They left to the Dordogne a tradition of living in caves that, in such troglodyte villages as Pas du Miroir, five miles out of Tursac, survived into modern times. They made stone lamps, and one was found at La Mouthe, decorated with an engraved head of an ibex. The valley of the Vézère was the thoroughfare for herds of cattle seeking southern pastures. Bison, deer, boar and elk were killed for their meat and skins; reindeer were providers of particularly succulent venison; rivers were fished for salmon, pike and trout; but lions, wolves and leopards were feared.

All these animals were carved and delineated deep inside caves in an astonishing naturalistic fashion. We have found the limestone slabs on which the Cro-Magnons ground their pigments, as well as the hollow bones in which the artists kept their paints. They used ochre for red and yellow, as well as manganese for black paint. Paint was applied in dots or with a bird's feather. On a ledge beneath an engraving was found the burin they had used millennia ago.

Not all prehistoric men and women were artists. The ancestors of those who have left us the necklaces, tools and curiously carved 'Venuses' came to the Dordogne from the less hospitable regions of eastern Europe something like a million years ago. We can see their descendants beginning to experiment with paint. At Font-de-Gaume one of them placed his hand against the cave wall and blew paint around it. Finally, in shelters and caves, these men and women, engraving and painting as they must have done entirely from memory, left for us works of art whose sensitivity has never been surpassed and which achieved a miraculous peak at Lascaux. As Georges Bataille wrote after visiting that cave, 'nothing supports the contention that we are greater than they were'.

Why did they paint? The most coherent theory was put forward by the Abbé Breuil. He suggested that Ice Age art was a form of hunting magic. Prehistoric man, according to Breuil, painted to invoke the supernatural, in an attempt to ensure 'plentiful game, which would breed and increase', and 'to make sure that enough would be killed'. Human figures such as the man painted on the wall of the Grotte de Villars, were in Breuil's view 'sorcerers', engaged in ritual magic, figuratively killing animals as a means of making sure that the hunters of the tribe would be successful.

The Abbé Breuil's theory had many merits. It explains why animals in many caves are painted over and why surfaces in the caves were re-used – often without any thought for what was already painted or engraved on them. Breuil suggested that prehistoric man painted deep inside caves and not where he normally lived because he regarded such mysterious localities as sacred. He interpreted the curious geometric patterns drawn on some walls as images of traps and snares. He also explained that the art disappeared 10,000 years ago because as the ice retreated the vast herds dispersed. Hunting magic was no longer needed.

Yet in spite of the coherence of Breuil's theory, two grave objections can be made to it. First, cave art is by no means all of a jumble, with animals superimposed on each other higgledy-piggledy. The unknown artists also painted friezes, grouped animals together, had a knowledge of perspective and, at Lascaux especially, were at times well aware of the possibilities of overall composition in a cave. Secondly, if the cave paintings are about hunting magic, why is the principal prey of Ice Age man – the reindeer – so rarely depicted? The French prehistorian André Leroi-Gourhan has calculated that the reindeer is represented by only 3.8 per cent of all the cave drawings. At Rouffignac, Leroi-Gourhan points out, there is a single reindeer, the last figure in the cave, drawn with a finger on the soft wall. At Lascaux, he adds, the bones that littered the floor of the cave, the debris of countless prehistoric meals, 'are almost exclusively of reindeer, while the walls could only produce a single and dubious image of this animal'.

Yet if Breuil's theory must be abandoned, it cannot be said that anyone else has produced a better explanation for these remarkable works of art. André Leroi-Gourhan has suggested that the animals in prehistoric cave art can be divided into two – representing the male principle and the female principle. He finds 'male' symbols predominating in the outer zones of caves and 'female' symbols chiefly in the central zones. For him a bison, for example, is a 'female' symbol, and a horse a 'male' symbol. Other scholars have asked why anyone should interpret the pregnant mares painted in several caves as somehow 'male'.

As the experts disagree the layman is tempted to suggest that our prehistoric ancestors may simply have loved to paint and carve and engrave. The man or woman who thousands of years ago saw two mammoths, their heads locked together, remembered the scene and painted it on a wall in the cave at Rouffignac, might have done so simply out of pleasure, to please others and perhaps even leave something for immediate posterity. It is this thought that gives you an exquisite *frisson* when confronted with Ice Age art. As Georges Bataille, writing of Lascaux, observed, these paintings constitute 'our earliest *tangible* trace, our first sign of art and also of man'.

All the more bizarre, then, is the phenomenon known as Lascaux II. When the Lascaux cave was opened to the public in July 1948, the response was remarkable. Soon more than 100,000 visitors a year came to Montignac in search of this prehistoric wonder. In August 1962, something like 1,800 persons a day visited the cave, their breath causing more damage to the paintings than they had suffered for 14,000 years and persuading the minister for culture, André Malraux, to close them for good.

Many refused to believe it. Every summer since then an average of a hundred people a day have arrived at Montignac and been turned away from the Lascaux cave. In response to this, the French government and the owner of Lascaux took the decision to build a replica. In an old quarry close by to Lascaux I, Lascaux II was slowly constructed. An underground skin of concrete and resin was created, eighty metres long. Inside this, layers of chicken wire supported by girders were covered in concrete whose contours reproduced those of Lascaux I. Then a team of artists set about recreating the original Lascaux, helped by French television, which filmed centimetre by centimetre the masterpiece of Ice Age man. In July 1983 Lascaux II was opened to the public.

The first example of prehistoric cave art to be discovered in the nineteenth century was at Altamira in Spain. So astonishingly 'modern' were the paintings that most prehistorians – led by Émile Cartailhac – dismissed them as fakes. What convinced scholars of the authenticity of prehistoric art was the excavation of the Grotte de La Mouthe in the Dordogne in 1895. La Mouthe contained not only a painted/sculpted bison but also a stone lamp by whose light the prehistoric artists might have fashioned the beast. In 1902 Émile Cartailhac admitted his error in a famous essay entitled '*Mea Culpa d'un sceptique*'. It is ironic that the same *département* which contained the evidence that convinced the scholarly world of the authenticity of mankind's earliest art should now possess – at a cost of £500,000 – its own stupendous fake.

❧ 7 ❧

The Cradle of Poets

Henry Miller described the Dordogne as 'the cradle of the poets'. Here 700 years ago the troubadours created what became the quintessential theme of lyric poety. They sang (as Charles Albert Cingria put it) 'not of happy, crowned and satisfied love, but on the contrary of love perpetually unsatisfied – and but two characters: a poet reiterating his plaint eight hundred, nine hundred, a thousand times; and a fair lady who ever says "No".'

According to Dante the greatest troubadour was Arnaut Daniel. 'In love songs and prose he excelled all the rest.' Dante placed him in purgatory, where Arnaut told him, 'I weep, but I continue to sing.' In real life Arnaut had transformed the purgatory of unrequited love into matchless poetry. He came of a noble family and was born in the château at Ribérac. His parents wished him to become a prince of the Church, but Arnaut chose the path of a poor minstrel, singing in vain for his lady. 'If I cannot return to her for whom my heart breaks and breaks,' he declared, 'I desire neither to be made Pope nor Holy Roman Emperor. Unless before the year is out she eases my anguish with a kiss, she will destroy me and I shall be damned.'

Blasphemously Arnaut dared say he loved his lady more than anyone could love God. 'I know no one – hermit, monk or priest – who worships God so constantly as I worship her of whom I sing.' For him the pain of unrequited love was exquisite. 'Desire for her has so greatly led me astray that I know not whether my heart dances or grieves.' He did know that such passion had transformed his world, and could do so for others, too. 'A man pursuing love must so surrender himself that to him even the cuckoo will seem a dove and the Puy-de-Dôme a plain.'

Arnaut may have written the finest lyrics in praise of an unattainable lady, but many others in the twelfth century shared such poetic grief. Aimeric de Sarlat became a wandering troubadour and remained passionately, jealously faithful to a lady who did not return his love. As if to ensure that their love remained unrequited, some troubadours deliberately addressed themselves to married women. Elias Carels, who was born in Sarlat around the year 1190, dedicated lyrics to the King of Aragon, to the Emperor Frederick II and, above all, to the Marquis of Montferrat whom he accompanied on expeditions and missions. He also declared his hopeless love for the marquis's wife Isabella, exulting over her 'blond hair like refined gold'. Bertrand de Born professed love for a married woman whom he called Maheut de Montagnac. 'Lady,' he lamented, 'since you refuse to think of me and drive me away without reason, I do not know where to find love.'

Passion of this kind overflowed into marvellous lyrical descriptions of these women. Bertrand de Born wrote of his beloved:

> A lady fresh and finely free,
> Gaily she goes, and gracefully;
> Ruby-shot gold her hair you see,
> More white her limbs than flour can be,
> Plump arms, and breasts spread firm for me,
> A rabbit's supple loins has she . . .

Did love need to be unrequited to produce such verse? Possibly not. Arnaut de Mareuil, a lowly born cleric of Château Mareuil, travelled the whole world for twenty years, singing, reading romances, losing money dicing and drinking. He finally married a fat, beautiful woman named Guillaumette Monja, and wrote for her a poem attributing his inspiration to their love: 'The great beauty and sure intelligence, the courteous words and fresh colour found in that lovely valorous woman, give me the skill and knowledge of my singing.'

These poets also reflected and even celebrated the darker side of the Middle Ages. The *Vita* of Bertrand de Born observes that 'Always he was at war with his neighbours and with the count of Périgord as long as he was count of Poitou. He was a good knight and a good warrior, as well as a shrewd and gallant man and a good troubadour.' But, the biographer adds, 'he always wanted the king of France and the king of England to be at war with each other . . . If there was the slightest truce, he strove and did all in his power to unmake the peace.'

Bertrand de Born became Lord of Hautefort by throwing his brother Constantine out of the château. Constantine appealed for help to Richard Cœur de Lion. Bertrand sought the support of Henry Court-Mantel, the son of Henry II. While Henry II was still alive, Henry Court-Mantel had been crowned as 'the young king' of England and made Duke of Normandy. Bertrand persuaded the young king to rebel against his father and helped him to lay waste part of Périgord. When the young king was killed, Henry II besieged Hautefort, captured Bertrand and condemned him to death. But Bertrand sang before the king a lament for his son:

> If all the misfortunes, the tears and the miseries
> Of this grievous century were gathered together,
> They would seem light alongside the death
> Of the young king of England.

Henry II wept, and forgave the troubadour, observing, 'My son wished only for your good. He loved you, and for love of him I shall give you your château, your fortune, your life and my friendship.'

If Henry II forgave Bertrand de Born, Dante did not. For persuading the young king to rebel against his father, Dante placed Bertrand de Born in hell, carrying in grisly fashion his own severed head:

> Io vidi certo, ed ancor par ch'io 'l veggia,
>   un busto senza capo andar sì come
>   andavan gli altri della trista greggia;
> e il capo tronco tenea per le chiome,
>   pesol con mano, a guisa di lanterna;
>   e quel mirava noi e dicea: 'Oh me!'
> Di sè faceva a sè stesso lucerna,
>   ed eran due in uno, e uno in due;
>   com'esse può, quei sa che si governa.
>
> Quando diritto al piè del ponte fue,
>   levò 'l braccio alto con tutta la testa
>   per appressarne le parole sue,
> che furo: 'Or vedi la pena molesta
>   tu che, spirando, vai veggendo i morti:
>   vedi s'alcuna è grande come questa!
> E perchè tu di me novella porti,

sappi ch'io son Bertram dal Bornio, quelli
che diedi al re giovane i ma' conforti.
Io feci il padre e il figlio in sè ribelli.

[Without doubt I saw and still seem to see passing before me a headless
trunk, just as the rest of that sad flock paced onwards. It carried its severed
head by the hair, as if it were a lantern hanging from its hand. It looked at
us and cried 'Oh me!' Thus it lit itself, and the two, though divided, were
one. How that could be, He knows who ordered it.

When it was directly at the foot of the bridge, it stopped, lifting the head
high so that we might hear what it said, which was: 'Now see this grievous
torment, you who are still alive and spy on the dead, see if there be any
sorrow like mine; and since you seek news of me, know that I am Bertrand
de Born, who gave evil counsel to the young king. I made father and son
rebels against each other.]

Yet Dante also recognized Bertrand de Born's genius in applying
the eloquence of a poet to the vicious art of war in a way no Italian
poet had yet done. War for pillage and booty was part of the economy
of feudal life. Bertrand de Born was a perfect feudal baron, who
dreamt of battles, money and personal vengeance, with love coming
only a close second. War released money, and Bertrand exulted in the
fact:

> I love to see the rich men brawl;
> Rich goods to serving-folk then fall,
> To castellans. Rich nobles all
> More generously their funds release,
> More easily in war than peace.

But I suspect that Bertrand and his fellow-troubadours also exulted in
war and bloodshed quite apart from any incidental benefit these might
bring to the general economy. Small wonder that they revered Richard
Cœur de Lion, even when fighting against him. 'Now I shall sing a
song, for Yea and Nay has come with plundering flames, and blood is
shed,' wrote Bertrand. Arnaut de Mareuil lamented Richard's death
in 1195 in a famous poem: 'The king is dead, the bravest king I've
seen, the bravest earth has seen these thousand years.'

Poets have usually welcomed the spring as quickening thoughts
of love. Bertrand de Born saw it as heralding a new season of
battles:

I love the gay time of spring, when the leaves and flowers
reappear;
And I love to hear the jubilation of the winds singing in
the bocage;
And I love to see tents and pavilions dressed on the
fields;
And I am filled with happiness to see knights and lords in
armour ranged in the countryside.

He confessed too that his heart was glad when he heard the neighing of
horses whose riders had been killed in battle and the groans of men
crying 'Help me! Help me!' He preferred his Périgord crimson to green.

In the twentieth century the fierce American poet Ezra Pound
warmed to this side of Bertrand de Born and even wrote a poem to
honour it:

Dante Alighieri put this man in hell for that he was a
stirrer-up of strife.
Eccovi!
Have I dug him up again? . . .
I have no life save when the swords clash.
But ah! when I see the standards gold, vair, purple opposing,
And the broad fields beneath them turn crimson,
Then howl I my heart nigh mad with rejoicing.

Most of us, I think, prefer the courtly lover to the bloodthirsty
knight. This is the Bertrand of the troubadour legends in Périgord. In
one such legend, Bertrand is singing and playing his music close by the
Château de Coulanges, when a beautiful woman appears. He begs to
entertain her. She tells him that she has not smiled for many years,
and welcomes him into the château. He sings a tender song, saying
that no flower can give off a scent comparable to hers. Then the
troubadour sees that the lady is weeping. 'I wanted to make you
happy,' he cries. She replies, 'Your music has indeed given me great
pleasure,' but the following morning she is still crying. She asks
Bertrand not to chide her, for if he does, she says, the château will fall
in ruins and she will die. Unable to hold the words back, Bertrand
cries, 'I love you as I have never loved anyone else.' Then he wakes
from his dream and finds himself among the castle ruins.

Yet to savour properly the literature of the Dordogne you must somehow hold together both the savagery and the sweetness of the troubadours. This was a literary mix that persisted in Périgord. In 1540 a nephew of Abbot Pierre de Mareuil of Brantôme was born in the nearby town of Bourdeilles, took the name Pierre de Bourdeille and is known to literature as Brantôme! Brantôme became a soldier of fortune, fighting not only in his own land but also in Malta, Italy, Morocco, England and Scotland. He was one who guarded Mary Queen of Scots when she was imprisoned at Leith. His amorous adventures were as varied as his military ones. Then in 1589 he fell so badly from his horse that he was permanently crippled.

Pierre de Bourdeille returned to Brantôme and, though a layman, became abbot of the monastery. There he wrote two famous works: his *Lives of Famous Men and Great Commanders* and *Ladies of Love*. The scurrilous nature of the second has helped to keep Brantôme's memory green in France. But the truth is that Pierre de Bourdeille, like Bertrand de Born before him, was enthralled as much by war as by love, as much by the warrior as by the courtesan.

For my part I infinitely prefer Brantôme's stories of fighting men (and women) to his tales of courtesans. Of the latter, two examples must suffice. First, an example of love turning to hatred:

I knew of a lady of considerable rank who gave an assignation to her lover to pass the night with her. He presented himself in his nightshirt, eager to do his duty; but, inasmuch as it was winter and very cold, he had become so chilled on his way that when he was abed he was good for nothing, and could think only of getting warm; wherefore the lady conceived a hatred for him and would have no more ado with him.

Secondly, a tale of the revenge of a cuckolded husband:

I have heard tell of one such husband who surprised his wife in her loves and gave her poison, whereof she languished more than four years and became dry as wood; and went often to see her, taking pleasure in this withering, and laughing at her, saying she had no more than she deserved.

Brantôme's *Ladies of Love* is filled with such profitless questions as whether a cuckolded husband should punish his unfaithful wife, her lover, or both of them; or why, of all the ladies at the court of Savoy, the French were the most charming. He also offers his readers such stale wisdom as:

> In the game of war
> and the game of love,
> For a single joy,
> a hundred griefs.

It seems to me, however, that in spite of his undoubted prowess in both, Brantôme found the game of war far more satisfying than the game of love. Certainly his writings on war, valour and fights crackle with life. I like best those illustrating the superior valour of the Spaniards over all other nations save the English, who, Brantôme rightly observes, always beat them. He published sixty-three delightful Spanish oaths, including: 'Yes: as true as these gashes in my face,' and 'Yes: by these whiskers, which owe their growth to cannon smoke.'

Even though the English always beat the Spaniards, he shows Spain fighting back. He dedicated his *Spanish Rhodomontades* to Margaret, Queen of France and Navarre, so our example is fittingly a fiery Spanish lady whose husband had been imprisoned by the English king. Since no ransom sufficed to secure his release, the lady wrote threatening to declare war herself on the King of England: 'And if I can find no captain, I'll take in hand the standard myself and come and fix it on the gates of London. And if I lack cannoneers, I'll fire off the artillery myself, so that the whole world shall say, "Jesu! What a warlike woman is this!" '

Generous as he was to the prowess of the English, Brantôme lost no opportunity of praising his fellow-Périgourdins. If it is bizarre to find an abbot celebrating courtesans and warriors, it is yet more so to come across one mocking the papal curia as well. But Brantôme tells the story of M. de Grignaux of Périgord, a friend of his father, who visited Rome at a time when Louis XII of France was at odds with the Pope.

There the Périgourdin saw five or six cardinals off to cast the devil out of a possessed man. M. de Grignaux knew that on such occasions the devil sometimes jumped out of one person straight into another. He therefore waylaid the cardinals and delivered himself of a magnificent insult. He offered to accompany them to the exorcism and there throw himself, fully-clothed, into a holy-water stock. Filling his mouth with the sacred liquid, de Grignaux promised to wait until he saw the devil emerge from the possessed man and then spout the water all over the fiend, 'plying him with it continuously, till he makes his way either out of a window or into the body of one of you, who are not a jot cleaner or better than I am, but rather worse; nay fouler than the devil himself, for you do nothing but trick, betray and impose upon the king my master'.

The Wars of Religion gave much scope for a soldier like Brantôme. Others in warlike Périgord paused for thought. The greatest of these was Michel Eyquem de Montaigne.

Born in 1533 in his father's château on one of the vine-covered hills of the Dordogne, Montaigne was the eldest son of a Gascon gentleman who remained a staunch Catholic. Three of Montaigne's brothers and one sister also remained Catholic, but another sister and two other brothers embraced Protestantism. Montaigne's personal experience of religious diversity was enriched by the fact that his mother was a Jewess. Huguenots flourished in the region of Bergerac where the Montaigne family lived. Before he was thirty years old they were engaged in a bitter struggle for existence which persisted intermittently throughout his life.

As a child Montaigne was brilliant. His father arranged for a German tutor who knew no French to bring the boy up speaking Latin as his first language. Latin fitted him to read medieval theology (and later to translate it into French), to read and enjoy the plays of the ancients when he was at school in Bordeaux (where he was taught by the Scottish humanist George Buchanan), and then to study law at the University of Toulouse. In the mid 1550s he became a counsellor in the Cour des Aides at Périgueux, a court which soon merged with the *parlement* of Bordeaux.

Before long Montaigne began to perceive the hypocrisy of the law as it was practised in Bordeaux. He spotted a judge writing out a judgment against an adulterer and then tearing a piece off the paper to send a billet-doux to a colleague's wife. And he was obliged to watch tortures that he found brutal, useless and absurd. In 1565 he married Françoise de Chassaigne. Of their six children only one survived infancy; but Françoise did bring him a large dowry. When his father died three years after the marriage, Montaigne took the opportunity of leaving the profession he now found distasteful. He sold his post as counsellor and retired to the family Château of Saint-Michel-de-Montaigne, just north of Montcaret.

Because of a disastrous fire in the late nineteenth century, all you can see today of the château as Montaigne knew it is the chapel on the ground floor, the tiny room where he said his prayers, and the tower where he wrote. Here you can still see fifty-four sentences in Greek and Latin which Montaigne had painted on the beams. These phrases sum up Montaigne's stoic, even cynical attitude to life: 'Neither wish for nor fear your last day'; 'Man is no more than a vase made of clay'; 'Why this rather than that?'; 'Mud and ashes, what have you to boast about?'; 'The wind swells empty goatskins and fame swells empty heads'.

But apart from a crisis of scepticism in the mid 1570s, Montaigne retained his faith. 'There is nothing so easy, so gentle, so favourable as the law of God,' he wrote. 'It calls us to itself, sinful and detestable as we are. It stretches out arms to us and takes us to its bosom, no matter how vile, filthy and besmirched we are now and will be in the future.' Montaigne remained a Catholic because he believed that continually calling authority into question pointed the way to complete disbelief. 'Once the vulgar see that some articles of religion have been called into question,' he judged, 'they will soon come to regard all other beliefs as equally uncertain and accept nothing at all on authority.'

Montaigne believed that the old religion was best, but his family history inclined him also towards tolerance. Around him he saw many, 'whom passion drives beyond the bounds of reason', advocating violence and injustice in the cause of true religion. 'I live in a time when we abound in incredible examples of cruelty,' he said. 'In the ancient histories we can see nothing more extreme that what we experience every day.' The former lawyer knew how men and women could disagree over the most trivial matters. 'No two men ever had the same opinion of the same thing,' he once declared. In Montaigne's view, one should accept and learn from disagreements, after the example of Socrates ('the most perfect man I ever heard of'). In his essay 'Of the Art of Discussion' Montaigne wrote, 'When someone opposes me, he arouses my attention, not my anger. I go to meet a man who contradicts me and thus instructs me.'

In Montaigne's day, however, few settled their religious disagreements by means of this Socratic method. After the massacre of St Bartholomew's day, 1572, when between 5,000 and 10,000 Huguenots were murdered, Montaigne made a vain attempt to mediate between the Catholic Henri de Guise and the Protestant Henri de Navarre. In 1580 he decided to escape for a while from his own strifetorn land, and travelled extensively in Switzerland, Bavaria, the Tyrol and Italy. The following year, while he was still in Italy, Montaigne was elected (without being told beforehand) to serve two terms, each lasting two years, as Mayor of Bordeaux. Reluctantly he took office. He ruled Bordeaux when a disastrous plague killed almost half the population. Doggedly he tried to reconcile Huguenot and Catholic, suffering attacks from both sides as a moderate.

For a man whose motto was '*Que sais-je?*', such obloquy from the bigoted was not easy to bear. Part of Montaigne's defence lay in his conviction that no one could read his innermost thoughts. We all need, he wrote, 'a room at the back of the shop' (*une arrière boutique*), where we can think for ourselves in secret, even though wise men will outwardly conform to the established order.

With such opinions he survived and even achieved happiness in those uncongenial times. The humour of the man shines through his essays. He savoured smells, though he held that 'the most perfect smell for a woman is to smell of nothing'. (In any case, he thought women shouldn't be noticed most of the time!) He rejoiced that his thick moustache could retain the smell of something he had eaten for hours afterwards. He did not like the smell of Venice or Paris, but he longed to learn of cooks who could fill dishes with incredible savoury aromas.

Montaigne insisted that a human being had the right to accept himself for himself, and not for any great attainment in this world. 'We are great fools. We say of someone, "He has spent his day in idleness." We say, "I have done nothing today." What? Have you not lived? That is the most fundamental and the most marvellous of all occupations.' The true aim of life, according to Michel de Montaigne, is 'not to win, or to write books, or to gain battles and lands, but to live orderly and tranquilly. To live properly is our great and glorious masterpiece.'

As W. H. Auden recognized in his lovely poem on Montaigne, views of this kind were almost revolutionary in sixteenth-century France. From his quiet tower in the Dordogne Montaigne preached tolerance to the bigoted, scepticism to the doctrinaire, self-knowledge to the hypocrite and self-fulfilment as the goal of life:

Outside his library window he could see
A gentle landscape terrified of grammar,
Cities where lisping was compulsory,
And provinces where it was death to stammer.

The hefty sprawled, too tired to care: it took
This donnish undersexed conservative
To start a revolution and to give
The Flesh its weapon back to defeat the Book.

When devils drive the reasonable wild,
They strip their adult century so bare,
Love must be re-grown from the sensual child,

To doubt becomes a way of definition,
Even belles-lettres legitimate as prayer,
And laziness a movement of contrition.

If Montaigne was a subversive, still more so was his greatest friend, Étienne de La Boétie. Étienne was born in 1530 in the most beautiful house in Sarlat, built in the previous decade by his father Antoine. He was ugly, as Montaigne later observed, and his soul was beautiful. By the time he was twenty-four the precocious Étienne was a counsellor in the *parlement* of Bordeaux. Two years later he met Montaigne, three years his junior. Montaigne judged him to be 'the greatest man of our century'. Then, in 1563, Étienne fell ill. Anxiously and despairingly Montaigne watched his friend die.

The citizens of Sarlat put up a statue to Étienne de La Boétie in 1892, but his real memorial is Montaigne's essay on friendship. Montaigne did not try to analyse why they loved each other or what spiritual consanguinity there might have been between them. Each was himself, and that was enough. 'I loved him,' wrote Montaigne, 'because he was himself and I was myself.' It was a friendship 'which together we fostered, so long as God willed, so entire and perfect that certainly you shall hardly read of the like and among men of today you shall see no trace of it. So many coincidences were needed to build up such a friendship that I should marvel if another were seen in the next three centuries.'

Étienne de La Boétie seemed to embody that tranquillity which Montaigne himself sought. He accepted the world, without submitting to its horrors. 'If he had been given the choice,' Montaigne said, 'he would rather have been born in Venice than in Sarlat – and with reason. But sovereignly imprinted in his soul was another maxim: to obey and submit religiously to the laws under which he was born.' But this did not lead him to accept blindly the fanaticism of the age. 'There never was a better citizen or one more devoted to the tranquillity of his country, or more hostile to the commotions or innovations of his time,' averred Montaigne.

'With death in his throat', Étienne de La Boétie bequeathed his papers to Montaigne. La Boétie was a Hellenist and had translated Plutarch and Xenophon; he also wrote sonnets for an ideal mistress, whom he dubbed 'Dourdouigne'. Montaigne had them published. In spite of Étienne's notion that he would have preferred to have been born in Venice, one of them at least speaks to me of the misery of not being in the Dordogne:

> Hélas, combien de jours, hélas, combien de nuits
> J'ai vécu loin du lieu où mon cœur fait demeaure!
> C'est le vingtième jour que sans jour je demeure,
> Mais en vingt jours j'ai eu tout un siècle d'ennuis.

[Alas, alas, how many nights and days have I lived far from where my heart would live! For twenty days I have lived homeless and in those twenty days have endured a century of tedium.]

But to love the Dordogne, to serve as a counsellor in the Bordeaux *parlement*, to write fine sonnets and to die at the age of thirty-two hardly qualifies Étienne de La Boétie as the greatest man of the sixteenth century. What I find remarkable about La Boétie is the extraordinary treatise on *Voluntary Servitude*, which he wrote at the age of eighteen and which Montaigne published after his death.

As its title implies, *Voluntary Servitude* asks why people willingly give up their liberty in order to serve others. In particular, Étienne asks, what makes men and women submit to a tyrant? He concluded that the basis of a tyrant's power is not the tyrant's own strength but the vast assembly of those who prop him up for their own tiny profit.

Étienne de La Boétie found it astonishing that so many people preferred such trivial rewards to their own freedom. He observed with sorrow that 'there are almost as many to whom tyranny is profitable as there are those to whom liberty would be agreeable'. In his own view, 'liberty is so great a good and so lovely that where it is lost all evils follow one upon another, and even the good which may remain loses its taste and flavour, being spoiled by servitude'.

If it is an anachronism to speak pejoratively of 'overlords' and 'underlings' in the Middle Ages, for such an attitude would scarcely have been understood by those who lived then, suddenly with Étienne de La Boétie the pretensions of unjustified power were revealed. In Étienne's eyes, those who accept tyranny of their own free will are as morally culpable as the tyrant himself. If they seemed to prosper in this world, they should suffer in the next. God, asserted La Boétie, 'must assuredly reserve some peculiar punishment in hell for tyrants *and for their accomplices*'.

Almost certainly the passion behind the cool prose of Étienne de La Boétie's treatise was inspired by the horror of the revenge taken by Henri II against the people of Bordeaux when they rebelled against the salt-tax in 1548. The rebels had assassinated the king's representative. Henri's response was to order a massacre. Montaigne's father, who was Mayor of Bordeaux at this time, succeeded in buying off the king only by distributing to influential personages at court much of the finest wine grown around his château.

The century that followed the publication of Étienne de La Boétie's attack on tyranny seems in retrospect to have been dominated by the absolutism of *le roi soleil*, Louis XIV. The treatise of the precocious Sarladais had its readers, but only with the radicals of nineteenth-century France did *Voluntary Servitude* play any major role in inspiring French political attitudes.

But the radical flame of Montaigne and Étienne de La Boétie could not be quenched. In the autocratic years of the seventeenth and eighteenth centuries it found expression in the life and writings of one of the most remarkable of all Périgourdins, François de Salignac de La Mothe-Fénelon, Archbishop of Cambrai.

A nineteenth-century British biographer described Fénelon as 'perhaps the most attractive and lovable (and if not the most saintly, he was certainly inferior to none in the beauty of holiness) among the many stars which shone in the Church's sky during the seventeenth century'. He was born on 6 August 1651 in the massive fifteenth-century château which lies on the left bank of the river Dordogne near the villages of Saint-Julien-de-Lampon and Sainte-Mondane, and there he spent his youth. The Salignac-Fénelon family expected preferment for such of their sons as went into the Church. Between 1567 and 1688, for all but twenty years, one of them was Bishop of Sarlat. But François, a thirteenth child, was exceptionally brilliant. After education at the newly founded seminary of Saint-Sulpice in Paris – a seminary especially concerned to train zealous clergy as teachers – Fénelon was ordained priest in 1675 and made head of a convent for the re-education of Protestant girls in the Catholic faith.

He was perfectly suited to this work – a born teacher, and a Catholic with Montaigne's tolerance. (The historian Jules Michelet slandered both by dubbing them men of 'floating beliefs'.) After Louis XIV revoked the edict of Nantes which had offered a measure of tolerance to Protestants, Fénelon undertook a three-year mission to Huguenots, attempting to convert them not by force but by argument and the beauty of his faith. His *Treatise on the Education of Girls* attracted attention, and in 1689 he was made tutor to Louis XIV's grandson, the Duke of Burgundy.

The duke was ugly, with a long nose, protruding jaw and twisted shoulder. He had neither wit nor charm. But Fénelon set about training him to be a just and Christian ruler. In that immoral court he taught the duke to detest adultery, and he wrote especially for him a brilliant educational novel, *Télémaque*. The theme of *Télémaque* is that one must be a good man to be a great king, as the legends of antiquity reveal. Fénelon used the tales of Ulysses, Hercules, Achilles, Antiope and the rest to demonstrate that 'there is in true virtue something open and ingenuous, which no art can counterfeit and which if looked for, can never be mistaken'.

This novel, though Fénelon never published it, was to be the occasion of his downfall. In the meantime he had formed a dangerous spiritual liaison with the French mystic Jeanne-Marie Bouvier de la Mothe-Guyon.

At the age of sixteen Mme Guyon had been married to an invalid twenty-two years her senior. She turned increasingly to mysticism, and after her husband's death began to wander about France along with her father confessor, preaching that the Christian soul can abandon itself to the love of God without the need for external observations, mortifications and such disciplines. In 1687 the two of them were cast into jail for heresy and suspected immorality. Mme Guyon's father confessor was not let out until 1699, but she herself was released as a result of the efforts of Mme de Maintenon (who had secretly married the king).

Mme Guyon's entry into court circles brought her teachings to the notice of Fénelon. They profoundly attracted him. They also profoundly offended the formidable Bishop of Meaux, Jacques Bénigne Bossuet. When Bossuet attacked Mme Guyon publicly, Fénelon defended her. She demanded to be heard at a theological commission, and in 1695 one was convened at Issy. Here again Fénelon defended her and Bossuet attacked her. Fénelon lost.

As Michael de la Bedoyere has written,

> History thinks of Bossuet and Fénelon as men born to differ and to clash . . . Bossuet, the 'Eagle', dominant, aggressive, sure of himself and of a world eternally ordered and shaped by Christian monarchy; Fénelon, the 'Swan', gently and dreamily floating along the tide, conscious of the strangeness and never-ending novelty of man and his world, contemplative, feeling his way, unsure of his goal, yet instinctively pursuing it in graceful circles.

There is truth in this, though as Michael de la Bedoyere points out, Fénelon had greatly admired Bossuet and learned much from him. But Fénelon's was the subtler mind. In consequence, as Michelet observed, this time justly, he was both the most religious man of his era and also almost a heretic. In the year the theological commission met at Issy he was consecrated Archbishop of Cambrai. Two years later he published forty-five articles setting out his distinctions between true and false mysticism. Bossuet managed to persuade the Holy See to condemn Fénelon's book.

Fénelon was now out of favour with the court. In 1697 King Louis XIV banished him to Cambrai. In 1698 he was deprived of his position as a royal tutor. The following year an enemy published *Télémaque* without the author's permission. It was instantly seen as an attack on the monarchy.

In vain Fénelon protested that he had not written a political satire. But *Télémaque* was one of those books which (in Étienne de La Boétie's words) 'recall the memory of things past to compare them with the present and make a judgement of the future'. Fénelon could not help contrasting the virtues of the past with the vices of the present. And in the radical tradition of Périgord, he clearly detested absolutism.

He was also indiscreet, not to say unworldly. Passionately desiring to reform the French court, he had once sent a letter to Mme de Maintenon pointing out that the king was 'scrupulous about little things and hardened to terrible evils'. Louis XIV, the letter continued, loved only his own glory and his own comfort. Inevitably the king and his courtiers now read the final sentences of *Télémaque* as a direct indictment of themselves:

Men are continually talking of virtue and merit, but there are few who know precisely what is meant by either; they are splendid terms indeed, but with respect to the greatest part of those who take a pride in perpetually repeating them, of uncertain significance. Justice, reason and virtue must be resolved into some certain principles, before it can be determined who are just, reasonable and virtuous: the maxims of a wise and good administrator must be known, before those who adopt them can be distinguished from those who substitute false refinement and political cunning in their stead.

Fénelon remained in disgrace in his diocese for the rest of his life. 'Whilst the world smiles on us and our way seems smooth,' he wrote, 'let us beware. Never are we better disposed for the next life than when things go badly for us in this one.' When the War of the Spanish Succession reached Cambrai, Fénelon ministered with equal kindness to wounded friends and enemies of his country. In 1715 he died prematurely of a fever contracted after a carriage accident.

But neither disgrace nor death could silence the opinions of this brilliant, meek Périgourdin. In eighteenth-century France his *Télémaque* went through 185 editions.

Fénelon longed for a good king, not for a republic. The Dordogne nurtured men and women who likewise remained royalist, even during the tumultuous years of the Revolution and Napoleon Bonaparte. The most famous was the philosopher and statesman, Maine de Biran, who was born in Bergerac in 1766. Two kilometres out of Bergerac on the road to Périgueux is a little stream known as the Cadeau. There a narrow road winds east through Pécharmant vineyards to the top of a plateau dominating the region, next to Saint-Sauveur, in whose churchyard Maine de Biran now lies. The road then winds through picturesque hamlets and *lieux-dits* with names like Rapaille, Touli-

faut, Chante-Alouette and Sans-Pareil, to the manor house of Grateloup which he loved. Maine de Biran's diary is full of affection for his
part of the Dordogne. 'Paris is not my lodging by preference, and I
long for the moment when I can quit it and return to live peacefully at
my Grateloup ... Sadly, again I said goodbye to my home, my trees,
my fields.'

In 1789 Maine de Biran was serving in the royal guard at Paris.
Wounded in 1791, he returned to Grateloup. Unable to live off his
land alone, he accepted the post of administrator of the Dordogne in
1795. He took part in the intellectual life of Paris and was a member
of the Committee of 500. Napoleon made him *Sous-préfet* of Bergerac.

Maine de Biran was an energetic administrator. He cleared land,
started a children's school on the principles of Pestalozzi and was an
enthusiastic vaccinator. He persuaded the doctors of Bergerac to set
up an association in order to improve their mutual skills. At the same
time he brooded and wrote about philosophy. He meditated on Fénelon as well as Descartes, and held that men and women could live on
one of three levels: submerged 'to all the appetites and impulses of the
flesh'; 'fighting against all the unruly desires of our animal nature by
moral force'; or 'absorbed in God'.

Philosophers frequently walk with their heads in the clouds and fall
into ditches. Maine de Biran's private life was not without problems.
In order to marry his sweetheart Louise Fournier he took advantage
of a Revolutionary law allowing her to divorce her émigré husband.
Unfortunately the husband unexpectedly returned in 1805. Louise died
of a brainstorm and Maine de Biran married one of his cousins.

Today Maine de Biran is remembered chiefly for his philosophy
and especially for his influence on the intuitionism of Henri Bergson.
But he was also an acute observer of the contemporary scene. He
disliked Napoleon, insisting that one so strong as the emperor ought
to exercise his power gently. He welcomed the return of the monarchy
but deplored the intolerance of the Restoration. He did not approve at
all of the success of the ultra-royalist party. He died in 1824 fearing
for the future of the monarchy.

By contrast the greatest nineteenth-century novelist of the Dordogne, Eugène Le Roy, rejoiced at the downfall of the monarchy and
all that it stood for. Eugène Le Roy was a republican and a freemason
who had suffered personally for his beliefs. He was born in 1836 into

a family that on his father's side had served the lords of Château Hautefort for generations. Eugène's mother also worked in the château, starting at the age of twenty as a chambermaid.

Eugène's parents wanted him to become a priest, and the Baron of Hautefort agreed to pay for his education. The Revolution of 1848 opened the boy's eyes to what he considered the servitude of his fellow Périgourdins, and he increasingly sought out peasants, listening to their memories of the outrages they had suffered in the past. He also learned business in Paris, before joining the finance department of Périgueux as a tax-collector.

Slowly he climbed in his profession. Posts at Champagne-de-Belair, Hautefort, Tocane-Saint-Apre, Domme and Jumilhac-le-Grand culminated in the position of tax-collector, third class, at Montignac. All the time Eugène Le Roy was exploring and learning more about his beloved Dordogne. At Domme he wrote, 'There was no track of our slopes, no wood, no coomb that I did not follow in my iron clogs, and not a cottage or château which I did not enter. I ferreted out every old hairy trunk, every archive in the town halls, every book in the dusty libraries.'

He also scandalized many people by giving an illegitimate son to Mlle Marie Peyronnet, who worked in the post office at Jumilhac-le-Grand.

Eugène Le Roy joined up to fight in the Franco-Prussian war of 1870 and was deeply dismayed at the defeat of his country. Then the blow fell. Le Roy's anti-clerical and republican views were anathema to the intensely conservative ruling class, who in 1871 would have brought back the monarchy if they could. Eugène Le Roy was dismissed.

He fought back, passionately defending his views in a series of articles in *Le Réveil de la Dordogne*. He was forced to live once again in the home of his parents, but in 1877 he defiantly married Marie Peyronnet in a civil ceremony and legitimized their son Hubert Yvon Laurent. The authorities were finally forced to relent, and Le Roy was reinstated as tax-collector, first class.

These bitter struggles provided the biting edge of Eugène Le Roy's masterpiece, *Jacquou le Croquant*, which he first published in 1899 as *La Forêt Barade*. Set for the most part in that deep wood of Périgord Vert, *Jacquou le Croquant* takes literary vengeance for the untold sufferings of the French peasant over the centuries.

Le Roy's very title is evocative, not only of the *Croquants* of the fifteenth and sixteenth centuries, but also of the *Jacquerie* who rose against the nobility of the Île-de-France on 28 May 1358 in protest against misery and poverty after the capture of the French king by the English. But Eugène Le Roy was also writing about his own century: the story of *Jacquou le Croquant* takes place between 1815 and 1830.

In 1815 the victorious allies exiled Napoleon; but the new king, Louis XVIII, attempted to preserve the achievements of the Revolution by retaining representative government, freedom of the press and the idea of a career open to talent. The first point of his charter of June 1814 was: 'Frenchmen of whatever title or rank are equal before the law.' Yet the peasants, lower clergy and most tradesmen were excluded from politics; and the ultra-royalists, many of them returning émigrés, led by the king's brother, the Comte d'Artois, were determined to restore the former privileges of the higher clergy and nobility. Almost immediately they succeeded in passing a law prescribing transportation as the punishment for 'sedition'.

The process of reaction accelerated with the accession of the Comte d'Artois as Charles X in 1824. The émigrés were paid 1,000m francs in compensation for estates confiscated during the Revolution. A new law of sacrilege threatened religious toleration and even the discussion of religion. The Jesuit order was readmitted to France and allowed to teach in state schools. The ministry of the religious fanatic Polignac in 1829 brought matters to a head, and in July 1830 a revolution in Paris, led by Thiers and Cavaignac, brought about the downfall of the king.

Against this background Eugène Le Roy tells the story of Jacques Ferral, known as 'Jacquou le Croquant', who is seven years old in 1815. Jacquou's father is a poor smallholder living in the Barade forest near Combenègre on the vast estates of the Count de Nansac. In face of harassment from Laborie, the steward of Château Nansac, he poaches game that the count claims belongs solely to him. When Laborie viciously kills the peasant's dog, Jacquou's father murders him in return, and then is hunted like an animal through the forest. Caught, he is sentenced to the galleys, and there dies. When the mayor casually tells Jacquou's mother, 'Your husband died a fortnight ago . . . If you wish you can have a mass said for him,' she replies: 'Poor people don't need masses. They live in hell in this world.'

Thrown out of their cottage, Jacquou and his mother take refuge in an abandoned kiln, where he watches her die. Jacquou tells the story:

Imagine a boy of nine, alone in a shack, lost in the middle of the forest, with his mother in agony. For several hours the poor unhappy woman fought against death, crazily beating her arms, trying to pull off the coverlet, completely lifting herself up in the throes of the fever, wild-eyed and panting, before falling back breathless on the bed and starting to breathe again only with a painful effort. Towards midnight or one o'clock the fever ceased, and I heard a hoarse sound coming from her chest: the 'rommeau' or rattle of death. It lasted half an hour. I was lying on the bench next to the bed, half-crouching and holding my poor mother's hand tightly against my breast. At the very end she became completely conscious. She turned her eyes towards me in agonized despair, and two great tears rolled down her thin brown cheeks. Then her lips moved. The rattle stopped. She was dead!

The local priest, judging that Jacquou's mother was a Huguenot because she rarely attended mass, refuses to pray for her soul and she is given a pauper's funeral. But Eugène Le Roy was not so unsubtle as to make every priest or nobleman a villain. Jacquou is taken in and educated by the kindly Abbé Bonal, his friend the aged Chevalier de Galibert and Galibert's sister. These characters become vehicles for Eugène Le Roy's Rousseauesque views, praising life led far away from corrupting cities: 'Eat the bread that you are proud of,' Galibert tells Jacquou, 'made from wheat you grew yourself.' But they are ultimately, in Le Roy's view, dying breeds. Galibert and his sister have no issue. The Abbé Bonal gives up his profession and becomes a peasant farmer. The old order has changed.

Jacquou, having vowed to avenge his father, now has also the death of his mother to add to his hatred of the great ones in the château. As a boy he has already begun to take revenge – beheading one of the dogs of the château, setting fire to the count's forests. Neither the gentle Abbé Bonal nor Jacquou's fiancée Lina can persuade him to renounce vengeance. The count has him flung into the 'oubliette' of the château, and Lina in despair drowns herself into the river Gour.

The Chevalier de Galibert eventually rescues Jacquou, who at last takes his revenge. He secretly stirs the whole countryside against those who live in the château. Following the example of the old *Croquants*, they burn it to the ground, Jacquou himself setting fire to the building.

The count, who destroyed Jacquou's father and mother and lost him his fiancée, is ruined. And in 1830 the brilliant advocacy of Jacquou's lawyer persuades the court at Périgueux to acquit him.

Eugène Le Roy possessed the ability to invest credible characters with enormous symbolism. As Jacquou is about to burn the château he learns that the count's fiery daughter Galiote will not come down from her room. He goes to rescue her, and she attempts to kill him with her dagger. Jacquou seized Galíote around her waist and carried the resisting girl out of the castle. As he did so, he was strangely moved.

In spite of all my hatred for the Count de Nansac, hatred which spilled over on to all his family, I was deeply stirred as I carried this beautiful creature through the rooms and corridors. Her breath on my face and the feeling of her superb body against me as she struggled to escape sent into my mind some of those brutal follies perpetrated by crude soldiers when they are taking a town by storm. The sight of blood, which fell from my cheek on to Galiote's forehead, intoxicated me.

Later he meets her in the forest, proudly surviving, hunting for her own food and kindling her own fires. He realizes that she too burns with desire for him and longs to seduce her. But he also realizes that she looks down on him, 'The blood of her race looked out from her eyes as she observed me from head to foot without the slightest embarrassment, just as she would have admired a handsome horse.'

Despite their obvious attraction to each other, in Galiote and Jacquou le Croquant the old régime and the new are at war. 'In spite of the passion which drove me towards her,' Jacquou reasoned, 'I was appalled by the thought of playing the role of despised lover. Against the arrogance of the young noblewoman I opposed my pride as a man.' So instead of living with Galiote, Jacquou marries Lina's sister Bertrille. Their dozen children, followed by grandchildren and great-grandchildren, in the words of Emmanuel Le Roy Ladurie, 'literally inundate Périgord' and (according to the hopes of Eugène Le Roy) lay the foundations for a better France.

Le Roy Ladurie makes another acute point about the relationship between Eugène Le Roy and his novel *Jacquou le Croquant*. Possibly the most odious character in the book is Laborie, steward of the château. 'Another steward haunted the childhood of the novelist,' observes Le Roy Ladurie:

simply his own father, steward of Château Hautefort in the Dordogne . . . In short, the father of the hero [of Jacquou] kills in the book the father of the novelist . . . The good father assassinates the bad father. Eugène Le Roy had an account to render, with the nobility certainly, but also with his own papa. He hated to think that this father, as a superior lackey of the nobility, could have simultaneously been humiliated by his masters and an oppressor of the humble poor.

Throughout *Jacquou le Croquant* Eugène Le Roy lovingly and richly describes the Dordogne. In 1877 he and a group of like-minded Périgourdins set up a society to study and disseminate the dialect of the *département*. In a solemn rite, they gave themselves patois names. Le Roy was called '*Bournai*', which means beehive. His novels are filled with such patois words as '*chien labri*' (sheepdog), phrases like '*ça me faisait crème*' (that upset me), and descriptions of local habits, such as '*tremper la soupe*' (to put slices of stale bread in the soup).

Le Roy remained the supreme regional novelist, from his first book, *Le Moulin du Frau*, which most movingly describes just such a village school as he first went to, through *La Belle Coutellière*, which celebrates the *bastide* Domme (under the pseudonym Montglet) to his last book, *L'Ennemi de la mort*, where he is still defending his views on social equality, respect for the labourer and the dream of a continuing social revolution.

All of Eugène Le Roy's books make the Dordogne a symbol of their own beliefs. In *La Belle Coutellière*, for instance, the *bastide* of Domme becomes a symbol of primitive egalitarianism:

In this small town in those days the distinctions of class were scarcely visible. Thanks both to its isolation and the difficulty of access which repelled strangers, something had survived of the original equality of the inhabitants, created by their early charters and by the way the land was parcelled out, and strengthened by the interlocking relationships of families that had frequently intermarried.

He believed that no one in Domme set himself up as superior to his fellow-citizens. When he worked there as a tax-collector, Eugène Le Roy felt himself among a people that could laugh together or good-humouredly at each other, even if by chance some had prospered a little more than their neighbours.

And in these novels there is little of the bitterness of *Jacquou le*

Croquant. But to my mind that bitterness, hovering always beneath the surface, controlled but only barely, is what makes *Jacquou le Croquant* Le Roy's masterpiece.

Le Roy's later years, spent in retirement at Montignac, were not happy. In 1902 his son Yvon, now a medical student, died suddenly, followed shortly by Marie. Apart from *Jacquou le Croquant*, his novels made little impact on national life – though he achieved momentary fame in 1904 when he refused the offer of the Legion of Honour ('to remain faithful to my principles') and was then dubbed the Dordogne Balzac.

If the writings of Eugène Le Roy are revered in Périgord and scarcely known anywhere else, it seems to me that Cyrano de Bergerac is a local hero cynically exploited by his own *département*. Throughout the region (and elsewhere in France, too) Cyrano peers from hoardings, sniffing wine and food with his enormous nose as if it no longer filled him with shame; in Edmond Rostand's famous play the grotesque nose revolts its owner.

The Cyrano made famous by Rostand's play in 1897 was based on a real Bergeracois who lived in the seventeenth century, wrote a novel about a voyage to the sun and the moon, attacked pedantry, and was famous for his satire, his love letters and his sorcery. As a true Périgourdin he believed in liberty – social, religious and philosophical. Discerning spirits admired him, though he was also a wastrel, fighter and adventurer, long before Rostand took him up. Théophile Gautier in 1844 declared that Cyrano's merit was as great as his nose.

Rostand, in alexandrine couplets, wove around this figure a sentimental tear-jerker that was an instant success. His Cyrano is both an amazing swordsman and a poetic genius. (In one celebrated scene he makes up a *ballade* while he is fighting a duel.) So brilliant is his swordplay that in Act I a handsome musketeer, after watching Cyrano fight, strides from the crowd and shakes him by the hand: it is D'Artagnan. But his gigantic nose makes Cyrano deeply conscious that no one can ever love him. He adores the beautiful Roxane, but uses his linguistic brilliance to woo her not for himself but for the handsome idiot Christian. The relationship between the sublime and the pathetic, the beautiful and the ugly, spirit and flesh, language and feeling, all the great themes of French romanticism, are deployed and (I think) cheapened in Rostand's melodrama.

In the end the playwright pulls his punches – which no doubt partly explains why *Cyrano de Bergerac* was such a roaring success. Roxane realizes that she loves not Christian's beauty but Cyrano's soul. Love triumphs over the bulbous nose.

Far from sentimental was the Christian philosopher Léon Bloy, born in Périgueux in July 1846 of French–Spanish parents. As a young man Bloy held opinions resembling those of Eugène Le Roy. He was anti-clerical and a freemason. An obscure religious experience transformed him into the exact opposite and he became a Catholic of such a virulent kind that he found even Pope Leo XIII wanting in religious backbone. In his two novels and his journals this mystical, truculent believer sometimes extolled the love of God, but mostly excoriated priests, other writers and anyone else he disliked or felt to be unworthy. It was as if the hatreds of the Wars of Religion had once again surfaced in the Dordogne.

Bloy's love of the poor was chiefly expressed in flaying the rich, even when the rich were behaving bountifully. In 1897 fire broke out at a charity bazaar in Paris, burning to death 117 upper-class do-gooders. Bloy felt that too few had died. 'The small number of victims limited my joy,' he wrote. 'At last, I thought, AT LAST, here are the beginnings of justice.'

'So complex, so virulent, so mysterious is Léon Bloy,' observed Georges Rocal in *Léon Bloy et le Périgord*, 'that I dread leafing at random on your behalf through the eight volumes of his diary, his novels, his philippics, his syntheses of history and faith.'

Bloy strongly believed in the value of suffering. In his view the only valid reason for making a pilgrimage to the miracle-working shrine of Lourdes was to ask for the gift of pain. According to one of his letters to his fiancée, Bloy seems to have been blessed by God with this gift: 'I asked Him to let me suffer for my friends and for Him both in body and soul. But I had envisaged noble and pure suffering which, as I now see, would have been only another form of joy. I had never dreamed of this infernal suffering that He has sent me and that has consisted in His seeming withdrawal from me, leaving me defenceless in the midst of my cruellest enemies.'

It is a relief to turn from Léon Bloy to a much less talented Dordogne writer, Alberic Cahuet, who lived at Fondaumier and wrote in 1937 the charming tale, *Pontcarrel*. Cahuet chronicles the life of Colonel

Pontcarrel, his love-affair with the beautiful Sybille in early nineteenth-century Paris and his death (as General Pontcarrel) on the battlefield in Algeria. But the real hero of the novel is the town of Sarlat, where the fiery General Fournier-Sarlovèze lives – the hussar of Waterloo and leader of the Périgord rebellion of 1816, now struck off the army list and under continual police supervision.

What most delighted Cahuet was the unchanging nature of Sarlat and Périgord Noir. 'Old Sarlat, the city of municipal consuls, bishops, priors and Étienne de La Boétie, appears not to have changed in any way,' he wrote. 'It is still the same Sarlat of the Middle Ages and the Revolution.' He affects to meet from time to time Mme Pontcarrel, now old and occupying 'one of those ruined mansions washed by the waters of the river Dordogne, that are to be found between Castelnaud and Vézac'. And he rejoices at the feuding of his neighbours, 'generation after generation inhabiting the country seats, their minds petrified under the dust of their ancient surroundings. I met people who were still at odds with each other over quarrels dating back to the Revolution or the Empire. Even though a century had passed, their feuds were still alive as if they had happened yesterday.'

Charming though he is, Alberic Cahuet is lightweight compared with Eugène Le Roy. Reading his over-delicate descriptions of the Dordogne, I soon find myself driven back to the massive, leisurely descriptions of the nineteenth-century master. In Les Gens d'Aube-roque, which he wrote in 1898, Le Roy imagined himself surveying from a great height the whole of Périgord:

The terrace revealed the most magnificent view of the Dordogne. Beyond the vast circle of hills, looking like an amphitheatre below us, one could see châteaux on the summits of steep rises, houses hung on the hillsides, villages nestling between them and coombs resting in the shade while the sun lit up the rooftops. On one side the Vézère flowed slowly, held back by a series of locks and gleaming like a massive snake with silver scales between its varied banks of green fields, bare bends and slopes bearing trees or vines. On the other side high hills, whose sides were covered with feudal dwellings, furrowed knolls and stony rises sown with copses and green oaks, marked the valley of the river Dordogne, over which floated a light mist. Next, wherever the soil was sufficient, thick copses grew on slopes and plateaux, making dark stains amidst the fallow land, the vineyards and the cultivated fields. Steeples on square towers and more modest ones pierced in the walls over the church doors were scattered as far as the horizon, dominating the houses clustered at their feet and scarcely visible in the distance. Here and there where the valley widened, trails of smoke indicated a small town or a village slightly more important than the rest.

This is the Dordogne that solaced André Maurois as he looked out of the Château of Essendiéras. 'The view across the valley of the Isle was beautiful, embracing a region of tenant farms with lovely names: Brouillac, la Guichardie, la Cerise. Two long converging alleys, one of oaks, the other of chestnut trees, led from the road up to the château. A rushing stream, the Loue (or Louve) ran along the foot of the hills and nibbled at the banks of the Essendiéras fields.' This is the Dordogne which, said Henry Miller, has been the refuge of poets and will be the cradle of poets to come.

For good measure Henry Miller added: 'France may one day exist no more, but the Dordogne will live on just as dreams live on and nourish the souls of men.'

❖ 8 ❖

A Gazetteer of the Dordogne

This part of my book aims at helping the motorist, cyclist or hiker, who sits down for a coffee in a village or town and wonders what there is of note to see in the neighbourhood. I hope, too, that it will help those passing through an apparently insignificant spot who suddenly see, say, a flamboyant château perched high amongst the trees and would like to know how it came to be there, when it was built, who once lived in it and whether the present owner welcomes visitors. Thirdly, it should be of service to those staying for a time in one part of the Dordogne who want to make that a base for exploring the region round about.

My gazetteer should obviously be used in conjunction with a good map. It is arranged alphabetically (ignoring 'Le', 'La' and 'Les', so that, for instance, LES EYZIES-DE-TAYAC comes after EYMET and before FAGES). A great many towns and villages in the Dordogne are named after Christian saints. These places appear in the gazetteer after SADILLAC. The female 'Sainte' comes after the male 'Saint', at least alphabetically. I have included separate sections on prehistoric CAVES and SHELTERS. The gazetteer dovetails with the rest of the book (Chapter 3, for example, is about the rich prehistory of the Dordogne), and occasionally at the end of an entry I refer you to the index of this book. Sometimes, too, I draw attention to nearby places of interest that might otherwise be overlooked. A cross-reference means that it is worth making a detour to a neighbouring place.

I have referred only skimpily to hotels, camp sites and *gîtes*. These change, whereas romanesque churches last for centuries. The French National Tourist Office, 178 Piccadilly, London WIV OAL, will provide endless information.

Inside the Dordogne itself, you can find information in Périgueux at the *Syndicat d'Initiative*, 1, Avénue de l'Aquitaine. In the same building is the *Centre d'Information Jeunesse*, offering virtually everything a young person touring in the area wants to know. For information about organized tours and much else in the Dordogne, visit the *Office Départemental du Tourisme*, 16, Rue Président Wilson.

Above all, make use of the local *Syndicat d'Initiative* in the centre of every sizeable place. Information about hotels, rooms to let and camp sites; about concerts, exhibitions and open-air theatre; about local châteaux, megaliths and guided tours; as well as maps, timetables and details of early closing days and public holidays, are all there at your fingertips. Alerted by local *Syndicats d'Initiative*, I have seen fireworks at Beynac-et-Cazenac, and at Chancelade Abbey superb *son-et-lumière*.

Supplemented, then, by a good map and the local *Syndicat d'Initiative*, this gazetteer will, I hope, show that there is no part of the Dordogne, from Bussière-Badil in the north to Biron in the south, from Terrasson in the east to Saint-Michel-de-Montaigne in the west, that is not crammed with delight, much of it virtually undiscovered.

ABJAT-SUR-BANDIAT lies on a splendid lake north-east of Nontron, close to the Limousin border. You can swim, fish or paddle a canoe under the shadow of the sixteenth-century Château Balleran. The other château at Abjat-sur-Bandiat, de la Malignie, is bulky, fortified, medieval.

The romanesque church, built in the thirteenth century, was restored and modified in the sixteenth and seventeenth centuries, and retains its old, dominating belltower. Market day at Abjat-sur-Bandiat is the last Tuesday of each month. See BUSSIÈRE-BADIL, NONTRON and SAINT-PARDOUX-LA-RIVIÈRE.

AGONAC: This charming town to the north of Périgueux possesses a fine example of a defensive Périgord church, dedicated to St Martin. The main body of this austere building was constructed in the eleventh century. Two domes were added over the sanctuary and the crossing a hundred years later. You can still see the corridor running round the base of the largest of these domes, allowing beleaguered citizens of Agonac to fire on invaders as they entered the choir of the church. In the sixteenth century, the citizens added another defensive room high up in the belltower, as a protection against warlike Protestants. The piers of this church are so massive that a passageway was pierced in them, giving the illusion of two side aisles. Today the fortress church seems out of place in a peaceful town whose chief economy is growing walnuts and truffles.

AILLAC: Near Sarlat, just off the road towards Grolejac, is the tiny village of Aillac, with its fourteenth-century romanesque church, obviously modelled on an older one in nearby Carsac.

AJAT: Just north of the route N89 leading from Périgueux to Thénon, Ajat possesses a fine church and a curious château. My guess is that the church was built in the twelfth century and the château in the sixteenth. Once the church had two domes, but these have long disappeared. What remains is two square bays, and a many-sided apse, surmounted by what the French call an 'oven-vault' and roofed in stone *lauzes*. Next to it the battlemented château looks as if it was once two separate buildings now joined together by a gallery.

If you have made the detour from the N89 to see Ajat, take the trouble to add three kilometres to your journey to see the lovely church of BAUZENS.

ALES-SUR-DORDOGNE: One of the great loops of the river Dordogne is known as the *cingle* of Trémolat. The view from the cemetery of Ales is one of the finest of this majestic sweep of water, as well as of the impressive cliffs of Limeuil. The cemetery also contains a romanesque church.

ALLAS-LES-MINES, close by Berbiguières on the road from Château Castelnaud, belies its name. The local quarries and mines are abandoned. Even the château, built in the fifteenth century, is in ruins. The once-reputed vines of this village were never replanted after the phylloxera disaster. But it still possesses a powerful fortified romanesque church large enough to protect the 200 villagers.

ALLEMANS, west of Ribérac, boasts a romanesque church with two domes and a modern belltower.

ANGOISSE, just inside the Dordogne on the route south from Saint-Yrieix in Limousin, has a fine château with two pepperpot towers. Try to get into the church to see its sixteenth- and seventeenth-century stone statues. See PAYZAC.

ANNESSE-ET-BEAULIEU, west of Périgueux and close by the river Isle, possesses a romanesque church. Inside is a carved altar and a statue of Jesus crucified, flanked by his mother and St John, sculpted in the seventeenth century. There are fine old houses in this district and, on a nearby peak, the Château of Puy-Saint-Astier, built in the fifteenth, sixteenth and seventeenth centuries. Beaulieu itself is five kilometres nearer Périgueux.

ANTONNE-ET-TRIGONANT, eleven kilometres east of Périgueux on the D705, possesses in the Château des Bories a beautiful example of a turning-point in Périgord architecture. Happily it is open to the general public in the tourist season. Today Les Bories stands at the end of a long alley of trees, perfectly symmetrical, with two splendid round towers wearing pointed caps. It was built in 1497 for Jeanne of Hautefort, widow of Jean of Saint-Astier, at a time when strong fortifications were still obligatory but it was increasingly possible to build for pleasure as well as defence. So renaissance windows pierce and lighten the walls. The entrance from the river Isle is finely landscaped and welcoming. A square tower on the south façade boasts a magnificent staircase – copied later by many a Dordogne noble. Château des Bories was completed in 1604 and very well restored in 1910. The interior is as splendid as the exterior, with an immense fireplace in one of the vaulted rooms.

This is château country. Near by is the fifteenth-century Château de Trigonant, and the severe, long Château d'Escoire, with its semi-circular rotunda, built at the end of the eighteenth century.

ARCHIGNAC, a village north of Salignac in Périgord Noir, has a lovely twelfth-century church with a dome, sculpted capitals and a fine romanesque doorway.

ATUR, eight miles south of Périgueux, has a good-looking church, carrying an oddly shaped dome and barrel-vaulting surviving from the twelfth century. But what adds interest to this village is its 'Lantern of the Dead', smaller than the one at Sarlat but equally mysterious, built in the twelfth century. Eugène Le Roy's Jacquou le Croquant ends his tale, 'I remain alone in the night, like the Lantern of the Dead in the graveyard of Atur, awaiting my own death.'

AUBAS, west of Montignac, is dominated by a château of the early six-teenth century, classical in style with attractive dormer windows and two high wings. The parish church contains lovely eleventh-century capitals and behind the altar a coloured carving of the Holy Family.

AUBEROCHE, a tiny hamlet, fifteen kilometres from Périgueux on the road to Brive, possesses a small romanesque chapel which was once part of a mighty fortress defending the capital.

AUDRIX is a pretty town south of Le Bugue, marvellously positioned on a high peak (200 m) giving a marvellous survey over the valleys of the Vézère and Dordogne. Its romanesque church was built in the fourteenth century. Near by is the prehistoric chasm of *Proumeyssac* (see CAVES).

AUGIGNAC, on the D676 north of Nontron, has a neat, domed romanesque church.

AURIAC-DU-PÉRIGORD lies five kilometres north of Montignac, under the shadow of Château de la Faye. The château was built around its twelfth-century keep between the fourteenth and the sixteenth centuries. In 1465 the lord of Château de la Faye built the little Chapel of Saint-Rémy, whose vaulted ogival arches are in delicate contrast to the fortified parish church of Auriac-du-Périgord, which was built in the twelfth century and fifteenth century, though the grimacing figures carved on the gables of the chapel add an earthier note. St Rémy was long reputed to be a great healer, and Eugène Le Roy amusingly described the annual pilgrimage from as far away as Limousin to Auriac-du-Périgord. The sick would take the little statue of the saint from his niche in the chapel and rub their affected parts with it – 'stomachs, arms, legs, thighs and as much skin as they could'.

AZERAT, thirty-six kilometres from Périgueux, on the road to Brive, is a curious town, set out in a square pattern like a *bastide*. Its gothic chapel, dedicated to Our Lady of Good Hope, was in the Middle Ages a centre of pilgrimage. Azerat possesses fine old houses and a town hall that was once a small château. The main château of the town was burnt down in 1903. It belonged to the family of Larochefoucauld-Liancourt, whose arms can be seen today in the little chapel. See in the index to this book *bastides*.

LA BACHELLERIE, on the junction of the N89 and the N704, thirty-eight kilometres east of Périgueux, derives its name from the lesser nobility (*les bas-chevaliers*) whose domaine it was in the Middle Ages. During the Hundred Years War the English left in ruins the town's old church, on the edge of the little river Cern, and ruined it stands today. But the chief claim to fame of La Bachellerie lies in its remarkable Château de Rastignac, built between 1812 and 1817 by

Mathurin Blanchard, an architect who lived at Mareuil. It uncannily resembles the White House. Joséphine Baker sent a postcard of it to John F. Kennedy on his election as President of the U.S.A., telling him that the château actually served as a model for his new home. The truth is that there is no direct connection between the two buildings. Château de Rastignac was burned down by retreating Nazis in 1944 and has been meticulously restored. Look out for the nearby honey museum (*musée de miel*). Further east is the fifteenth-century Château de Peyraux at Le Lardin-Saint-Lazare. See AZERAT.

BADEFOLS D'ANS derives its curious name from the lords of Ans in Flanders, one of whom married a daughter of Château Hautefort in the fourteenth century. The village of Badefols, just south of Hautefort, was part of her dowry. Its fifteenth-century château, burned down in 1944, has been restored, with careful attention to the alterations made to the original in the eighteenth century. Badefols d'Ans also possesses a fine, domed twelfth-century church, and holds a fair on the third Monday of each month. See COUBJOURS.

BADEFOLS-SUR-DORDOGNE lies on the river twenty-five kilometres east of Bergerac. Its château, built in the twelfth and fifteenth centuries, once controlled the river traffic out of Périgord. Today it is a picturesque ruin, destroyed in 1794. This is tobacco-growing country, but tourism is well catered for, and the river here is not too dangerous for fishing and some swimming.

BALOU is a hamlet on the D31, three kilometres north-west of Rouffignac in the Barade forest. Here a road to the left leads to the ruins of the infamous Château de l'Herm. Built in 1512 by Jean III de Calvimont, it was the scene of the assassination of his granddaughter at her husband's command. The ruin remains impressive, with its doorway carved in the flamboyant gothic style, its huge ruined chimneys and its spiral staircase. The unsavoury reputation of this château and its ruined condition prompted Eugène Le Roy to use it as the home of the evil Comte de Nansac in his novel *Jacquou le Croquant*. It is burned to the ground by Jacquou in revenge for the deaths of his parents.

BANEUIL, a hamlet twenty kilometres east of Bergerac and north of the D660, has a domed twelfth-century church, and a fifteenth- and sixteenth-century château (built around an earlier tower), open to the public in summer. See COUZE-ET-SAINT-FRONT, LALINDE and LANQUAIS.

BANNES is a château dominating the valley of the river Couze three kilometres north of Beaumont. It was constructed on the site of an older château by Armand de Gontaut-Biron, Bishop of Sarlat, in the fifteenth century. (The older château had been captured on behalf of the English in 1409.) In Château de Bannes, which is unfortunately not open to the general public, the decorations and carvings are exceptionally fine. Fleurs-de-lis and ermine represent kings Charles VIII and Louis III. The letters L and A represent Louis XII and his consort Anne de Bretagne. A drawbridge crosses a dry moat from the terrace, leading to the main château, with its pepperpot roofs and great circular towers.

BARA-BAHAU, see CAVES.

BARADE FOREST, south-east of Périgueux, though still a substantial stretch of woodlands, is no longer the almost impenetrable, massive forest of the past, haunt of felons, poachers, the poor and the mad. Until the Revolution it was popularly called 'the enclosed forest', since the lords of the local châteaux claimed all its game for themselves. Eugène Le Roy made it the scene of his *Jacquou le Croquant* (the novel was first called *La Forêt Barade*). Jacquou speaks of its old state: 'Today it is easy to pass through the forest; but in the days I am speaking of it was much larger than it is now. Much has been cleared during the past twenty-five years, but then there were no well-marked routes, save two wide though poor roads skirting the edge, flooded and cut into gullies by the winter rains, and the paths in the woods used by charcoal-burners and poachers.' And in those days the traveller at night went in fear of both highway robbers and wild boars.

BARDOU, a village seven kilometres east of Issigeac in south-west Périgord, has a sturdy twelfth-century church, its belltower rising from the wall over the doorway, and a restored château – a conglomeration of different styles from the fifteenth to the seventeenth centuries – standing happily in a fine park. See ISSIGEAC.

BARS, a village north-west of Montignac, today marks the edge of the Barade forest, and offers the tourist a pretty church and a splendid panoramic view of the region.

BASSILAC stands almost on the confluence of the rivers Isle and

Auvézère, eleven kilometres south-east of Périgueux. There in the sixteenth century the almoner of Henri I V built Château de Rognac, re-routing the river to cover its flanks. The château, well-restored in this century, stands next to a seventeenth-century mill. In the domed romanesque church of Bassilac, which was reshaped at the time of the Renaissance, is a carved seventeenth-century retable.

LA BASTIDE: Twenty-five kilometres west of Monbazillac (and lying on the D16) is a tiny village which – as its name implies, was built as a fortified town by the English. Alas, only a corner of this *bastide* remains. See CUNÈGES.

BAUZENS, three kilometres north-east of Ajat, possesses a beautiful romanesque church. Its west façade is delightfully unusual. The crossing is domed.

BAYAC, see LALINDE.

BEAUMONT-DU-PÉRIGORD was founded in 1272 by Lucas de Thanay, who was Seneschal of Guyenne and a servant of King Edward I of England. His aim was to build a fortified *bastide*, of which many impressive traces remain. The massive Luzier gateway, built in the early thirteenth century, still stands, the grooves of its portcullis readily traceable. If broached, invaders had to run along a narrow passage before coming up against a second fortification. All *bastides* were granted a market by charter, and the market square and market hall of Beaumont preserve much of their ancient aspect. The fair still takes place on the second Tuesday of each month. The streets are straight and wide, crossing each other at right-angles, where you can often find a gothic house.

The last refuge of an invaded *bastide* was its fortified church. Although the interior of the Church of Saint-Front, Beaumont, was much restored in the nineteenth century (and some of its military features removed), the exterior is still that of a huge defensive building as well as a house of prayer. Constructed at the end of the thirteenth and beginning of the fourteenth centuries, Beaumont church managed to combine beauty with security. Three of its walls are severe, but the west façade makes up for the rest. The porch is finely carved, surmounted by a gothic balustrade and sheltering a sculpted frieze which contains carvings of the four evangelists, a siren, a stag hunt and the head of a king (possibly Edward I).

Beaumont-du-Périgord is on the so-called '*bastide* circuit', lying north of Monpazier (another English *bastide*, built thirteen years later) where the D676 meets the D660. Its environs are well worth exploring. North of the *bastide*, left of the road to Bergerac, is the little chapel of Belpech, built in the romanesque style at the end of the eleventh century as part of a priory owing allegiance to the Abbey of Cadouin. Belpech became a staging post on the pilgrimage route to Santiago de Compostela in Spain. Some three kilometres south of Beaumont on the D676 you can see on the left the Dolmen de Blanc, one of the finest prehistoric megaliths in Périgord. Medieval legend Christianized the site with the story of a young girl, caught in a terrible storm, who prayed for help to the Blessed Virgin, at which these great stones miraculously arranged themselves as a long sheltered corridor. See also BANNES, MONTFERRAND-DU-PÉRIGORD, SAINT-AVIT-SÉNIEUR and SAINTE-CROIX-DE-BEAUMONT and, in the index, *bastides*.

BEAUPOUYET, south-west of Mussidan, has a twelfth-century church, of which the choir alone remains, with fine decorated capitals.

BEAURONNE, see MUSSIDAN.

BEAUSSAC, a village off the beaten track north of Mareuil, possesses not only a church built in the twelfth and thirteenth centuries, but also three renaissance châteaux – de Bretagne, d'Aucors and de Poutignac.

BELCAYRE is an astonishing château, built in the fifteenth and sixteenth centuries high on a rock which juts out like the prow of a ship over the river Vézère. Château de Belcayre is best seen from the D706 just north of Saint-Léon-sur-Vézère. See THONAC and, in the index to this book, Château de Belcayre.

BELET is a château of the fifteenth and sixteenth centuries to the left of the D709 sixteen and a half kilometres east of Ribérac.

BELEYMAS, a village north of Bergerac (on the way to Villamblard), has a romanesque church altered in the seventeenth century, with the distinction of possessing the only contemporary carving of St François de Sales (taken from the Chapel of the Visitation in Périgueux).

BELVEDÈRE-DE-SORS, four and a half kilometres east of Trémolat, offers one of the finest panoramic views of the Dordogne valley, encircled by a great loop of the river.

BELVÈS, a lovely old medieval town on the D53 north of Monpazier, is built on a promontory giving splendid views over the valley of the Nauze. This is walnut country *par excellence* (see DOISSAT), and the Saturday market of Belvès, held near the fifteenth-century market hall, specializes in them. (Belvès also holds a fair on the first Saturday in July and on 14 August.) The ring road follows the old walls of the town, protecting the château with its square twelfth-century keep, the fifteenth-century belfry, and its medieval and renaissance houses. Oddly enough, the church was built outside the town in the thirteenth century, as a Benedictine priory. It was much reconstructed in the fifteenth and seventeenth centuries. Don't miss the chain still attached to one of the pillars in the market place, where miscreants were punished in the Middle Ages.

BERBIGUIÈRES, a lovely village five kilometres from the Château de Castelnaud in the valley of the river Dordogne, consists of fine houses clustered around a great seventeenth-century château whose walls are guarded by watchtowers.

BERGERAC, the commercial centre of south-west Dordogne, is today a modern city, with its medieval and renaissance past peeping through. Here the Dordogne river was bridged, north–south roads crossed east–west routes, the river was deep enough to create an important inland port and the fine vineyards around the city gave it an international fame. It remains a commercial centre while increasingly serving tourists, with its hotels, camping, sports and aerodrome.

The spirit of the old days lives on on market days (every Wednesday and Saturday for farm produce; for animals, the first and third Tuesday of each month). Farmers sell direct to the public in the shadow of the cathedral church of Our Lady, with its slender gothic belltower. Inside the cathedral are pictures of shepherds and magi adoring the Christ child (attributed respectively to Pordenone, an Italian of the school of Giorgione, and to a pupil of Leonardo da Vinci named Ferrari).

In the sixteenth century Bergerac became the capital of Périgord Protestantism, as opposed to Périgueux, the capital of Catholicism. The Protestants rebuilt the ramparts of the city using stones from Catholic convents. In the seventeenth century Richelieu demolished these ramparts. These ravages happily failed to destroy the Recollects convent, built in brick and stone over five centuries. Today it is open to the public, as is the unique tobacco museum in the town hall. And the northern quarter of the city, with its narrow twisting streets, its medieval and renaissance houses, its pilgrim church of St James (now much restored) and its covered market – built on the site of a Protestant church destroyed in 1681 – require very little imagination to charm the tourist into the past. Bergerac is filled with fine restaurants. I like the Hôtel de Bordeaux (38, Place Gambetta); Restaurant 'Le Cyrano' (2, Boulevard Montaigne); La Flambée (Route de Périgueux); and La Crémaillère (36, Place Gambetta).

LES BERNARDIÈRES, château dominating the valley of the river Nizonne, ten kilometres from Mareuil, is built around a square fourteenth-century keep. Well worth a visit, it is open to the general public in the tourist season. The main buildings date from the seventeenth century, though the vast wall and dry moat are obviously earlier. Small wonder that even the mighty Du Guesclin, who besieged the château in 1377, failed to take it.

BERNIFALS, see CAVES.

BESSE, see VILLEFRANCHE-DU-PÉRIGORD.

BEYNAC-ET-CAZENAC is a tiny picturesque village on one of the finest stretches of the river Dordogne. But the visitor scarcely looks at it, overawed by the immense, brutal château perched 150 metres high on a rock above the river. The history of this formidable place – splendidly restored and today open to the public – is as martial as its aspect. It was begun in the twelfth century, but its lord left for the Crusades in 1147 and returned in 1194 to die in Périgord. Richard Cœur de Lion then gave the château to another courtier-soldier, who ravaged the surrounding countryside. In 1214 Simon de Montfort, on his way to fight the Albigensian heretics, razed the château, but the lords of Beynac rebuilt it. Beynac became one of the four baronies of Périgord, defending itself by means of a double rampart, a double moat and a barbican. For five centuries Château Beynac was embellished; today it possesses a beautiful vaulted great hall, a romanesque church with a stone, *lauze* roof, a fifteenth-century chapel with a fresco of the Beynac family and another depicting the Last Supper, and a splendid Florentine staircase made in the seventeenth century.

During the Hundred Years War Beynac remained a stronghold of the French. From its ramparts can be seen châteaux Marqueyssac, Fayrac, La Malartie and, not least, the great Château de Castelnaud on the other side of the river, held by the English throughout this period.

It is a relief to drive down from this overpowering place to look at the fifteenth-century church at Cazenac. Near by are the caves of Cro-Bique, filled with stalagmites and stalactites formed long before the warring Middle Ages. See CASTELNAUD, FAYRAC and LES MILANDES.

BEYSSAC: Ten kilometres outside Les Eyzies, on the D47 leading to Sarlat, you can make out on the left, towering over oak forests, the much-restored though still impressive Château de Beyssac, with its sixteenth-century machicolated tower. At the foot of this château are some desolate forges dating from the seventeenth and eighteenth centuries, evidence of an abandoned rural economy. Just over a kilometre further on, a path to the right leads up to the famous Gaulish village of Breuil, a group of small stone cabins unchanged since Neolithic times.

BIRAS, a small village off to the right of the D939 south of Brantôme, possesses a good, domed romanesque church.

BIRON: Eight kilometres or so south of Monpazier on the D150, the magnificent bulk of Château Biron dominates the view. Situated on a steep hill, it served as the home of the Gontaut-Biron family – who became chief barons of Périgord – until our own century. Now, restored with money from the State, Château Biron is open to all.

Its history vividly recalls the turbulent past. Generation after generation added to its bulk, beginning with the twelfth-century keep, building walls and a great round tower in the fourteenth century, adding a massive yet somehow graceful tower to guard the entrance two hundred years later. The renaissance buildings, the great pavilion, its stables and its eighteenth-century cloister add charm and lightness to a fortress that once had to withstand the assaults of soldiers like Simon de Montfort. To the south a superb sixteenth-century loggia is entered by an arch delicately shaped like the handle of a basket and supported on four slender pillars. The double chapel, built at the beginning of the sixteenth century, is the masterpiece of Château Biron. In the upper chapel, designed for the great ones of the château, lie the tombs of Pons de Gontaut-Biron and his brother, Armand, Bishop of Sarlat. The lower chapel was designed to serve as the villagers' parish church, even though they already possessed the little twelfth-century Church of Notre-Dame-de-Sous-Biron.

BLANC: For this megalithic dolmen, see BEAUMONT-DU-PÉRIGORD.

BOISSEUILH: This village north of Hautefort has a lovely romanesque church with a couple of bells and a classical porch.

BORIES. For the Château de Bories, see ANTONNE-ET-TRIGONANT.

BOSCHAUD ABBEY lies one kilometre from Puyguilhem. In spite of restoration work to stop it falling down altogether, it will now never be anything other than one of the most evocative ruins in Périgord. Founded by Cistercian monks in 1154, the abbey church was given two domes; today one, half destroyed, hangs perilously in the air (the second has gone for ever). The convent scarcely survived the Hundred Years War and was cruelly despoiled during the Revolution. The cloister and other priory buildings are open to the public.

BOULAZAC, south of Périgueux on the N89, has a much-restored château of the fourteenth and fifteenth centuries: a simple quadrilateral with great circular towers at each corner.

BOULOUNEIX, see Château de RICHEMONT.

BOURDEILLES, seat of one of the four great baronies of Périgord, is a marvellous combination of feudal fortress and renaissance palace, the whole beautifully situated high over the river Dronne ten kilometres south of Brantôme. The medieval portion is paradoxically known as the 'new château', since it was built by Géraud de Maumont to replace an earlier twelfth-century fortress. He started building in the early thirteenth century. A superb keep was added soon after. During the Hundred Years War this part of Château Bourdeilles was much fought over and the fifteenth-century buildings are mostly ruined. In 1481 the rightful owner had to buy his château back from his enemies for 4,000 gold *écus*. But for a while peace prevailed, and his daughter-in-law, Jacquette de Montbron, as Châtelaine of Bourdeilles was able to commission the renaissance buildings which now so stunningly complement the medieval. Her brother-in-law, Pierre de Bourdeilles, was the soldier of fortune who became Lay Abbot of Brantôme and wrote stories of scandalous ladies and short-tempered fighting-men. Jacquette's contribution to Château Bourdeilles included the famous 'golden chamber', decorated by Ambroise Le Noble of the school of Fontainebleau.

In the twentieth century the Bourdeilles descendants, unable to keep their château, offered it to the State, which has restored the buildings, organizes concerts in them and welcomes visitors. Unlike many French châteaux, Bourdeilles is filled with furniture – not, on the whole, Périgordian, but Spanish, with items from Burgundy, Flanders and other parts of France.

Another delight at Bourdeilles is simply to look down from the ramparts of the château at the exquisite medieval bridge over the Dronne and the old water mill built like a ship. In the village is a twelfth-century domed church, and near by can be found the prehistoric shelters of La Chèvre, Bernoux and the 'Devil's Furnace'.

LE BOURDEIX, a tiny village between Nontron and Bussière-Badil, has a romanesque church with a dome whose crown has disappeared and a nave that was gothicized in the fifteenth century, standing next to a twelfth-century keep which, very oddly, is also domed.

BOURG-DES-MAISONS, on the D99 south of Mareuil, was once rich enough to build itself a romanesque church with three domes and later unwise enough to add a nineteenth-century gothic west façade.

BOURG-DU-BOST, on the D20, twelve and a half kilometres west of Ribérac, boasts a romanesque church, well worth entering to see its grey and gold retable and its statue of the infant Jesus worshipped by a princess, both carved in the 1600s.

BRANTÔME is lovely, a medieval and renaissance town with charming cafés and hotels, embraced by the river Dronne which divides to do this. Charlemagne founded an abbey here and gave to it the body of one of the infants murdered on the orders of King Herod. In the eleventh century the Normans sacked Charlemagne's abbey, but the monks rebuilt at the foot of the rocks close by the river. Among their first buildings was the splendid belltower, set apart from the other buildings, soaring like a graceful pyramid above the rest. The abbot's garden, now the *jardin publique*, contains a renaissance pavilion. Where the monks lived is now the town hall, its eighteenth-century wing reflected in the placid river. Inside rises a magnificent seventeenth-century staircase. Earlier buildings include the renaissance pavilion where the lay Abbot Pierre de Bourdeille wrote his famous, sometimes scandalous works.

The monks utilized the caves in the rocks behind their abbey as kitchens and a wine-cellar, and there, in the sixteenth century, they carved a bas-relief of the crucifixion, with Jesus flanked by his mother, St John and other watchers and worshippers, as well as another huge bas-relief of the Last Judgement. There are also fine carvings inside their abbey church, which was restored by the architect Abadie in the nineteenth century. The baptistry houses a lovely fourteenth-century carving of Jesus's own baptism, while near by is a thirteenth-century bas-relief of the martyrdom of the Holy Innocents.

The narrow streets of Brantôme give way occasionally to wide squares, but offer shelter if the sun is too hot, along with coffee, bakeries, gothic chimneys and renaissance windows. Market on Tuesdays. Look out for the summer Dance Festival. Good food at Les Frères Charbonnel. See LA GONTERIE-BOULONEIX and RICHEMONT.

BREUIL, Gaulish village. See BEYSSAC.

BRIDOIRE: The fifteenth-century Château de Bridoire, south of Château Monbazillac on the D107, suffered greatly during the Wars of Religion and was restored ('a trifle generously', as the art historian Jean Secret puts it) in the nineteenth century. None the less, its grey walls and huge machicolated towers give an impression of grandeur. Charles de Foucauld lived here for a time. After a dissipated life as a French cavalry officer, he became a servant of the poor and a hermit in Algeria, where, in 1916, he was murdered by the Tuaregs. The *Mission de Charles* and the *Association Foucauld* keep his spirit alive.

LE BUGUE, at first glance an unprepossessing city on the river Vézère near its confluence with the river Dordogne, has in fact much to offer the tourist. Not only has the town provided excellent sporting facilities and camp sites for its visitors; it also possesses several fine eighteenth-century houses, a romanesque gateway and a fine monumental fountain. Close by are the splendid prehistoric caves of Bara-Bahau and Proumeyssac (see CAVES). Le Bugue also offers the pleasures of a Dordogne market every Tuesday and every Saturday morning, and a fair on the third Tuesday of every month; there are also two great fairs each year: on 25 August and 30 September (unless these days fall on a Monday or a Wednesday, when for some reason the fair is transferred to the nearest Tuesday). Try eating at L'Albuca. See SAINT-ALVÈRE.

LE BUISSON-DE-CADOUIN, just off to the west of the D31 after it has crossed the river Dordogne south of Le Bugue, is a sizeable town with fine camping sites and excellent beaches for those who wish to swim in the Dordogne or sunbathe beside it. See CADOUIN.

BUSSIÈRE-BADIL, an old medieval town situated almost at the northernmost tip of Périgord Vert, offers the tourist fishing, hunting, tennis and also – as its proximity to Limousin would explain – fine ceramics. It also possesses a beautiful eleventh-century romanesque church, restored in the fifteenth and sixteenth centuries. Over the crossing is a pretty, octagonal belltower. But the glory of Bussière-Badil church is its massive west façade, supported at each corner by heavy buttresses and divided into three by two even more powerful ones. Above the porch is a rose window. The three arches of the porch are splendidly carved. Inside the church is a sixteenth-century coloured statue of the Virgin and Child, carved by Mathieu Dyonise of Le Mans. See also PIÉGUT-PLUVIERS.

CADOUIN, situated on the D2 in Périgord Noir, became famous in the Middle Ages because it was thought to possess a holy kerchief that had covered the face of Jesus in the tomb. The claim was recently proved false. Yet the Cistercian abbey, founded by Géraud de Sales in 1115 and now a historic monument, remains supremely attractive. The depredations of the Hundred Years War meant that the monks built a new flamboyant gothic cloister in the fifteenth century. The buildings suffered from but survived the Wars of Religion, but the Revolution forced out the monks and greatly endangered the whole structure. Fortunately, the State took over in 1839 and the partly ruined buildings are beautifully preserved, the frescoes and sculptures of the sixteenth century are no longer in danger, and a museum of religious art has been set up beside the abbey.

Close by are camp sites, fine hotels, water sports and a lovely old people's home, built in the old Périgord style. See MOLIÈRES.

CALVIAC, near Carlux in Périgord Noir, possesses a fine twelfth-century church, once an abbey and later embellished (in the fifteenth century). Here lived the monk Sacerdos, later Bishop of Limoges and patron saint of Sarlat, who was beatified for curing leprosy. Grouped around the church are pretty houses, and Calviac is much favoured for camping and for walks along the river Dordogne.

CAMPAGNE, south of Le Bugue on the D705, possesses a fairly desolate fifteenth- and sixteenth-century château in a fine park, as well as a pretty romanesque church.

CANCON, on the N21 forty kilometres south of Bergerac and almost in the *département* of Lot-et-Garonne, is a sizeable town excitingly perched on the side of a hill, topped by the ruins of a thirteenth-century château. The upper parts of the town consist of narrow ancient streets with sixteenth-century stone houses.

CANTILLAC, close by Brantôme, displays in its eighteenth-century domed church just how long traditional architecture could survive in the Dordogne.

CARLUX, slightly north of the river Dordogne, halfway between Sarlat and Souillac, is noted, apart from its cuisine, camping and fine walks, for a fourteenth-century château left in ruins by the English during the Hundred Years War, and – on a splendid hill site in the forest to the south – for the sixteenth-century Château de Rouffilhac. See also SAINT-VINCENT-LE-PALUEL and SAINTE-NATHALÈNE.

CARSAC-AILLAC is a 'must' for anyone in the region of Sarlat. Situated in a charming little grove of trees east of the main route from Sarlat by way of Grolejac to Gourdon, the church of Carsac is a perfectly restored medley of styles of architecture and religious art from the eleventh to this century. The nave was not originally vaulted but was given a dome over bays. Attacked during the Hundred Years War by marauding English, it was restored in the late 1400s, when the ogive-vaulted chapels of the south side were created. The Renaissance added its characteristic bas-reliefs, including the head of the architect, Antoine de Valette. Don't miss the renaissance capital of the infant Hercules fighting serpents or the bust of a woman to whom Cupid offers a bouquet.

The whole church was carefully restored in the early 1940s. You can see traces of medieval paintwork, and also a renaissance wood-carving of God the Father. (The Holy Spirit and God the Son have been stolen.) Modern works of art include a stained-glass window of the patron saint of Carsac, St Caprais, and an engraving on stone of St Teresa by Léon Zack. Léon Zack also made the modernistic, fascinating Stations of the Cross in Carsac church, to which he added texts from *The Way of the Cross* by Paul Claudel, some of which are extremely moving. (*Rendez-moi patient à mon tour du bois/que vous voulez que je supporte./Car il nous faut porter la Croix/avant que la Croix nous porte.*)

Leaving the church by its five-arched doorway, you notice the fifteenth-century buildings opposite and then turn back to admire the stone *lauze* roofs of the nave and pointed belltower. See also GROLEJAC, Château MONTFORT and VITRAC.

CARSAC-DE-GURSON lies on the D33 at the western extremity of the Dordogne near Villefranche-de-Lonchat. From miles around you can see the ruins of Château de Gurson, which King Henry III of England gave to his seneschal, Jean de Grailly. Ruined in the Hundred Years War, the château was restored and once again fell into ruin. The romanesque church at Carsac-de-Gurson is, by contrast, in robust health. Few marauders could batter down its massive tower, and inside the carved capitals are delightful. See MONTPEY-ROUX.

LA CASSAGNE, see SAINT-AMAND-DE-COLY.

CASTELNAUD: Château de Castelnaud, founded in the twelfth century on a promontory dominating the rivers Céou and Dordogne nine kilometres south-west of Sarlat, peers across at its rival Château Beynac, held by the French throughout the Hundred Years War while the English occupied Castelnaud. In the early thirteenth century the owners were heretics, and Simon de Montfort drove them out. But instead of destroying the château, as was his habit, he restored it. The French took it from the English in 1405, but two years later Castelnaud was retaken and held by the remarkable soldier Raymond de Sort for twenty-five years. The English added a barbican and a powerful keep, before ceding Castelnaud.

Then came its decline. Stones were used for building elsewhere. Roofs were allowed to fall in. The cluster of beautiful Périgord cottages and houses at its feet no longer needed the protection of the château. Fortunately the château is under restoration today, ready for opening to the general public. See also châteaux de FAYRAC and des MILANDES.

CASTELS: The old romanesque church of Castels, near Saint-Cyprien, is a sad ruin, but its eighteenth-century Château d'Argentonnesse is intact in a pretty park.

CAUDON, see CÉNAC-ET-SAINT-JULIEN.

CAVES: Chapter 6 of this book (page 100) is devoted to the meaning and delight of the prehistoric caves (mostly known as *grottes*) and shelters (*abris*) of the Dordogne. They form the finest group so far known to mankind.

Go early when you want to visit a cave. The delicate nature of the paintings and engravings as well as the narrow passages mean that tours are conducted only in small parties. (Ever since I started visiting the cave of Font de Gaume, near Les Eyzies, a comical notice there has announced that parties will be limited to twenty persons and that reductions are offered to groups of twenty-five.) You can book yourself on a tour for later in the day and then in the meantime visit a shelter or take lunch. Not all caves are yet open to the public. Here, as always, the local *Syndicat d'Initiative* offers valuable up-to-date information.

Take a woolly pullover, even on hot days, for it gets cold deep inside the earth. And take some reasonable walking shoes (for the underground paths can be fairly irregular), save to Rouffignac, where you ride on a little electric train – the ideal cave for the elderly or unsteady, or young children. Here then is a list of pre-historic caves, some open to the public, some not.

Bara-Bahau lies two kilometres from Le Bugue. Discovered by the prehistorian Norbert Casteret and his daughter Maud in 1951, the cave, 120 metres long, was created by an underground river. Its engravings of horses, oxen, bison, rhinoceros, and its human finger marks were made perhaps 20,000 or 30,000 years ago. Open in summer.

Bernifals, near Meyrals, on the D47 south-west of Les Eyzies, was discovered in 1902 by Denis Peyrony. A narrow passageway reveals fine paintings and engravings of animals, as well as 'tectiform' patterns, perhaps 20,000 years old. Open to the public.

Carpe Diem is near the village of Manaurie on the D47 north of Les

Eyzies. The cave runs 180 metres deep into the rock to reveal exquisite stalactites, well-lit. Open save in winter.

Les Combarelles, on the D48 west of Les Eyzies, was discovered in 1901 and prehistorians recognized its importance, for it reveals the art of our prehistoric ancestors at its finest. Several hundred engravings, often superimposed on each other, cover more than 300 metres of cave. They include images of men as well as the animals he hunted (and possibly domesticated). A finely traced lion has become famous. Here, too, tools and other traces of prehistoric people have been found. Open almost all the year.

Commarque: South of the D48, seven and a half kilometres west of Les Eyzies, rises the majestic ruin of Château Commarque. Close by is the tiny Grotte de Commarque, decorated with very early prehistoric sculptures and engravings.

Cro-Bique, see BEYNAC-ET-CAZENAC.

Domme: In the market hall of this *bastide* is the entrance to 450 metres of underground cave (also known as the Grotte du Jubilé). The people of Domme almost certainly sheltered here during the Wars of Religion. The cave contains well-illuminated stalagmites and stalactites. Open from April to September. A second cave at Domme, not open to the public, has revealed traces of prehistoric painting and engraving.

Font-de-Gaume: Scarcely a hundred metres outside Les Eyzies, a path leads from the D47 to this cave, which after Lascaux and Altamira contains the finest collection of multi-coloured prehistoric paintings so far discovered. The cave was known long before the Abbé Breuil and Denis Peyrony spotted its importance in 1901. (Some drawings had even been disfigured.) Visitors are shown thirty or so of the paintings, though 200 have been catalogued, including eighty bison, forty horses and twenty-three mammoths. Closed 25 November to 25 December.

Gabillou: A little-known cave, near Sourzac on the N89 north-east of Mussidan, containing fine prehistoric engravings.

Grand Roc: Scarcely three kilometres north-west of Les Eyzies on the D47, the cave, created by an underground river, offers a vast variety of crystalline structures as well as stalagmites and stalactites. Open for most of the year.

La Grèze lies five and a half kilometres west of Les Eyzies on the D48. This small cave contains the engraving of a bison. Sometimes open. The famous 'Venus' of Laussel, now in the Bordeaux museum, was discovered near by. (There is a replica in the museum at Les Eyzies.)

La Mairie, near Teyjat, north of Nontron. The Grotte de la Mairie was explored by Denis Peyrony and the Abbé Breuil in 1903. They concluded that its fifty or so engravings were around 30,000 years old. Deer, stags, reindeer and horses, indecipherable to the inexperienced eye, leap into life as the guide traces them out. Open in summer.

La Mouthe, on the D706 south of Les Eyzies. The historical importance of this cave derives from the fact that its evidence finally scotched all doubts about the authenticity of prehistoric art. In 1895 E. Rivière discovered here not only engravings and coloured paintings of horses, stags and bison but also a prehistoric lantern by the light of which they may well have been painted. The Grotte de la Mouthe contains a unique drawing, in red and black, of a prehistoric hut. Open to the public.

Lascaux, the world-famous cave discovered at Montignac in 1940, containing the most remarkable groupings of prehistoric animal paintings ever discovered, has been described in Chapter 6 of this book (page 100). The paintings were done between 20,000 and 10,000 years before Christ. Today the cave is closed to all but a handful of visitors; but a replica, painstakingly executed, is open to the general public (see MONTIGNAC). See also *Regourdou* under SHELTERS.

Proumeyssac: The Gouffre de Proumeyssac, three and a half kilometres south of Le Bugue, offers fine translucent stalagmites and stalactites, as well as other curious concretions. Open during the tourist season. A stream running through the *gouffre* helps to feed the present stalactites and to create new ones for the future.

Rouffignac, ten kilometres north-west of Les Eyzies, makes life easy for the speleologist by taking the visitor along four kilometres of underground passages by electric train, pausing to trace out prehistoric engravings of horses, rhinoceros, bison, ibex, mammoths, and so on. Finally the train reaches a large chamber: many horses, painted in ochre, black and brown, sport in abandon on the ceiling. The cave has been known to modern man since the time of the Renaissance, though its importance was only spotted by Professor L. R. Nougier in 1956 and this chamber is slightly disfigured by graffiti. Visits most of the year.

Sorcier: As its name implies, the Grotte du Sorcier at Saint-Cirque-du-Bugue (midway between Le Bugue and Les Eyzies) contains one of the rare prehistoric representations of a human being, dubbed a 'sorcerer'. Recently opened to the general public.

Villars: Four kilometres north-east of Villars, off the D82, is the splendid Grotte de Cluzeau. Exquisite stalagmites, stalactites and other translucent concretions are delightful. In addition, the cave contains very early engravings and paintings, including one 'sorcerer'. Archaeologists have excavated at the mouth of the cave the blackened hearth of a prehistoric family or tribe. Open most of the year.

See also LES EYZIES, prehistoric SHELTERS, THONAC, and Chapter 6 of this book.

CAZELLE: Approaching the valley of the river Beune on the D6 from Marquay, you pass by the rocks of Cazelle, where medieval men lived in caves.

CELLES, north-east of Ribérac on the D99, possesses a good, fortified twelfth-century church, inside which is a seventeenth-century painting of St Catherine and St Radegunde (a Thüringen princess who fell into the hands of the Franks and founded a nunnery at Poitiers in the mid sixth century), the two brought together no doubt because both preferred virginity to a forced marriage.

CÉNAC-ET-SAINT-JULIEN, lying at the foot of the massive rock on which Domme is built, is noted for its splendid camp sites and for swimming in the river Dordogne. The village itself, which straggles along the main road, possesses two romanesque churches. The one in the village (on the road leading up into the cliff-side) is the least interesting – though its original apse, separated from the rest by pillars, is fine enough.

Just over half a kilometre from the village centre, on the road to Saint-Cybranet, lies the Priory of Saint-Julien, which remains one of the most remarkable of all Périgord romanesque buildings. Aquilanus, the Abbot of Moissac, bought land to build this priory in Cénac in A.D. 1090. The building was finished in the first quarter of the twelfth century. Its history was by no means tranquil. During one religious quarrel a prior refused to allow the Bishop of Bordeaux to enter the priory. In the early fourteenth century this bishop became Pope Clement V, and excommunicated the prior. During the Wars of Religion, Geoffroi de Vivans, having captured Domme for the Protestants, descended to Cénac and destroyed all but the eastern end of the priory. The whole was restored in the nineteenth century, but the smooth, massive, machine-cut stones readily distinguish the new part from the original.

None the less, the original remains one of the most important pieces of romanesque architecture, above all for the carvings inside it. The tops of capitals are decorated not only with carvings of leaves and plants, but also with such animals as lions, long-eared rabbits, salamanders, monkeys and birds with their prey. These form one of the two finest collections of animal carvings in the whole of romanesque Périgord. (The other is in the church of Sadillac.)

Even more exciting are the carvings of human beings. Human figures scarcely ever appear in romanesque Périgord sculpture. In the priory of Cénac, Daniel is depicted in the lions' den; a monkey-trainer scratches the neck of one of his charges and the back of the other; Lazarus is raised from the tomb (while two women watching hold their noses against the stench); shepherds (or wise men – the sculpture here is mutilated) praise the infant Jesus; angels cense Christ; men and women dance, some naked, some clothed, while a man beats a drum between his legs; and a snake between two naked women castigates the sin of lust.

As if this romanesque bestiary and biblical pageant were not feast enough, the visitor should go into the vast graveyard to view the carvings on the outside of the apse. Flowers and birds, as well as patterned mouldings, imitate carvings inside the priory. But here nature is more frightening. Whereas inside, Daniel actually puts each of his hands into lions' mouths (while others vainly snap at him), outside a lion eats his prey and a pig eats two human heads. And – in the medieval fashion – in order to scare off evil spirits, a contortionist turns his backside to the outside world and a man and a woman lewdly embrace.

On Tuesdays Cénac holds its own regular market, and each August arranges a wine festival in the main street. The bread shop at Cénac is one of the best for miles around. Cénac also provides the best approach route to another famous church, the slightly eerie troglodyte church of Caudon. Take the road from the centre of the village towards Grolejac. Drive or cycle for 4.2 kilometres. On the left is the office of the camp site of the French gas and electricity workers. On the right a short road leads up to the medieval church, constructed out of a cave, with its own troglodyte belltower and bells. See DOMME and VITRAC.

CENDREIX, on the D2 north-west of Le Bugue, has a massive domed church, whose belltower resembles the keep of a castle. The building was reordered in the eighteenth and nineteenth centuries.

CERCLES, just north of the D2 below La Tour-Blanche, has a pretty church, once a priory, with fine romanesque capitals and delicate ogive vaulting added at the end of the sixteenth century.

CHALEIX, west of the N21 en route from Châlus to Thiviers, has an imposing château with three towers – two square and one round, built in the sixteenth century. In the village are remains of a Gallo-Roman forge.

LE CHAMBON, see Château de Sauvebœuf at AUBAS.

CHAMPAGNAC-DE-BELAIR, on the D83 north-east of Brantôme on a promontory overlooking the river Dronne and its valley, holds an important market on the first Monday of each month. Its seven-teenth-century Château de la Borie-Saulnier replaces one destroyed by the Huguenots in 1569. Its fine buttressed church dates from the sixteenth century, and possesses an interesting porch and a classical seventeenth-century retable. Food at the Hostellerie Moulin du Roc (an old walnut-oil mill) is altogether splendid. Sheep fair, last Sunday in August. See CONDAT-SUR-TRINCOU.

CHAMPAGNE-ET-FONTAINES, on the D24 south-east of Mareuil, has a sixteenth-century château (de Clauzurou) built in the renais-sance style with an eighteenth-century entrance. The Revolu-tionaries of 1789 knocked off the tops of its towers. Next to the château is a twelfth-century church which was fortified during the Wars of Religion.

CHANCELADE, six kilometres north-west of Périgueux, was founded as an Augustinian priory in 1129. The priory suffered greatly during the Hundred Years War and the Wars of Religion, but some of the original buildings remain and the monks continued to build valiantly for many years. Today a museum of religious art has been established at Chancelade, and the exquisite belltower, the fine romanesque Chapel of St John, as well as what remain of the monks' lodgings, make for a rewarding visit. English tourists will warm to a fresco depicting St Thomas à Becket. See also MERLANDE.

LE CHANGE: The village nestles beautifully on a corner of the river Auvézère, seventeen kilometres east of Périgueux, its houses clustering round a fifteen-century manor (with battlemented tower), a sixteenth-century château (also protected with towers) and the romanesque church, happily in good condition. Near by is the ruined oratory of Saint-Michel-d'Auberoche. From the bridge across the river can be seen the charming ancient mill.

LA CHAPELLE-FAUCHER, on the D3 east of Brantôme and south of Champagnac-de-Belair, offers one of those stunning views of a château perched above a river that characterize the Dordogne. Here the river is the Côle. The château, partly ruined by a fire after it was struck by lightning, has two battlemented towers that are still inhabited, and was first built in the fifteenth century. A twelfth-century domed church completes the scene. See JUMILHAC-LE-PETIT.

LA CHAPELLE-MOURET, see COLY.

CHÂTEAU-L'ÉVÊQUE, eleven kilometres north of Périgueux on the N939, was built by Adhémar de Neuville, Bishop of Périgueux in the fourteenth century, and modified over the next hundred years by successive bishops. Today, though a hotel, its defensive aspect speaks of the dangerous life led even by a man of God in the late Middle Ages. It is said that St Vincent de Paul was ordained priest in the parish church in 1600.

CHAVAGNAC, on the D60 south of Larche, has a keep that once belonged to a thirteenth-century château, and a domed twelfth-century church.

CHENAUD, on the river Dronne near the western border of Périgord, has a domed romanesque church with a stone pulpit dated 1615.

CHERVAL, twenty-six kilometres south of Mareuil on the D102, boasts a fortified twelfth-century church with no less than *four* domes (see GENIBLANC). The French historical monuments commission has splendidly restored it. Nearby Gouts-Rossignol has two eighteenth-century châteaux: de la Vassaldie and de Jaurias.

CHERVEIX-CUBAS, on the D704 north of Hautefort, boasts one of the three 'Lanterns of the Dead' in the Dordogne (see ATUR and SARLAT): a column 20 feet high, topped by a cone and pierced by four rectangular openings. The town itself is far from dead. The twelfth-century Church of Saint-Martial-Laborie, built by the Templars, contains a late fifteenth-century statue of St Valérie, and once held the miracle-working statue of St Rémy (known in Dordogne patois as 'St Remedy') till it was mysteriously stolen from Cherveix-Cubas. The last *curé* of this church represented the Périgord clergy in the Estates General of 1789. Cherveix-Cubas prides itself on its fishing in the Auvézère and its welcome to tourists. There is also excellent canoeing. It holds a regular fair on the fourth Monday of each month.

CLERMONT-DE-BEAUREGARD, on the D21 north-east of Bergerac, has the splendid Château de la Gaubertie, built in the fifteenth century and restored in the twentieth, almost hiding a tiny chapel dated 1676. This is strawberry-growing country.

COLOMBIER, just east of the N21 five kilometres south of Bergerac, possesses a château which Henri IV gave to Gabrielle d'Estrées at the end of the sixteenth century. Restoration in the nineteenth century proved unsympathetic to the original. The romanesque church at Colombier was given a splendid renaissance porch in the sixteenth century.

COLY takes its name from the little river Coly, nine kilometres long and said to be crammed with fish. Situated on the D62 south of Le Lardin, the tiny village contains vestiges of a château once belonging to the monks of Saint-Amand-de-Coly. Two kilometres east of Coly is the even tinier village of La Chapelle-Mouret, with its own church and ancient stone-roofed houses. See SAINT-AMAND-DE-COLY.

COMMARQUE is an incredibly noble, frightening, complex ruined château, in the forest east of Les Eyzies and opposite the prehistoric shelter of Cap Blanc; it was built in the thirteenth century, but despoiled by the English in the fourteenth century. See CAVES.

CONDAT-LE-LARDIN, just south of Le Lardin on the D62, contains fine remains of the medieval Knights Hospitallers: their church, their battlemented lodgings, their fine houses. The village now makes paper for its livelihood and (being at the confluence of the rivers Coly and Vézère) is sometimes called Condat-sur-Vézère.

CONDAT-SUR-TRINCOU, just south of Champagnac-de-Belair, has a fine romanesque church with powerful buttresses and a comical belltower, situated in an old cemetery. See LA CHAPELLE-FAUCHER.

CORGNAC-SUR-L'ISLE, south of Thiviers on the D76, boasts what must be the last great château built solely for defence in the Dordogne, without any concession to comfort. Perhaps for this reason Château de Laxion, almost entirely a sixteenth-century building, is now sadly dilapidated.

COUBJOURS, south-east of Hautefort, through Badefols-d'Ans and on to the D71, is worth a pause to see the sixteenth-century wood-carving of the *pietà* in the parish church. The romanesque church at nearby Saint-Robert was fortified in the fourteenth century.

COULAURES, on the D705, six and a half kilometres south-west of Excideuil, is a village once important for commanding the confluence of two rivers (the Isle and the Loue): hence its two châteaux – de la Cousse, built in the sixteenth and seventeenth centuries; and de Conti, a château reconstructed in 1830 around a much older, square machicolated tower. The whole village is lovely, with two churches: a well-restored romanesque church with two domes, a fine porch and inside a fourteenth-century fresco; and the seventeenth-century Church of Our Lady. See MAYAC.

COULOUNEIX, south-west of Périgueux on the D4, is guarded by a ruined sixteenth-century château. See COURSAC.

COURSAC, still further south than Coulouneix on the D4 (i.e. the countryside route from Périgueux to Bergerac), is guarded by the Château de la Jarthe, battlemented, slightly inhospitable.

LE COUX-ET-BIGAROQUE: Bordering the river Dordogne on the D705 south of Le Bugue, Coux possesses a romanesque church, while nearby Bigaroque, as well as boasting its own twelfth-century church, was the site of the now ruined château of the archbishops of Bordeaux, a site carefully chosen in medieval times in order to tax the boatmen plying their trade on the river.

COUZE-ET-SAINT-FRONT, on the D660 east of Bergerac and near the English *bastide* Lalinde, may well have been the birthplace of St Front, the missionary of Périgord. Many paper-mills – some dating back as far as the fifteenth century – reveal the origins of what is now the most important paper-making centre of the Dordogne. In summer you can join organized courses learning the traditional methods of producing handmade paper. Couze-et-Saint-Front holds a market every Monday. See BANEUIL, LALINDE and LANQUAIS.

CUNÈGES, on the D16, twenty-two kilometres west of Monbazillac, has a church with a fine twelfth-century porch. Se LA BASTIDE.

DAGLAN is a bare village on the D57 south-west of Domme. Here is the fortified Château de Peyruzel, built in the seventeenth century in the odd shape of a Greek cross; the town hall and the village school in a manor with a round tower and a sixteenth-century doorway; a fine house dated 1788 alongside an eighteenth-century chapel: in all an unexpected surprise. The porch to the church was carved in the twelfth century.

DALON: For the ruins of this Cistercian abbey, see SAINTE-TRIE.

DOISSAT, south-east of Belvès on the D34, is the site of the ruined château where the Huguenot captain Geoffroi de Vivans was buried. Part of it is now a walnut museum.

DOMME, the most beautiful *bastide* of Périgord, is situated on a rock high above the river Dordogne, slightly east of the D46. The great walls are pierced by three gates: the Porte de Tours, flanked by two massive semi-circular towers; the Porte del Bos, still grooved for its portcullis; and in between these the arch of the Porte de la Combe. I should like to see the walls properly excavated; for those with energy and interest, they still repay a scramble to discover little crevices and medieval alterations.

Founded on the orders of the French king, Philip the Bold, in the early 1280s, Domme, because of its irregular site, could not quite follow the classic rectangular pattern of a *bastide*. Even so, the plan succeeds remarkably well, with narrow and wider streets crossing each other at right-angles almost throughout the town. The *barre* (or 'bluff') gives an astonishing panoramic view of the river

Dordogne and much of Périgord Noir. The houses are a perfect ochre. Although Domme did not remain impregnable, either during the Hundred Years War or the Wars of Religion, it has survived remarkably well. The market hall is supported by stone pillars, and faces the house of the governor, with its corbelled tower. (The façade was altered in the seventeenth century.) The Protestant leader Geoffroi de Vivans burned down most of the original church of Domme. I find the rebuilt one less than charming, though it has a fine renaissance porch. To explore the side streets is exceptionally rewarding: the houses are exquisite. The Rue de l'Abbaye contains the remains of a fifteenth-century cloister. The old town hall has a restored thirteenth-century façade. The oldest house in Domme has an inscription telling you it was once the royal mint.

Domme now cleverly combines the life of a Dordogne town with a generous welcome to tourists. Butchers, a general store, and the Thursday morning market combine with a hotel and restaurant, bars, and shops selling Périgord wine and specialities. (Fine food at the Hôtel l'Esplanade. Try *la truite braisée au Bergerac sec*.) The Paul Reclus Museum displays objects such as mammoths' teeth, found in local prehistoric sites. The public gardens provide picnic places and the chance to play the local variant of bowls. And, fittingly placed in between the church and the graveyard, is a beautifully built old people's home and hospital. See CAVES, CÉNAC-ET-SAINT-JULIEN, SHELTERS and, in the index to this book, Jacques de Maleville, Henry Miller and *bastides*.

DOUBLE, the forest between the rivers Isle and Dronne, was planted by the monks in the Middle Ages, chiefly of oak, and soon became the haunt of robbers and outlaws. The most famous, grisly tale of the Double records the bodies of several Girondin deputies, discovered there in 1793, mysteriously eaten by wolves. Today the forest is tamer, and pine is slowly replacing the oak trees.

DOUZILLAC, on the D3 north-east of Mussidan, is worth a detour for its pretty romanesque church (with sixteenth-century vaulting) and the Château de Mauriac, built in the 1500s and situated imposingly over the Isle valley. The view over the valley here is beautiful, and in the local cemetery is a monument erected in 1964 by the French Foreign Legion to their last surviving hero of Camerone, Corporal Louis Maine.

DUSSAC, on the D707 to the west of Lanquaille, possesses a pretty, domed romanesque church and an elegant château built in 1778. See PAYZAC.

ENFER: For the Gorge d'Enfer, see SHELTERS.

ESSENDIÉRAS, see EXCIDEUIL.

EXCIDEUIL, on the D705 in Périgord Vert, is an imposing and yet somehow altogether charming town. In the eleventh and twelfth centuries the viscounts of Limoges replaced a wooden keep with a stone one, and then used the château to consolidate their claim to land contested by the counts of Périgord. A second keep was built in the twelfth century and a curtain wall joined the two. Three times in 1182 the army of Richard Cœur de Lion failed to take the château. Luck, alas, did not hold. The English besieged and took Excideuil in 1356. After Du Guesclin had recovered it, the two keeps were rebuilt with battlements. During the Wars of Religion, the Huguenots captured the château and held it for a short time. In 1582 Henri III, badly needing money, sold Excideuil Château to François de Cars for 150,000 *livres*. François's fortune (derived from his wife's dowry) was not exhausted, and he proceeded to transform part of Excideuil Château into a splendid renaissance home. It is this combination of stern medieval fortress and turreted renaissance delicacy, of massive wall and graceful steps, that impresses the visitor, as the château is first glimpsed in the distance and then, bit by bit, in its total magnificence.

The rest of the town is filled with interest too. The Rue des Cendres commemorates the fire which devastated Excideuil in 1420. The Place Bugeaud honours the town's greatest nineteenth-century son, Marshal Bugeaud, conqueror of Algeria. (A statue of Bugeaud on the rock of Saint-Martin, sent back by the former colony, shows that the Algerians take a different view of the marshal's achievements.) The triangular market place is filled with local produce every Thursday and becomes the scene of a full-scale fair on the first Thursday of each month. Bugeaud gave the fountain still playing there. St Thomas's Church, once a romanesque Benedictine priory, was much altered in the fifteenth century, when a splendid flamboyant doorway was added. Inside is a romanesque statue of John the Baptist, a sixteenth-century *pietà* and a seventeenth-century retable.

The Avenue Eugène Le Roy leads to the sixteenth-century turret and casement windows that remain from the old Cordeliers' sacristy. The hospital outside the walls of Excideuil was once a Cordeliers' convent, founded in 1260. The ramparts afford superb views and still support the gardens of seventeenth-century noble houses. And the Hôtel de Vendeuil in the shopping arcade retains its fine eighteenth-century façade and courtyard.

At Saint-Médard-d'Excideuil, a little way out of the town to the north-east along the D705, is a domed romanesque church with a seventeenth-century retable. Close by Saint-Médard is the Château d'Essendiéras. Here was the summer home of Émile Herzog (1885–1967) who, under the pen name André Maurois, wrote a brilliant series of novels, essays, histories and biographies and was in 1938 both elected a member of the Académie Française and made a Knight of the British Empire. See CHERVEIX-CUBAS, COULAURES, LANQUAIS and, in the index to this book, Marshal Bugeaud and André Maurois.

EYBENÈS, see SALIGNAC-EYVIGNES.

EYMET: An unexpected delight just before you leave the Dordogne at its south-west tip by the D933, Eymet on the river Dropt is a lovely medieval *bastide*. Founded in 1271 by Alphonse de Poitiers, brother of King Louis VII of France, the *bastide* was spared neither during the Hundred Years War nor during the Wars of Religion; but many of its houses were rebuilt in the fifteenth century in stone or wattle and daub and still stand. Unusually for a *bastide*, Eymet possessed a château, built in the fourteenth century, of which the square keep alone remains, along with an annex which now houses a museum of local history, prehistory and palaeontology. The château's keep is known locally as the '*tour Monseigneur*'.

Every Thursday Eymet holds a market in the fine Place des Arcades with its seventeenth-century fountain, where fine conserves from six surrounding factories can be bought. This industry, as well as the profit from locally grown cereals and plums, have brought a certain prosperity to this ancient *bastide*. See MONBOS and, in the index to this book, *bastides*.

LES EYZIES-DE-TAYAC, on the river Vézère where the D47 crosses the D706, is the centre of French prehistory. Close by here in 1863 Edouard Lartet and Henry Christy discovered in the village of La Madeleine part of a mammoth's tusk apparently carved and chiselled, and postulated the existence of 'Magdalenian' man contemporary with that mammoth. Five years later workmen digging out the route of the new Périgueux–Agen railway uncovered at a nearby spot called Cro-Magnon the remains of three prehistoric men, a woman and a foetus. 'Cro-Magnon' man, his wife and child, living perhaps 35,000 years ago, had been discovered.

The Vézère valley proved astonishingly rich in prehistoric finds and Les Eyzies became the capital of French prehistory. The town possesses a château built by the lords of Beynac in the eleventh and twelfth centuries under an overhanging rock on the cliff-side. Denis Peyrony founded here a museum of prehistory which now belongs to the French nation and is internationally renowed, its priceless collection (drawn from many other places as well as this region) in part on display to the general public, in part open only to scholars.

Les Eyzies combines the role of prehistoric capital with that of host to the many tourists who want to sail, swim in or camp alongside the rivers Beaune and Vézère, which meet at this point (a combination of tourism and prehistory bizarrely summed up to English ears in the name of a local hotel: 'Cro-Magnon'). Near the railway station is a powerful fortified church, built in the twelfth century, its belfries crenellated for defence, the interior as mighty as the exterior. The only jarring note in this attractive town seems to me the ridiculous statue of Cro-Magnon man sculpted by Paul Dardé in 1930. See CAVES and SHELTERS. See also MARQUAY and MARSAC, as well as Chapter 6.

FAGES, château, see SAINT-CYPRIEN.

FANLAC, a virtually deserted village west of Montignac, is celebrated as the home of the kindly Abbé Bonal and the equally attractive old Chevalier Galibert in Eugène Le Roy's *Jacquou le Croquant*. The choice was apt. Fanlac possesses both a fine twelfth-century church (modified in the seventeenth century) and the Château d'Auberoche, built between the fourteenth and the seventeenth centuries. There is an attractive cross outside the church and also an effigy of Jean de Lajalage, sergeant-at-arms, who lived at Fanlac in the late fourteenth century. The houses of the little village are built out of the beautiful stone of this neighbourhood. See in the index to this book *Jacquou le Croquant*.

FAYOLLE, château, see TOCANE-SAINT-APRE.

FAYRAC: Château de Fayrac stands on the banks of the river Dordogne on the D52 just north of Castelnaud, under whose suzerainty it lay. The château, built between the fourteenth and the seventeenth centuries, was restored in the nineteenth, and very well, too. Two great round towers, with pepperpot roofs, balustraded and buttressed curtain walls, crenellated side walls of the great hall, and smaller towers (square and round), build up to a very satisfying whole, all surrounded by a double moat. See also CASTELNAUD and LES MILANDES.

FÉNELON: The D50, as it runs beside the river Dordogne south-east of Sarlat, leads to the village of Sainte-Mondane. Two kilometres from Sainte-Mondane is the splendid Château de Fénelon, built on a succession of rocky terraces in the thirteenth and fourteenth centuries and partly rebuilt some 300 years later. Today the château houses a small museum devoted to the famous Archbishop Fénelon of Cambrai, who was born here in 1651 and spent his childhood here; it also houses a larger exhibition of vintage motor-cars. Château de Fénelon has not lost its warlike aspect, ringed by a triple series of defences and fortified doorways. The two great towers and stern pavilion on the east side (containing a chapel, though you would not guess so from the outside) retain their ancient stone *lauze* roofs. The north side is slightly gentler, with its seventeenth-century gallery, terrace and balustrade, graceful steps and drawbridge. The interior is equally noble and the views are stunning. See CARLUX, CARSAC-AILLAC, GROLEJAC, SAINT-JULIEN-DE-LAMPON, VEYRIGNAC and, in the index to this book, Fénelon, Archbishop of Cambrai.

FESTALEMPS, see VANXAINS.

LA FLEIX, see VÉLINES.

FONT-DE-GAUME, see CAVES and LES-EYZIES-DE-TAYAC.

LA FORCE, nine and a half kilometres west of Bergerac on the D34 once played an important role as a Protestant stronghold during the Wars of Religion. Here the Huguenot leader Jacques Nompar de Caumont-La Force, ally of Henri IV in his Protestant days, built a huge château, now completely destroyed. See SAUSSIGNAC.

FOSSEMAGNE, halfway between Périgueux and Brive on the N89, apart from inviting speculation about the origin of its name (was there a great ditch here, or even once a communal grave?), is a spot to pause at and ask whether there is time for a brief detour from the main road. See AJAT, BAUZENS, LIMEYRAT.

FOUGUEYROLLES, six kilometres north of the *bastide* of Sainte-Foy-la-Grande on the D708, has a restored twelfth-century church with a retable dating from the sixteenth century. Near by are the ruins of Château de Ségur.

GABILLOU, see CAVES.

GENIBLANC, south of Mareuil en route to Ribérac, has a fortified twelfth-century church with four domes. You must drive 800 metres to the right to find it.

GENIS: If you take the D5 north of Cherveix-Cubas to travel along the breathtaking banks of the Auvézère river, you come across the scarcely pretty village of Genis, which none the less boasts a domed romanesque church. Genis holds a fair on the second Monday of each month. Further north is Saint-Mesmin, with its romanesque church (containing a seventeenth-century retable) and impressive site.

LA GONTERIE-BOULOUNEIX, north-west of Brantôme (and west of the D939) is notable for its pretty romanesque church (with carved capitals) and its sadly ruined priory of Belaygue.

GOUTS-ROSSIGNAL, see CHERVAL.

GRAND-BRASSAC can be found by taking the main route between Périgueux and Ribérac (the D710) and turning north at Tocane-Saint-Apre to pass through Montagrier. It really is worth the trouble. The church of Grand-Brassac was started in the twelfth century with just one dome. The following century saw the addition of an overpowering fortified belltower and two more domes. The Protestants destroyed part of the church during the Wars of Religion. Antoine de Montagrier repaired it, adding a new apse. (The date 1599 can be seen on one of the beams.) The vaulted choir dates from this era. On the eastern face of the belltower you can see where defenders climbed in.

The whole, in spite of its diverse styles, seems to form a unity. Even more remarkable is the decoration of the west façade, where a group of sculptures of different dates have been combined into a harmonious, impressive pattern. See Grand-Brassac in the index to this book. Near by are the Château de Marouatte and the Château de Montardy, both built between the fourteenth and the sixteenth centuries.

GRANDE-FILOLIE: For this château, see MONTIGNAC.

LES GRAULGES, directly north of Mareuil on the edge of the Dordogne, possesses a fine romanesque church with carved capitals.

LA GRÈZE, see CAVES.

GRIGNOLS, in the green valley of the river Vern on the D107 south-west of Périgueux, boasts a château which in the twelfth century belonged to the barons of Périgord. Its church also dates from this time, and was once rivalled by a chapel dedicated to St Valery, now a private house but detectable by its vault and two outside columns. See NEUVIC-SUR-L'ISLE and VILLAMBLARD.

GROLEJAC, on the road from Carsac-Aillac to Gourdon in the Lot, though approached by the ugliest bridge to span the river Dordogne, has charm, good swimming, hotels and a splendid camp site. The village, formerly a Gaulish site and seemingly strung out along the road, is in reality set back on either side. On the left, over the ugly bridge, narrow medieval streets wind up to the romanesque church with its stone *lauze* roof, standing next to a fine classical château. Inside the church are eighteenth-century woodcarvings. Further on along the road to Gourdon, troglodyte caves can be seen in the cliffs on the left of Grolejac. (For excellent, reasonably priced food, try the Hôtel du Pont, just over the bridge.) See CARSAC-AILLAC and VEYRIGNAC.

HAUTEFORT: The outstanding château dominates the charming village in Périgord Vert, east of the D705 and visible for miles around. All that remains of the twelfth-century château is the drawbridge. The present château was constructed between 1640 and 1680 by two successive architects (Nicolas Rambourg and Jacques Maigret, a Parisian who took over after Rambourg's death in 1649). Their patron was Jacques-François de Hautefort. Jacques Maigret also built a hospital in the form of a Greek cross, with a huge dome similar to the four great domes on the château, and this is now the parish church of the village.

Much of Château Hautefort is now open to the general public, who can explore the great terrace, the 'court of honour', the fine dormer windows and the fashion in which the architects used battlements and other military features to enhance what is chiefly a luxurious residence for a rich seigneur of the Grand Siècle. Inside are fine furniture and seventeenth- and eighteenth-century tapestries, as well as a museum devoted to the memory of Eugène Le Roy, whose father was steward at Hautefort. See in the index of this book Bertrand de Born and Eugène Le Roy, as well as Hautefort.

The village of Hautefort is geared to tourism and camping, and its environs include the placid lake Coucou. Market day at Hautefort is the first Monday of the month. There is a fascinating exhibition of textile-weaving in the old church, July–August.

HERM: for the Château de L'Herm, see BALOU.

ISSAC, on the river Crempse (and the D38) south-east of Mussidan, is the site of the splendid Château de Montréal – in the words of Jean Secret, the 'architectural prince of this region'. Set on a great rock, dominating the old route between Bergerac and Mussidan, Château Montréal preserves some of its great double rampart dating from the eleventh century. Its bulky medieval lodgings, curtain walls and round tower contrast with the renaissance living quarters, boasting delicate windows, columns and medallions. In the early 1500s François de Pontbriand built a fine chapel, with a spiral staircase in a tower and stone statues of the Apostles, the Virgin and her Child. He married three times and now lies inside in a tomb with one of his wives.

Montréal gave its name to the capital city of Canada. Claude de Pontbriand, accompanying Jacques Cartier on his second visit to Canada, was heard to observe that the St Lawrence river came second only to his own beloved river Crempse. See MUSSIDAN and VILLAMBLARD.

ISSIGEAC, beautifully situated in south-west Périgord where the D21 crosses the river Banège, is a lovely medieval town, with overhanging timber-framed houses, twisting streets and the occasional larger gothic hôtel. The bishops of Sarlat made it their holiday home. Between 1498 and 1519 Bishop Armand de Gontaut-Biron built the gothic parish church with its octagonal belfry and its buttresses. The Huguenots set it on fire, but the citizens rebuilt it. Then in 1699 another bishop of Sarlat (one of the Salignac-Fénelon family) built the sombre 'Jansenist' palace with its square towers, now converted into the town hall. Here the bishop received his nephew, the famous Fénelon. Close by the court of Issigeac sat in the great sixteenth- and seventeenth-century 'Prévôté', with its huge, angled pavilions.

Today Issigeac prospers on wine, cereals and fruit-growing (especially plums). Market day is Sunday. Good food at the Hôtel des Voyageurs. See BARDOU.

JAVERLHAC-ET-LA CHAPELLE-SAINT-ROBERT is situated in northern Périgord on the D75 from Nontron to Angoulême where the road crosses the river Bandiat. Javerlhac possesses its own church; but the religious pride of the village is a nearby abbey church which the monks of Vigeois built and dedicated to St Robert (a former abbot) after a rich bourgeois named Frotaire de Terrasson had left them much land. This thirteenth-century building is beautifully simple, as is the imposing Château of Javerlhac, built in the following two centuries and consisting of a rectangular great house dominated by a massive machicolated round tower with a pointed cap. Javerlhac also boasts a dove-cot with 1,500 nests. Round about the village are the remains of ancient forges, once the renown of Périgord and Limousin. Javerlhac prides itself on its hotels and restaurants with rooms to let, and each month holds a fair on the second Monday. See CAVES (*La Mairie*).

JAYAC, see SALIGNAC-EYVIGNES.

JUMILHAC-LE-GRAND in Périgord Vert, sitting on the river Isle (and the D78) halfway between the N21 and the D704, has the most astonishing château in the Dordogne. In 1579 the Chapelle de Jumilhac family acquired a thirteenth-century fortress built by the Knights Templars and proceeded to add a fantastic skyline consisting of pointed and pepperpot turrets roofed in slate. This was a region of great forges, and on top of the turrets are forged metal motifs – birds, an avenging angel, cupid, the sun and the moon. In the seventeenth century two classical square wings were added, and behind the château a fine balustraded terrace. Next to the château is the old feudal chapel, now the parish church. To sit in the huge square opposite and gaze at Jumilhac-le-Grand Château is a deeply satisfying architectural experience (except, of course, on market days – the second and fourth Wednesday of each month). The château is floodlit in the tourist season, and visitors are welcome to go inside and look at the great chimneys, the fabled room of the spinning maiden (*La Fileuse*) and so on. The great Dordogne novelist Eugène Le Roy gave a child to a girl who worked in the post office here and later married her. See in the index to this book Eugène Le Roy and Jumilhac-le-Grand.

Behind the château the road drops steeply past newer houses and then runs through delightful countryside and hamlets on its way towards Thiviers.

JUMILHAC-LE-PETIT, near La Chapelle-Faucher (which lies on the D3 east of Brantôme) has a romanesque chapel built by the Templars, and a fortified house.

LADORNAC is a pretty village south-east of Terrasson (close by Chavagnac-la-Fauconnie) with a thirteenth-century church, remodelled 300 years later and containing an eighteenth-century water-stoup.

LADOUZE lies in a commune of ponds, twenty kilometres south of Périgueux on the D710. To the north, just outside the village, is its interesting church, built in fifteenth-century gothic. The belltower is huge. Inside, the stone altar bears carvings of Christ crucified, adored by Pierre d'Abzac (Lord of Ladouze) and his wife Jeanne de Bourdeille. Their escutcheons are carved on the stone pulpit, as is a representation of St Paul. The church fonts are made from what was once a Gallo-Roman column. See Ladouze in the index to this book.

LAFORCE, on the D4 west of Bergerac, was once a Huguenot stronghold. The Protestant church built by the lords of Laforce still stands, but the triangular château they constructed was razed during the Revolution. The site of its ruin offers fine panoramic views of the river Dordogne and its valley.

LALINDE, the *bastide* founded in 1270 by King Edward III of England near a ford across the river Dordogne, suffered so greatly during the Wars of Religion that today the only traces of the *bastide* are the pattern of its streets, vestiges of ramparts and the western gate (or Porte Romane – so-called because it was constructed out of stones originally quarried by the Romans).

Lalinde today lies between the river and its adjacent canal. It is a busy town of 3,000 or so inhabitants, catering with hotels and camping for tourism, and holding a market on Thursdays which turns into a fully fledged fair on the second Tuesday of each month. It retains numerous old houses. The Maison du Gouverneur dates from 1597. The stone cross was erected in the market place in 1351. From its public garden you have a magnificent view of the Dordogne as it flows from the great *cingle* of Trémolat down to Bergerac. Near by are the twelfth-century Chapel of Saint-Front; the splendid Château of Laffinoux, with its pepperpot towers built on a powerful square base in the fifteenth century to which the eighteenth century added charming pavilions; and the château at Bayac (south on the D660) with its machicolated towers, built in the sixteenth century. See BANEUIL, COUZE-ET-SAINT-FRONT, and LANQUAIS. See also in the index to this book *bastides*.

LAMONZIE-MONTASTRUC, north-east of Bergerac, just off the D21 south of Montastruc, is worth a brief detour to see its fine seventeenth-century château. See CLERMONT-DE-BEAUREGARD and LIORAC-SUR-LOUYRE.

LAMOTHE-MONTRAVEL: You have almost reached the westernmost tip of the Dordogne, close to Castillon-la-Bataille, where the defeat of John Talbot, Earl of Shrewsbury, on 17 July 1453 marked also the defeat of England and the end of the Hundred Years War. A monument south of the D936, west of Lamothe-Montravel, marks the spot where Talbot was axed to death. A happier recollection is the fine Montravel vintages of these parts. In 1307 Cardinal de Sourdis lived in a château in Lamothe-Montravel, the only remaining vestiges of which are the medieval towers of the *Mairie* and some romanesque features in the old neighbouring walls. See MONTCARET and SAINT-MICHEL-DE-MONTAIGNE. See also wines in the index to this book, as well as Chapter 4.

LANQUAILLE, see ANGOISSE, DUSSAC, PAYZAC and SAVIGNAC-LÉDRIER.

LANQUAIS: Cross the river Dordogne by the bridge at Saint-Capraise-de-Lalinde on the D660 and go south for four kilometres to visit the refreshing Château de Lanquais, open to the general public from May to October (except Thursdays) and sometimes floodlit at night. The château is a clear mixture of medieval and renaissance, readily distinguishable. The medieval part, substantially of the fifteenth century, is defensive, with a huge machicolated tower and narrow windows. The renaissance half has wide, regular decorated windows, and jolly dormers, with a taller square end to match the round tower. Unlike many châteaux, the interior is fully furnished, and it is possible that Italian artists designed the fancy chimneys.

Lanquais is on a splendid site. Its village is filled with old build-

7. Geese and a pigeon-loft, Sainte-Nathalène.

8. *Market place at Monpazier.*

9. *Fortified twelfth-century abbey church, Saint-Amand-de-Coly.*

10. *Gaulish huts, Breuil, near Les Eyzies-de-Tayac.*

11. *The fortifications of a bastide, Porte des Tours, Domme.*

12. *Aerial view of Périgueux with the river Isle and Saint-Front Cathedral.*

*13. The twelfth-century apse of the abbey church
of Cénac-et-Saint-Julien.*

ings, including a restored romanesque chapel with domes. Near by is the fifteenth- and sixteenth-century manor of Laroque. See BANEUIL, LALINDE, VERDON and also Lanquais in the index to this book.

LE LARDIN-SAINT-LAZAIRE, see LA BACHELLERIE.

LASCAUX, see CAVES and also in the index to this book Lascaux.

LAUGERIE-BASSE and LAUGERIE-HAUTE, see SHELTERS.

LAUSSEL: Château de Laussel, built in the sixteenth century, is on the D48 west of Les Eyzies. See COMMARQUE, LES EYZIES-DE-TAYAC, MARQUAY, and in the index to this book Venus of Laussel.

LEGUILLAC-DE-CERCLES, see MAREUIL.

LEMPZOURS, see SAINT-PIERRE-DE-CÔLE.

LIGUEUX, on the D24, lies west of Sorges (on the N21 south of Thiviers). Here in the twelfth century Géraud de Sales founded a convent for Benedictine nuns. Their church, austere and beautiful, remains, domed, buttressed, virtually as it stood when it was built in 1185. The stern pavilion to the west was built for the abbess in the seventeenth century. During the Revolution much was despoiled, but some seventeenth-century stalls were saved (and are in the cathedral of Périgueux) as well as a retable and pulpit (which are now in the church of Mareuil).

LIMEUIL, on the D51 at the confluence of the Dordogne and the Vézère, was not surprisingly once a mighty fortress town. You can still see parts of its ramparts and three great gates, as well as the esplanade of the old château. The panorama is splendid. The town has preserved many delightful renaissance elements in its buildings. The domed Church of St Martin was built in 1194. The other church in Limeuil possesses a statue of the Virgin carved in the sixteenth century. Today's peaceful pursuits here include fishing, canoeing and swimming.

LIMEYRAT, north of Fossemagne between Périgueux and Terrasson, has a fine twelfth-century domed church. Near here the stones to build the Paris Opéra were quarried. See AJAT and BAUZENS.

LIORAC-SUR-LOUYRE, on the D52 north-east of Bergerac, dominates the forest in which it lies and the river Louyre that gives it its charm. The twelfth-century church has a fortified belltower, and the village is surrounded by charming old manor houses. See LAMONZIE-MONTASTRUC.

LISLE, positioned on the D78 near the river Dronne, has exerted itself to welcome those who like to swim, fish for trout and camp. Its annual fête, once confined to the Sunday after 15 August, now stretches for four days. The Wednesday market (selling principally veal, fowl and walnuts) is delightful. The church has a sixteenth-century gothic vault on a romanesque original. See CHANCELADE and TOCANE-SAINT-APRE.

LOSSE: For the château, see THONAC.

LA MADELEINE, see SHELTERS.

LA MAIRIE, see CAVES.

MANAURIE, on the D47 north-west of Les Eyzies, has a domed romanesque church that seems to have been modified over the years by later builders. Near by is the Grotte de Carpe-Diem. The D47 continues to Mauzens-Miremont, which possesses a fortified romanesque church. The ruins of an old château rise above the village. The remains of prehistoric men and women have been found in the debris under overhanging rocks throughout this area. See, under CAVES, *Carpe-Diem*, and *Les Eyzies-de-Tayac*.

MAREUIL (or MAREUIL-SUR-BELLE), situated on the N130 on the borders of the Dordogne, lay on the route of Roman soldiers marching to Angoulême. It became the seat of one of the four baronies of Périgord, and a magnificent sixteenth-century château, defended by a deep moat and a drawbridge, was built here, after the earlier twelfth-century buildings had been partly destroyed during the Wars of Religion. The flamboyant gothic chapel is a jewel. In fact, much of the château is a careful restoration dating from the mid 1950s, for château Mareuil was abandoned in 1770 and suffered grievously at the Revolution and afterwards from neglect. Today the general public can admire its repaired walls, rooms and gardens, its keep, its underground prisons and its Louis XV furniture.

The romanesque Church of Saint Pardoux-le-Mareuil was re-vaulted in ogives in the sixteenth century, when two gothic chapels were added. The church retains its dome and boasts a splendid three-tiered belltower.

Mareuil is surrounded by châteaux: Beaulieu, Beauregard, Montbreton and Le Repaire. Fifteen kilometres south-east on the D939 is Vieux-Mareuil, whose thirteenth-century church has three domes and fourteenth-century fortifications. Twenty kilometres north-west, at the confluence of the rivers Lizonne and Manoure, is La Rochebeaucourt-et-Argentine, which has two lovely churches: that of La Rochebeaucourt itself, built by the monks of Cluny in the thirteenth century; and the romanesque, slightly inaccessible church of Argentine. (Try La Bonne Auberge, at La Rochebeaucourt-et-Argentine.)

And north-east of Mareuil on the D708 lies Saint-Sulpice-de-Mareuil, whose domed romanesque church has a fine carved porch.

Mareuil has a fair on the 28th day of each month, and La Rochebeaucourt-et-Argentine, not to be outdone, holds one on the first Thursday of each month. See NONTRON and LA TOUR-BLANCHE and, in the index to this book, Arnaud de Mareuil.

MAROUATTE, Château de, see GRAND-BRASSAC.

MARQUAY, a village due east of Les Eyzies, is close by Château de Puymartin, a lovely late-medieval building with two turrets and battlemented walls, set peacefully in a field today but once the headquarters of the Catholic general who attacked Protestant-held Sarlat during the Wars of Religion. In summer you can get inside to see its Flemish tapestries, its seventeenth-century furniture, its eighteenth-century wall-paintings and its small chapel.

The village of Marquay boasts a fortified domed romanesque church. See also *Cap-Blanc* under SHELTERS.

MARSAC: The Château de Marsac is the one you spot high on the left, obviously built between the fourteenth and the sixteenth centuries, as you leave Les Eyzies on the D706 for Montignac.

MARSAC-SUR-L'ISLE, is a pretty village situated on the river four kilometres west of Périgueux, with a small twelfth-century church. See MONTANCEIX.

MARTHONIE: Château de la Marthonie, see SAINT-JEAN-DE-CÔLE.

MAUZENS-MIREMONT, see MANAURIE.

MAYAC lies just off the D705 (south-east) between Coulaures and Savignac-les-Églises, in a bend of the river Isle, and possesses a romanesque church with a delicate twelfth-century porch as well as a seventeenth- and eighteenth-century château. See ANTONNE-ET-TRIGONANT and SARLIAC-SUR-L'ISLE.

MERLANDE Priory is not easy to find. The Augustinian Priory of Chancelade is six kilometres north-west of Périgueux. From Chancelade the D2 winds north, and the first reasonable road to the left leads to Merlande. Founded by the canons of Chancelade, the priory first possessed two domes, but the English destroyed one in 1170, and the builders replaced it with broken barrel-vaulting. The Wars of Religion led them to fortify their church in its present striking fashion. Finally, the whole priory was ransacked at the time of the Revolution. Of all the monastic buildings, only the impressive gaunt church remains; inside its lovely twelfth-century capitals depict monsters whose madness scarcely competes with the violence shown by human beings to this place over the centuries. See CHANCE-LADE.

MEYRALS: The village, which is approached by travelling due south-east on the D48 from Les Eyzies and then taking a minor road left, is graced by the picturesque Château de la Roque, a delightful triangular-shaped building of the fifteenth and sixteenth centuries, set high on a rock. In the church of Meyrals is a retable given in the eighteenth century by an archbishop of Paris. See *Bernifals*, under CAVES.

LES MILANDES: At the point where châteaux Beynac and Castelnaud dominate the river Dordogne, a shady road travels south along the river past Château de Fayrac to the village of Les Milandes and the Château des Milandes. Its very origins are as romantic as its history. François de Caumont, Lord of Castelnaud, married in 1478 and built for his wife a charming renaissance château here, with terraces and gardens leading to the river. The Caumonts kept the château until the Revolution (at one point turning Protestant and yet continuing to worship undisturbed in the renaissance chapel at Les Milandes). Happily, the Revolution spared Les Milandes, and it was considerably extended during the nineteenth century. In the twentieth century the cabaret artist Joséphine Baker bought and beautified it as a home for her international orphans, the 'rainbow children'. During the tourist season Les Milandes is well worth a visit. The interior is furnished and the chimneys and carvings are sumptuous. The grounds and terrace are a delight. See BEYNAC-ET-CAZENAC, CASTELNAUD, FAYRAC and, in the index to this book, Les Milandes and Joséphine Baker.

MOLIÈRES, west of Cadouin in Périgord Noir, is an English *bastide* begun in the thirteenth century and never finished. It boasts a fine gothic church.

MONBAZILLAC: Just the kind of château you would make as a child's model, Château Monbazillac, seven kilometres south of Bergerac on the D13, was built by François d'Aydie, Viscount of Ribérac, in 1550. Its turrets, its solid grey stones and jolly brown roofs, its crenellations and its battlements form a perfect whole. The white wine of Monbazillac is perhaps the best-known wine of the Dordogne, and Château Monbazillac now belongs to (and has been restored by) the Union de Coopératives Vinicoles de la Dordogne. The Union has made it partly into a museum of wine, partly into a museum of French Protestantism and partly a museum of local furniture. There is a restaurant and the chance to taste wine, with guided tours throughout the year. See Chapter 3.

MONBOS, near Sigoulès in south-west Dordogne, has a romanesque church with delightfully carved capitals. See EYMET.

MONPAZIER, along with Domme, is the best preserved of the *bastides* of the Dordogne. Lying in a plain above the river Dropt where the D660 from Lalinde meets the D53 from Belvès, Monpazier was founded in 1284 by Jean de Grailly, Seneschal of King Edward I of England, with the intention of dominating the road from the south into Périgord. The rectangular plan of the streets remains, with scarcely a stone changed since the Middle Ages. The great gates and their towers are still there. The main square contains, as in other *bastides*, a covered market hall with, at Monpazier, the measures for grain still intact. Here today Monpazier holds a fair on the third Thursday of each month. The covered arcades running round this square are exquisite, as are the houses in the side streets.

Monpazier church is fortified, as befits a house of God in a *bastide*. The nave dates from the time of the founding of Monpazier. The apse and its surrounds were added in the fifteenth century, and the tympanum and porch in their present form were constructed in the seventeenth. Don't miss the inscription carved on the tympanum at the time of the Revolution, declaring that the people of France believe in a Supreme Being and the immortality of the soul.

Monpazier changed hands many times during the Hundred Years War and suffered during the Wars of Religion. Freda White tells a fine story from the annals of Henri IV's General Sully:

The citizens of Villefranche had formed the plan of surprising Monpazier, another little town nearby. They chose for this attack the same night as the men of Monpazier, without knowing anything about it, had decided upon trying to capture Villefranche. It so chanced that as both troops took different paths, they did not meet. All was carried out with the more ease, because on one side and the other the walls were left defenceless. They looted, they were laden with booty; everyone thought himself in luck; till the day broke and both towns realized their mistake. The terms of peace were that everybody went home and returned everything to its own place.

But war was not always waged in so gentle a fashion. When a revolt of *Croquants* broke out in 1637, their leader was broken alive on the wheel in the market place of Monpazier. See BIRON, VILLEFRANCHE-DU-PÉRIGORD and, in the index to this book, *Croquants* and *bastides*.

MONTAGRIER, a small village across the river Dronne north of Tocane-Saint-Apre (which lies between Périgueux and Ribérac on the D710), has first of all a tremendous panoramic view of the region with a useful '*table d'orientation*'; and secondly a twelfth-century church with a complex apse, much restored in the nineteenth century. Montagrier, perched on its rock, was once fortified. See GRAND-BRASSAC, LISLE and TOCANE-SAINT-APRE.

MONTANCEIX: Six kilometres south-west of Périgueux on the N89 lies this village, with its mill on the river Isle, dominated from a rock by the medieval/renaissance château. See MARSAC-SUR-L'ISLE and SAINT-ASTIER.

MONTCARET lies on the D936 just before the border of the Dordogne and Bordelais. In 1827 the construction of a public wash-house uncovered beautifully preserved Roman mosaics – fish, fruit and abstract patterns – dating from the second and fourth centuries A.D. Objects found near by from what was once an extensive Roman villa are now in the Montcaret museum. A fountain runs into the start of a Roman aqueduct. And if you step into the romanesque church next to the mosaics, you find that the Christians re-used Gallo-Roman sculptures to decorate the apse. See LAMOTHE-MONTRAVEL, SAINT-MICHEL-DE-MONTAIGNE and, in the index to this book, Montcaret.

MONTFERRAND-DU-PÉRIGORD: The D2 from Cadouin leads you south to the river Couze, where a right turn leads to Montferrand-du-Périgord, a beautiful medieval village on the slopes of a hill, enhanced with some renaissance houses and the eighteenth-century market hall. In spite of its setting in the cemetery, the romanesque chapel is worth seeing. High over the village are the majestic ruins of its medieval château, where the (fake) holy kerchief of Cadouin was hidden when the Huguenots were trying to destroy it. See CADOUIN, SAINT-AVIT-SÉNIEUR, and SAINTE-CROIX.

MONTFORT: Château Montfort must be the best known of all the châteaux of the Dordogne, if only because of its romantic aspect, perched high on a sheer rock where the river Dordogne makes a huge loop around the tiny village of Turnac. Part of its charm lies in the blend of styles that go to make up Château Montfort. On a medieval base, renaissance motifs and patterns lead upwards to classical features. And machicolations, turrets and dormer windows add their charm.

All this mixture derives from the sometimes savage history of this château. In 1214 Simon de Montfort took the château from Bernard de Casnac, burned it down and, ironically, gave it its name. Rebuilt, the château passed into the hands of the Turenne family, took its part in the Hundred Years War, and was captured by the English after three sieges. Pons de Turenne, who recovered Montfort, was exiled for having insulted the king, but his successors managed to hold on to the château and to resist a royal order to demolish it. In the Wars of Religion, the Turenne family turned Protestant and made Montfort into a Huguenot stronghold. After the wars were over, Henri I V revoked the orders of the former Catholic monarchs that Montfort should be razed to the ground.

The fine gardens of the château and the château itself are not open to the general public, though there are restaurants in the little village where you can eat in its shade. (You eat well at Chez Robin.) Perhaps the most breathtaking view of the château is from the road between Vitrac and Carsac-Aillac. See CARSAC-AILLAC, CÉNAC-ET-SAINT-JULIEN, GROLEJAC and VITRAC.

MONTIGNAC, situated where the D706 and the D704 meet at the river Vézère, began to gear itself seriously for tourism with the discovery of the Lascaux caves. But the town had a long and active history before that time. The river here was a source of trade, and the charming buildings that flank it were built to pursue that trade. Montignac still holds a Wednesday market which turns into a fully fledged fair on the second and last Wednesday of the month. The old priory church, built in the twelfth century, was embellished in the fourteenth and again in the seventeenth. The counts of Périgord had a château here, partly destroyed in the fourteenth century. South-east of the town along the D704 is the fascinating Château de la Grande-Filolie, a remarkable blend of fortified fifteenth-century house and renaissance manor, linked by a polygonal tower.

Lascaux is now closed to the general public, but its replica, Lascaux II, is open. (To find Lascaux II, go to the centre of Montignac and follow the signs.) At the prehistoric shelter of Regourdou is a small museum of prehistory. Eugène Le Roy ended his days in Montignac in the Rue 14 juillet. A museum in the Rue septembre commemorates his life and writings. See AUBAS, FANLAC, SAINT-AMAND-DE-COLY, *Regourdou* (under SHELTERS), THONAC and, in the index to this book, Lascaux I and Lascaux II.

MONTPEYROUX, on the western edge of the Dordogne, south of the D32, pleasingly sets side by side its pretty church (with a twelfth-century apse, 'oven-vaulted', as the French say, and a lovely fifteenth-century chapel) and the seventeenth- and eighteenth-century Château de Matecoulon. See CARSAC-DE-GURSON and SAINT-MICHEL-DE-MONTAIGNE.

MONTPON-MÉNESTÉROL, west of Mussidan on the N89, has a romanesque church, restored in the sixteenth century, with seventeenth-century woodwork (including the fine organ case). Four kilometres north-east is an ancient Carthusian house of Vauclaire, with a gothic chapel, now a psychiatric hospital. Markets and fairs on alternate Wednesdays.

MONTRÉAL: For Château de Montréal, see ISSAC.

LA MOUTHE, see CAVES.

MUSSIDAN: On their royal tour of 1564 to 1566, Charles IX and Catherine de' Medici found Mussidan *une belle petite ville*. Today, standing athwart the river Isle on the N89, Mussidan is an industrial town with 3,200 inhabitants, specializing in ceramics. (During the tourist season you can join ceramics classes.) In the past Mussidan paid dearly for its Huguenot sympathies. In 1944 after partisans had attacked a train, the Nazis killed fifty-three citizens in reprisal. See SAINT-MARTIN-L'ASTIER.

NANTHEUIL-DE-BOURZEC, see THIVIERS.

NANTHIAT, see THIVIERS.

NEUVIC-SUR-L'ISLE, on the N89 south-west of Périgueux, is an industrial town boasting a splendid early renaissance château. In the Middle Ages the Talleyrand family owned the château here, which they sold to the Marquis of Fayolle. His son Annet rebuilt it between 1520 and 1530. Today it stands close by the river in a fine park, substantially as he left it – two great rectangular buildings making up a formidable square, mullioned windows in the façade, round towers with pointed caps high up on each corner and sturdy dormer windows in the roof. Annet embellished the château with his initial interlaced with that of his wife Charlotte d'Abzac.

Neuvic has a market on Tuesdays and Saturdays, and a great grain and agricultural fair on the third Saturday in September. See GRIGNOLS.

NONTRON, on the D675, is the sub-prefecture of Périgord Vert, a busy city that welcomes tourists and offers camping, fishing, hotels and restaurants. The old city is picturesquely perched on a promontory between the steep valley of the river Bandiat and an adjacent ravine. Its ramparts are powerful and impressive. The eighteenth-century château (containing a museum of – among other local objects of interest – ancient dolls) is beautifully sited, though the historian Jean Secret eloquently laments the passing of the older building it supplanted. ('Adieu, the keep which withstood the attacks of the English; adieu, the lodging that was a part of the dowry of Françoise de Bretagne, Viscountess of Limoges, when she married Alain d'Albred, a lodging which Élie de Colonges bought for Henri IV and which belonged for many years to the Pompadours!') Nontron is surrounded by placid lakes, and by bizarrely shaped rocks (some of which have been given names, such as Poperdu and Caisse-noisette), making this excellent country for walks. There are markets on Wednesdays and Saturdays and a fair on the 18th of each month (or the day before, if the 18th falls on a Sunday). The annual fête is on 13 August. Eighteen kilometres to the east the waters of the Dronne form the Chalard waterfall. See ABJAT-SUR-BANDIAT, BUSSIÈRE-BADIL, JAVERLHAC-ET-LA CHAPELLE-SAINT-ROBERT and SAINT-PARDOUX-LA-RIVIÈRE.

ORILIAGUET is an isolated hamlet east of Sarlat and south of Salignac whose romanesque church contains a twelfth-century font and an eighteenth-century carved Virgin and retable.

PALEYRAC, see URVAL.

PAYZAC: Those entering the Dordogne by way of Saint-Yrieix in Haute-Vienne and the D704 can find at Payzac, on the D75 east of Lanquaille, a domed twelfth-century church. The bridge is a century older. See ANGOISSE and DUSSAC.

PÉRIGUEUX, capital of the Dordogne, is a gem of a city. Even the dusty route south, which passes through dull streets and tedious intersections, offers glimpses of the remarkable Cathedral of Saint-Front and the pre-Christian Tour de Vésonne and passes by the mutilated Church of Saint-Étienne. Those tempted to stop and explore further will not be disappointed.

The Tour de Vésonne is one of the most remarkable Gaulish remains left in the whole of France, a pagan temple 27 metres high and almost the same size in diameter, built in honour of the goddess Vesunna, protector of the ancient tribes known as the Petrocorii (from whose name we derive both 'Périgueux' and 'Périgord'). We do not know whether the tower was once covered or was permanently open to the sky. Legend has it that St Front, who converted Périgord to Christianity, banished a demon from the pagan temple with such force that the demon smashed through the wall on his way out – hence the incomplete circle of the tower. In fact the temple opens here to the rising sun and may have been built deliberately like this. The Petrocorii built with taste, decorating the top section of Vesunna's temple with little brick arches over openings that (I think) once supported beams. Round the tower you can see the remains of other temple buildings.

Being no match for the Romans in war, the Petrocorii soon decided to live quietly under their conquerors. Cross the Rue de Vésonne and you find the excavated Villa Pompeia, a luxurious Roman town house built in the first century. This sumptuous home was once enriched with colonnades and frescoes. In need of entertainment, the Romans would walk past the present site of the Church of Saint-Étienne to their amphitheatre (the Jardin des Arènes), built in the first century, which could seat 20,000 spectators. It lies just north of the church. This spot, stained with the blood of animals, gladiators and Christian martyrs, is now a children's playground. Close by is the fourth-century Gallo-Roman wall of Périgueux. Walk from the amphitheatre over the Rue de Turenne and you pass under the one surviving Roman gateway to the 'old city', the Porte Normande.

The turbulent Middle Ages persuaded the citizens to strengthen their Roman wall with towers. One remains to this day – the Château Barrière, built in the thirteenth century, ruined by the Protestants in 1575.

All this is south-west of the modern city of Périgueux. We are in fact in the oldest of two separate townships that later came to make up Périgueux. Here St Front erected a church on the ruins of the old temple of Mars, dedicated to St Stephen (Saint-Étienne), the first Christian martyr. In the eleventh and twelfth centuries the church was rebuilt magnificently. Four domes now covered what was the cathedral of the city. Inside, a beautifully carved romanesque arch guarded an octagonal sculpted font. Only the gate of Mars to the west retained a memory of the old pagan religion.

Then in 1575 the Protestants of the area, disguised as peasants, made their way as if to market in Périgueux and took over the city. The tomb of St Front was despoiled. Half the Church of Saint-Étienne was demolished. Protestants occupied the city for no more than six years. But in 1699 the citizens of Périgueux decided that a half-demolished church with no surviving belltower was not fit for the bishop's seat. Saint-Front in the new city became the cathedral of Périgueux. None the less, if I were to choose the one great treasure of Périgueux, it would be this magnificent church, again despoiled by the Fronde in the seventeenth century, secularized at the time of the Revolution, reconsecrated and now peaceful and cool. Against the south wall is a fine, carved baroque reredos. The beautiful romanesque font and arch are still there.

Throughout the Middle Ages Périgueux suffered. First the Barbarians terrorized the inhabitants. The population slowly declined. Only pilgrims around the shrine of St Front to the north-east of the old city brought some wealth and trade. The two communities wasted their substance in savage rivalry until in 1251 they decided to unite and take the name Périgueux. In the fourteenth and early fifteenth century, apart from pilgrims the most characteristic inhabitants of Périgueux were beggars and vagabonds, battening on the noble families, the churchmen and the butchers and bakers, prosecuted by the lawyers and pursued by the *sergents*. Yet this impoverished city remained fiercely devoted to the kings of France. Ceded to the English by the Treaty of Brétigny in 1360, Périgueux instantly declared herself loyal to Charles V of France. A draper named Tendon Deltorn, who planned to betray the city to the English for 3,000 *écus*, was beheaded and his quartered body displayed on the city gates. Outside the city, near a château called Lieu-Dieu, the English and the French set thirty-nine champions from each side against each other. The French cut the English champions to pieces. You can still see Château du Lieu-Dieu at Boulazac, south-east of Périgueux on the N89, with its drawbridge, tower and turret, and massive machicolated walls.

Périgueux survived, in part because of the faithfulness of its citizens (whose motto is still *Fortitudo mea civium fides*: 'my strength lies in the loyalty of my citizens'), partly owing to its great wall, which boasts twenty-nine towers. One of these, the Tour Mataguerre, built in the thirteenth century, destroyed and rebuilt in the fifteenth century, still stands. You can climb to the top for a splendid view of the city. Carved on the tower is, fittingly, the fleur-de-lis of the royal house of France.

And at the beginning of the Renaissance, during the reign of François I, Périgueux was granted a respite from its wars that enabled the citizens to build in the new part of their city a number of houses of great delicacy and beauty. These buildings, in the narrow twisted streets of the 'safeguarded sector' of Périgueux, are today almost all marked out by the enterprising city fathers with notices in French, English and German.

The best way of approaching this lovely medieval part of the city is to make the cathedral your point of reference. Then divide the city into three: north of the cathedral, west and south. (The east end points to the river Isle.)

The narrow streets directly opposite the great north doors of the cathedral are almost always deserted. To explore them is a pleasure reserved for the fit and active, for these alleyways are steep and irregular under foot.

But at every twist and turn is revealed some new piece of architectural wonder, usually succinctly identified by a little notice.

Sometimes the way is through a dank passage where the sun can scarcely ever have shone – a reminder that medieval and renaissance life easily combined a certain squalor with elegance. Alleys and turrets, exquisite courtyards with renaissance staircases, moulded doorways, ancient corbels, balconies and elegant steps reveal exactly what was the entrancing environment of renaissance urban life in south-west France when for a moment war had ceased. Périgueux has restored much of this ancient quarter without adding modern charcuteries or bars. You can turn right and walk down to the Boulevard Georges-Saumande on the bank of the river Isle. There at the end of the steep Rue Barbecane the fine façade of the seventeenth-century Hôtel de Foyolle overlooks the water. A little way south is the fifteenth-century 'Maison des Consuls', and just over the bridge a quaint mill, perched on the city wall, is buttressed by ancient wooden beams.

If you go back to the cathedral and pass on through the Place (and Avénue) Daumesnil – where the famous Yrieux Daumesnil (who lost a leg at the battle of Wagram) was born – you find yourself in a modern city that has managed to incorporate old streets and houses without destroying their charm or displaying the meanness that often characterizes twentieth-century architecture. The main market at Périgueux is held every Wednesday and Saturday at the other side of the cathedral, in the Place de la Clautre; but just beyond the Avenue Daumesnil in the Place du Cloderc a small covered and open-air market is held every weekday morning. Here are little streets with fine cafés, restaurants, cake shops, alongside modern statues and fountains. The Rue Limogeanne, the Rue de la Constitution and the Rue de la Miséricorde all contain richly decorated renaissance hôtels.

François I's salamander symbol appears everywhere in these streets, as well as the Italianate renaissance he fostered. I also like coming across quaintly carved panels on the stairs and ceilings of courtyards (such as Venus laying down her arms in No. 1, Rue de la Sagesse; further along the same street a naked Eros; and Adam and Eve eating of the tree of knowledge, carved on a staircase in the Rue du Plantier, while the serpent peeps out at them, its tail curled round the tree trunk). Proud of their city, the twentieth-century inhabitants of Périgueux tend to leave the front door of their fine houses open, allowing the tourist to peep into the courtyards and admire the marvellous twisting stairs. There is a peculiar pleasure in making use of the shops and bars of, say, the Rue de la Clarté, whose tall overhanging buildings were once the lodgings of the great ones of Périgueux and their servants.

The south side of the cathedral equally repays the explorer. The Place de la Clautre was once the scene of executions as well as the city's chief graveyard. Today, especially on market days, it presents a colourful contrast to the white soaring belltower of Saint-Front Cathedral. Here the houses are mostly eighteenth century, though not without a few turrets and arched doorways of an earlier age. Instead of taking the wide straight Rue Taillefer down to the modern part of the city, bear left into the Rue des Fargues. Here is the oldest house in Périgueux, the twelfth century 'Maison des Dames de la Foy'. Here the English governor lived after the Treaty of Brétigny, until Constable Du Guesclin expelled him from Périgueux and took over his lodgings. Later the Knights Templars made it their headquarters. Although the house has been spoiled by modern additions, twelfth-century domestic buildings are rare enough to merit a special visit. And on the same street is a museum dedicated to the military exploits and glory of the Dordogne.

Near by is the Rue Aubergerie, throughout charming and containing two celebrated fine houses: the Hôtel de Sallegourde, with its battlements, machicolations and polygonal staircase; and the Hôtel d'Abzac de Ladouze, built almost entirely in the fifteenth century, with an octagonal tower and fine balustrades. You can return to the cathedral by way of the Rue Saint-Roch (No. 6 is a house with two romanesque bays) and by the twisting narrow Rue du Calvaire, which (it seems to me) is too narrow for anyone to fight in, yet is equipped with mini-fortifications in a couple of its houses.

The streets of Périgueux are shady. In any case, should the sun make an extensive walkabout irksome, they are not short of places for food and refreshment. But the coolest, most inviting interior is that of the Cathedral of Saint-Front, now splendidly restored. A glance at engravings of the cathedral before the restoration was accomplished indicates the importance of the task and the achievement of those who carried it out.

Saint-Front was built to honour and shelter the bones of the saint who converted Périgord. Pillage, fire and neglect had brought it by the nineteenth century to a sad state. Yet part of the old church still remains. It was built towards the end of the tenth century and consecrated in 1074. Then, as pilgrims flocked to Saint-Front on their way to the tomb of St James at Compostella in Spain, a great domed sanctuary was built, in the shape of a Greek cross and almost certainly modelled on the Church of the Holy Apostles in Constantinople.

Today you can see all that remains of the church of 1074 at the western end of Saint-Front Cathedral. On either side of this old building are two 'confessionals', as they are called, which incorporate even older elements. These may date back even to the eighth or ninth centuries. The 'confessional' on the north side is the older one. Today no one remembers the saints to whom they were dedicated. But there is a nobility and an austerity about them that is still impressive; and the faith of the past glimmers through a thirteenth-century fresco in the south 'confessional' depicting the hand of God in blessing.

You can visit not only these two ancient parts of the cathedral, but also, with the help of a guide, the crypt and the south-facing cloister. Here again much of the past has been preserved, from romanesque times until the seventeenth century. The arches are not so delicate as those at, say, Cadouin, and yet these cloisters are as romantic as any in Périgord.

There is nothing to compare with the astounding restored Cathedral of Saint-Front, not even Sacré-Cœur de Montmartre in Paris, which is modelled on the cathedral of Périgueux. The great Viollet-le-Duc wanted to restore the ruin. Instead the architect Abadie was chosen. He was bold enough to see that virtually a new start was needed, faithful to the old without remotely trying to be a replica of a romanesque original. Five great new domes, topped by cupolas, were built. More cupolas peep out in between these domes. The interior is massively bare, with huge 'Byzantine' chandeliers designed by Abadie. Incorporated in the cathedral today are treasures from other centuries. St Bernard and St Benedict appear in two lovely fifteenth-century paintings. The pulpit is seventeenth-century baroque, as is the retable. The altar in the south apse was made out of Italian marble in 1761 for the Charterhouse at Vauclaire, and brought to Saint-Front after the Revolution. But essentially the sweep of the cathedral derives from Abadie. He aimed at a grandeur that depends on space and purity. The walls of his cathedral are almost completely bare. Some decoration is provided by the Stations of the Cross created in 1860 by the Périgourdin artist J.-E. Lafon. The stained-glass artist Didron provided windows depicting saints and episodes in the life of the patron saint of Périgueux cathedral. In front of Abadie's great east apse are seventeenth-century stalls taken from the Benedictine abbey of Ligueux. Hidden in recesses are some sculptures and frescoes from the earlier building. Yet all of this virtually disappears in the inspired open spaces of the cathedral.

Size obsessed Abadie and his successors as they restored the Cathedral of Saint-Front. The five great domes are each 13 metres in diameter and 27 metres high. (At your own risk a guide will take you up to the vertiginous rim of one of them.) They rest on twelve huge white pillars, each 6 metres square. And joining the 'old church' and the new is the massive belltower, 64 metres high. Here the restorers remained most faithful to the original, though Abadie had to reinforce part of the 'old church' to take the weight of the great tower. You can almost *see* its weight. The bottom storey of the tower has two great round 'blind' arches on each side. The next has four square Corinthian columns. The third storey has on each side four great round columns. And from this a series of steps leads to a splendid, unique pomegranate of a dome, supported on forty-three round columns, each 8 metres high.

Abadie brilliantly replaced the old weathercock on top of the belltower with the present stone angel. (The weathercock today is in the Périgord museum, on the Cours de Tourny, along with much else – Gallo-Roman remains, romanesque sculptures from Saint-Front, and so on.) He wished to recreate not just a civic monument but a house of prayer. The very size of Saint-Front, in his vision, was to contribute to this aim. And indeed, in a cathedral 145 metres long and 60 metres wide, it is possible either to join in a great act of worship or to remain hidden, at peace and alone.

The people of Périgueux are proud of their history and the great figures of their past. The Place Bugeaud is properly dominated by the statue of Marshal Bugeaud, a replica of the one sculpted by

Auguste Dumont in 1853, erected in Algeria and sent back by the Algerians when they claimed their independence. In 1873 General Daumesnil was honoured by his fellow-citizens with a statue in the Cours Michel-Montaigne, depicting him pointing proudly at his wooden leg. The citizens still erect statues. Although I personally do not much like the 1980 statue of a fat lady masquerading as a fountain in the Place Saint-Louis, I have found much pleasure taking a coffee there with friends and watching the world go by.

The city fathers show a characteristic wit in the names of some of their streets. The Rue Berthe-Bonnaventure was named in 1966 after a lady who had left 250,000 francs to the local hospital under the mistaken belief that she had been born there. Rue Professor Pozzi was named in 1915 after a celebrated medical man, a member of the French academy of medicine and a senator, who was assassinated in his surgery by a madman.

And the city is blessed with a fine philosophy, sometimes enshrined in its architecture. One famous house, the 'Maison du Patisseur', stands in the Rue Eguillerie. Built in the fifteenth and sixteenth centuries, it displays gay motifs of the Italian renaissance. But the inscription on its wall is authentically Périgourdin. It expresses a fervent desire, after centuries of troubles, to live at peace with your neighbours – at least the ones you can trust when your back is turned!

> *Souviens-toi qu'il faut mourir –*
> *Celui qui aime a dénigrer la vie des absents*
> *Qu'il sache que cette maison lui est interdite –*
> *La plus grande gloire est déplaire aux méchants.*

[Remember that we must die. Those who love to vilify the life of absent ones should know that they are not welcome in this house. The greatest glory is to displace wicked ones.]

In the Rue Littré (which took its present name in 1890 from the celebrated creator of the Dictionary of the French Language) is another inscription, on the Chapel of the Visitandes (formerly the Cordeliers) which was demolished during the Wars of Religion in 1575, rebuilt in the seventeenth century, abandoned at the time of the Revolution and restored in 1847. Over the door are the famous lines:

Petra si ingratis, cor amicis, hostibus ensis
Hoec tria si fueris Petra-cor-ensis eris.

[Stony to the disagreeable, your heart for friends, iron to enemies: if you are these three, you're a Périgourdin.]

Among many fine restaurants try the Restaurant Léon (18, Cours Tourny), especially for its *filets de truite saumonée au Monbazillac*.

See BOULAZAC, CHANCELADE, MARSAC-SUR-L'ISLE, MERLANDE and MONTANCEIX. See also in the index to this book Bugeaud, Daumesnil and Périgueux.

PEYZAC-LE-MOUSTIER, on the D706 north of Les Eyzies, near where the little stream of Le Moustier joins the Vézère, is known best for its prehistoric shelters; but don't miss its fourteenth-century church (in the cemetery), or the romanesque church of Moustier, with its seventeenth-century woodcarvings. See SHELTERS.

PIÉGUT-PLUVIERS, a thriving town twelve kilometres north of Nontron, once possessed one of the four great châteaux defending the way south into Périgord. In 1199 Richard Cœur de Lion attacked and dismantled its defences, but the twelfth-century keep, 23 metres high, still dominates the surrounding countryside. Piégut also has a twelfth-century church (and close by is the tiny hamlet of Reilhac, with its own romanesque church, boasting a crudely carved entrance). Wednesday is market day at Piégut, and the people here pride themselves on their excellent *cèpes*. They hold an annual fair on the Wednesday of the second week in September.

PIERRE-LEVÉE, is the name of the best-preserved dolmen in Périgord, just east of Brantôme.

PLAZAC, in the lovely Villemont valley north of Les Eyzies, has a curiously Provençal aspect, with its splendid pine forest and, in the cemetery, a huge church tower dating from the twelfth century. The presbytery, built in the fourteenth century, was once a bishop's summer residence. The Chapel of Our Lady of Pity contains sixteenth-century frescoes. The villagers hold a market on the third Thursday of every month. You can fish for trout in the little stream or in the nearby lake, or walk round the Château de Chabans, built in the sixteenth and seventeenth centuries.

POISSON, see SHELTERS.

POMPORT, north of Sigoulès (west of the D933), stands amidst vineyards and has a restored romanesque church, with a fine belfry, on a little stream known as 'La Gordonnette'.

PRATS-DE-CARLUX, just off the D479 east of Sarlat, is a charming village, with a church, the fifteenth-century Château de Sirey (battlemented) and fine manor houses.

PRATS-DU-PÉRIGORD, north of Villefranche, has a twelfth-century church, powerfully fortified 400 years later during the Wars of Religion. The nearby château was built in the sixteenth century. See VILLEFRANCHE-DU-PÉRIGORD.

PROUMEYSSAC, see CAVES.

PUYGUILHEM, a magnificent château west of Thiviers and north-east of Brantôme, was almost lost to the French nation. In the early sixteenth century Mondot de la Marthonie, first president of the *parlements* of Bordeaux and Paris, started to rebuild an old château, using brilliant sculptors whose names have been forgotten. 168 metres above sea level, the château was completed by Mondot's son Geoffroy around 1530. The great circular tower, bas-reliefs, fine polygonal staircase, splendid dormers and the later, eighteenth-century pavilion, were in such a state of ruin that the State took over the château in 1939 and restored it after the Second World War. Today it is open to the public and, happily, has been furnished from other French châteaux belonging to the State. See BOSCHAUD ABBEY and VILLARS.

PUYMARTIN, situated just off the D47 north-west of Sarlat, is the château that sheltered the Catholic general deputed to rescue Sarlat from the Huguenots during the Wars of Religion. Today it is open to the general public during the tourist season. Round towers and a huge machicolated keep contrast with less fearsome buildings, including a small chapel, all built in the fifteenth and sixteenth centuries. Furnishings include Aubusson tapestries. See MARQUAY.

QUEYSSAC, west of the N21, north-east of Bergerac, has a fine domed twelfth-century church. Look inside for the carved capitals.

QUINSAC, see VILLARS.

RASTIGNAC: For Château de Rastignac, see LA BACHELLERIE.

REILHAC, see PIÉGUT-PLUVIERS.

RIBAGNAC, see BRIDOIRE.

RIBÉRAC, former Sub-prefecture of the Dordogne, at a crossroads on the river Dronne, west of Périgueux, was described by Charles IX and Catherine de' Medici on their tour of 1564–6 as 'a beautiful and large village, with a château, on the mountainside'. With 4,000 inhabitants today it retains its charm, set on a slope covered in cypress trees. Here lived the troubadour Arnaut Daniel, though the château where he was born has now disappeared. Ribérac has two churches of particular interest: one romanesque, massive, thickset; the other quasi-Byzantine in appearance. At Villetoureix, north of the river, is a well-preserved Gallo-Roman tower, similar to the Tour de Vésonne in Périgueux, and now incorporated into the Château de la Rigale.

Ribérac caters for tourism in an area often neglected, filled with fine walks and lovely villages. It also remains an important agricultural centre, with a market every Friday, a fair specializing in wickerwork and baskets every Wednesday from May to September, and great fairs on the first Fridays of July, August, September and October. Not content with all this, Ribérac stages an important agricultural fair during the third week of August. See in the index of this book Arnaut Daniel.

RICHEMONT: Château de Richemont was built between 1550 and 1580 by the adventurer, author and lay Abbot of Brantôme, Pierre de Bourdeille, in the little village of Saint-Crépin-de-Richemont near the river Boulou (north of Brantôme, on the D98). The château is open to the general public during the second half of July and during August. The two long wings of the château and its solid square tower are impressive. Inside the decorated chapel is the tomb of Pierre de Bourdeille (1610). If you have visited Richemont, take the trouble to look at the lovely nearby village of Saint-Félix-de-Bourdeilles. See in the index to this book Pierre de Bourdeille.

LA ROCHEBEAUCOURT-ET-ARGENTINE, see MAREUIL.

LA ROQUE-GAGEAC: An extraordinary village, set under towering cliffs seven kilometres south of Sarlat on a lovely bend in the river Dordogne. The strategic position of La Roque-Gageac in the past, when the river transported wine to Bordeaux, is immediately apparent. Today it is a tourist paradise, with its lovely ochre houses reflected in the water and, high up, houses built partly into the rock itself. At the western end of the village, Château de la Malartrie turns out to be a nineteenth-century imitation of a fifteenth-century château. Narrow streets lead up into the cliffs (and to the twelfth-century church). La Roque-Gageac resisted the English during the Hundred Years War under the direction of the Bishop of Sarlat. You can see where the rockface occasionally falls, killing citizens and burying their houses. Don't miss the excellent pottery, with its old kiln, a kilometre or so to the south of the town.

LA ROQUE-SAINT-CHRISTOPHE, near to the D76 north of Les Eyzies, is close by a troglodyte village (known as Pas de Miroir) where men, women and children have lived in caves from Gallo-Roman times to our own century. There are guided tours in the tourist season.

ROUFFIGNAC: The village of Rouffignac on the D6 due north of Les Eyzies was almost completely burnt to the ground by retreating Nazis in 1944. Only the beautiful church was spared. The romanesque apse is a modern reconstruction. The rest is a lovely example of renaissance and gothic, unusual in the Dordogne. The porch, built in the first half of the sixteenth century, has Corinthian capitals and renaissance sculptures. Inside is ogive vaulting ranging from the simple to the delightfully ornate. Rouffignac today holds a market on the second and last Mondays in the month. This is strawberry country, and during the season (mid May to mid July) you can buy them every day in the market place between 12.30 and 1.30. The annual fair is on 21 August. See BALOU and CAVES.

ROUFFIGNAC-DE-SIGOULÈS, see BRIDOIRE.

ROUFFILHAC: Beautifully sited, high among the trees where the bridge crosses the river Dordogne between Carlux and Saint-Julien-de-Lampon, is the restored sixteenth-century Château de Rouffilhac.

SADILLAC: Due south of Bergerac on the D107, Sadillac boasts a fine, domed twelfth-century church and a neighbouring sixteenth-century château.

SAINT-AGNAN, three kilometres from Hautefort boasts a restored twelfth-century church. If you can get inside, there is a sixteenth-century *pietà*.

SAINT-ALVÈRE, north-west of Le Bugue on the river Louvre, retains the ruins of a thirteenth-century château. Market day is Monday.

SAINT-AMAND-DE-COLY, a small village east of the D704 south of Montignac, contains the finest fortified church in the whole of the

Dordogne. Built by monks for their own protection and to protect the villagers whose houses nestle around it, the twelfth-century church suddenly looms massively over a huge defensive wall, pierced by an archway. No windows open into the enormous keep-like belltower, save for some holes far out of reach. Inside you can see where beams could be placed giving a secure retreat up inside the belfry. Running round the nave and choir near the roof is a pathway from which beleaguered villagers could fire down on their attackers. And yet the church has lovely proportions; its domed roof is graceful; it remains a house of God. The Huguenots captured it in 1575; but the Augustinian monks later returned and survived here till the Revolution. See in the index to this book Saint-Amand-de-Coly.

SAINT-ANDRÉ-ALLAS, close by Sarlat, well signposted on the road to Les Eyzies, boasts a romanesque church of the twelfth century, roofed in stone, almost invariably locked. The corner of the churchyard was the scene of the execution of the partisan Emmanuel Perera on 26 June 1944, as the plaque observes, 'mort pour la France'. Near by is the lovely renaissance Château du Roc. But continue beyond Saint-André-Allas to the immaculately preserved Gaulish hamlet of Breuil-de-Bousseyrial, with its tiny stone huts: fascinating.

SAINT-ANTOINE-CUMOND: Leaving the Dordogne for Charente by the D20 east of Ribérac, you can turn off to have a last look at an example of a domed, twelfth-century church (developed in the eighteenth and nineteenth centuries), with an absolutely splendid decorated doorway.

SAINT-ANTOINE-D'AUBEROCHE, north-west of Fossemagne on the N89, has a fortified church with an eighteenth-century retable. See AJAT and LIMEYRAT.

SAINT-AQUILIN, see SAINT-ASTIER.

SAINT-ASTIER is situated on the D3 south-west of Périgueux on the banks of the river Isle. Its peaceful aspect conceals a turbulent past. The renown of its patron saint led to the establishment here of an abbey church, destroyed by the Normans in the ninth century. The present church was founded in 1013 (though little of that era remains) and Saint-Astier continued to attract both pilgrims and pillagers. In the early thirteenth century the monks decided to fortify their church. During the Hundred Years War the English besieged

the town and held it from 1339 to 1351. During the sixteenth century
the town and church were attacked and suffered as a result of the
religious wars. The armies of the Fronde pillaged Saint-Astier in
1652. In spite of all this the monks did not cease to repair and
elaborate their church, enlarging it in the fifteenth century, adding
gothic chapels in the sixteenth, somehow managing to preserve the
romanesque sculptures of Jesus with six of his apostles on the
façade.

Today the town's prosperity derives partly from its cement
works, partly from farming and partly from tourism. It stands in
ideal fishing and camping country. Thursday is market day. The
town is worth exploring for its renaissance houses.

To the east is Château de Puyferrat, built in the sixteenth and
seventeenth centuries, rectangular, with two huge circular towers.
And the D43 winds north to Saint-Aquilin (where there is a fortified
gothic church) and on past fine châteaux: du Belet, built in the
fifteenth and sixteenth centuries; de la Martinie, a fifteenth-century
building adorned later in the style of the renaissance; and de Fayolle,
built in the seventeenth century in a severely classical style. See
ANNESSE-ET-BEAULIEU.

SAINT-AULAYE, on the D5, high up over the river Dronne and once
a *bastide* guarding the entrance into Périgord from Charente, boasts
an imposing though much-restored château (now its town hall) and
a splendidly decorated romanesque church. The *bastide* was
founded in 1288. Its market is held on the last Tuesday of each
month and an annual fair on 10 September.

SAINT-AVIT-SÉNIEUR, on the D25 between Cadouin and Beaumont, was the spot where a sixth-century hermit, St Avitus, in-
stalled himself in a cave and built a chapel dedicated to the Blessed
Virgin. The Normans pulled it down in the ninth century. By this
time a colony of Augustinian canons had been established on a
nearby hill (where excavations have revealed the pattern of their
abbey), and they decided to rebuild. As a result this small village
possesses an outrageously huge fortified church, with a doorway
strong enough to resist an army and two colossal towers on either
side. Most of the fortifications date from the fourteenth century,
the ogive vaulting inside from the thirteenth, after the Albigensian
heretics had destroyed the domes of the church.

Apart from the charm of the medieval village itself, the surviving bits of the abbey are worth seeing; and a local museum houses excavated treasures. See SHELTERS and, in the index to this book, Albigensians.

SAINT-CAPRAISE-D'EYMET, due south of Bergerac, not far from the southern border of the Dordogne, has a domed romanesque church with fine sculpted capitals, a seventeenth-century pulpit and eighteenth-century wood-carvings.

SAINT-CAPRAISE-DE-LALINDE, see Château de LANQUAIS.

SAINT-CIRQUE-DE-BUGUE, see CAVES.

SAINT-CYPRIEN, north-west of Beynac-et-Cazenac on the D703, was, according to tradition, founded by the saint himself in the sixth century. His disciples are said to have drained the land to make it fertile. Certainly a medieval abbey was founded there. Today the fine abbey buildings of the sixteenth century are used as headquarters of the tobacco industry. Among the attractive buildings of Saint-Cyprien is the Maison Beaumont, built in the eighteenth century. The fourteenth-century church is protected by an earlier massive belltower. Near by is Château de Fages, despoiled and renovated in the sixteenth century. Sunday is market day at Saint-Cyprien, and there is a fair on the second Tuesday of each month.

SAINT-FÉLIX-DE-BOURDEILLES, see RICHEMONT.

SAINT-GENIÈS, lying on the D64 ten kilometres north of Sarlat, retains the ruins of Château de Pelvery, where King Louis VII, first husband of Eleanor of Aquitaine, once stayed on his way to visit the monastery of Cadouin. This small village also boasts the gothic chapel of Cheylard (decorated with fine fourteenth-century frescoes) as well as a romanesque, stone-roofed church with a sixteenth-century fortified belltower. See in the index to this book Louis VII.

SAINT-GEORGES-DE-MONTCLARD, on the D21 north-east of Bergerac, has the sixteenth-century Château de Lascoups, a thirteenth-century house with what they call an 'English gallery', an eleventh-century chapel and a lovely rustic market hall of the same date.

SAINT-JEAN-DE-CÔLE, on the D707 west of Thiviers, is a stunning village, grouped around its remarkable twelfth-century church, where a lovely old bridge crosses the river Côle. The citizens tried again and again to stop the ambitious dome of their church from falling down; but after successive rebuildings they gave up. None the less, the building is lovely, almost circular, containing several stone carvings and boasting a fine belltower. The eighteenth-century cloister is now in private possession. Although this can be readily seen from over the bridge, it is now impossible to examine closely the polygonal apse and its splendid carvings. A small museum near the church is excellent. The village itself is filled with charming houses, with picturesque roofs, as well as the colonnaded 'house of the carpenter'.

Open to visitors in July and August is the Château de la Martonie. All but its two fourteenth-century towers was burnt down during the Hundred Years War. Mondot de la Martonie (see PUY-GUILHEM) rebuilt it in the sixteenth century. In the following century a wing and a fine monumental staircase were added.

Camping, restaurants and rooms-to-let combine with concerts in the church to make Saint-Jean-de-Côle an enterprising tourist centre. In the tourist season you can join pottery classes here. See in the index to this book Saint-Jean-de-Côle.

SAINT-JULIEN-DE-LAMPON is an attractive village in Périgord Noir, across the river Dordogne south of Carlux, and situated on a crossroads. There is a tree-lined square at the side of the gothic church. Try to get inside to see the strap-worked font, and also the sixteenth-century frescoes depicting God the Father, the four evangelists and several prophets. See FÉNELON and VEYRIGNAC.

SAINT-LÉON-SUR-VÉZÈRE is situated where the river Vézère bends gracefully near the D706 between Montignac and Les Eyzies, at the foot of the Côte de Jor, a peak 225 metres high giving magnificent views of the surrounding countryside. The church, too, is magnificent, its belltower reflected in the river, part of its walls built on to old Gallo-Roman constructions, its round chapels and apse roofed with pointed stone caps. Inside are traces of frescoes, some as early as the twelfth century. The domes are lovely. Just outside the village is the local cemetery, with its own fourteenth-century chapel that once served as a 'Lantern of the Dead' (see ATUR and SARLAT). Surrounding châteaux (de Clérans, first built in the sixteenth century, with fine towers and machicolations; de la Salle, with its massive stone keep dating from the fourteenth century; de Chabans, built between the sixteenth and the seventeenth centuries and standing today at the end of its great row of cypresses) make the whole setting of Saint-Léon-sur-Vézère especially romantic.

SAINT-MARTIAL-VIVEYROL, on the north-west border of the Dordogne (on the D1), due east of Brantôme, is a village with yet another powerful, gaunt, fortified church of the twelfth century, its belltower like some battle-scarred bruiser.

SAINT-MARTIN-L'ASTIER, three kilometres north-west of Mussidan, boasts the only twelfth-century church in the Dordogne with an octagonal choir. The D3 follows the river Isle ten kilometres west to Saint-Laurent-des-Hommes, a pretty village whose gothic church contains a coloured seventeenth-century retable.

SAINT-MARTIN-LE-PIN is a pretty village six kilometres north-west of Nontron, with a rustic romanesque church, domed and elaborate without the sophistication of, say, Thiviers.

SAINT-MÉDARD-D'EXCIDEUIL, see EXCIDEUIL.

SAINT-MESMIN, see GENIS.

SAINT-MICHEL-DE-MONTAIGNE: North of Montcaret, near where the D936 runs out of the Dordogne, the famous essayist Michel Eyquem de Montaigne (1533–92), was born, lived and died. In 1884 a fire destroyed almost all of his château, and it was rebuilt in the gothic style. But the tower where Montaigne wrote his essays remains. He described it himself: 'My library is circular in shape, with no flat wall save the one taken up by my desk and chair. Since it is round, I have at my fingertips all my books at once, arranged on five tiers of shelves.' The room itself is a literary document of the first order, for Montaigne inscribed melancholy, humanistic texts in Latin and Greek on its beams: 'Don't be cleverer than you ought to be: be soberly clever', and so on.

Montaigne's chapel lies beneath the tower. His heart is buried in the romanesque church of his village, where today those who love camping and the wines of Bergerac will be made entirely happy. See in the index to this book Michel de Montaigne.

SAINT-PARDOUX-DE-MAREUIL, see MAREUIL.

SAINT-PARDOUX-LA-RIVIÈRE, situated on the river Dronne, on the D707 south-east of Nontron, eight kilometres downstream from the Saut du Chalard waterfall, preserves the ruins of a Dominican convent founded in the thirteenth century by Marguerite of Limoges. The lakes around Saint-Pardoux-la-Rivière add to its charms, as do the three châteaux of Saint-Front-la-Rivière (two kilometres south): du Pommier, Saulmier and de la Renaudie, all built in the fifteenth and sixteenth centuries. Château de la Renaudie was the home of the Huguenot leader Jean de Barry, whom the Catholic Guises hanged from the bridge of the Château d'Amboise.

There is a fair at Saint-Pardoux-la-Rivière on the second Tuesday of each month.

SAINT-PIERRE-DE-CÔLE, on the D78 east of Brantôme, guards the ruins of Château du Bruzac, whose domaine once stretched as far as Limoges. Du Guesclin took it in 1371 and Marshal Boucicaut in 1387, when the château was demolished. On its ruins was erected a renaissance château, of which only seven round or octagonal towers now remain. A chapel, known as 'des Ladres' dates from the time of the old château, still bearing the holes through which lepers received the sacraments of the church. In the village is a much-restored romanesque church. South-east is the village of Lempzours, its romanesque church still carrying two of its three original domes.

SAINT-POMPONT: During the Hundred Years War the English managed to reach as far south as this village south-west of Domme on the river Lousse (and the D60), staying long enough to build a château of which only the machicolated tower remains. Saint-Pompont's many old houses match its romanesque/gothic church with its enormous square belltower. Two medieval châteaux are still standing here: de Saint-Pompont and du Mespoulet.

SAINT-PRIVAT-DES-PRÉS is defended by a magnificent fortress church, well able to shelter every inhabitant of this village south-west of Ribérac. The dome is impressive, the west façade formidable, with a door sunk in the darkness behind a massive porch, over which nine blind round arches menace the enemy.

SAINT-RAPHAËL: Here, in a romanesque church south of Excideuil, is the final resting-place of the body of the healing saint, Rémy (known as St Remedy in the Dordogne), whose very statue was said to work miracles (see AURIAC-DU-PÉRIGORD, CHERVEIX-CUBAS and SAINT-RÉMY-SUR-LIDOIRE). The village commands splendid views.

SAINT-RÉMY-SUR-LIDOIRE: The fame of St Rémy reached from Cherveix-Cubas as far south as Saint-Rémy-sur-Lidoire, south of Montpon-Ménesterol, where the D705 meets the D35. Since the saint's body is at Saint-Raphaël and his miracle-working statue has found its way at various times to Auriac-du-Périgord and Cherveix-Cubas, Saint-Rémy-sur-Lidoire has to make do with a fountain dedicated to its patron. The church of this village, resting by a lovely small river, has a further curiosity: an altar taken from the church of Verdun.

SAINT-ROBERT, see COUBJOURS.

SAINT-SAUVEUR, a little village east of Bergerac, whose cemetery contains the tomb of Maine de Biran. The cemetery church is gothic in style and pretty. See in the index to this book Maine de Biran.

SAINT-SULPICE-DE-MAREUIL stands on the D706 north-east of Mareuil. Its romanesque domed church has an elegant twelfth-century porch in the south wall. The Château de Faye stands in its own park, with a sixteenth-century cross guarding the entrance. The great ruined tower near by is virtually all that is left of the twelfth-century Château de la Vergne. Saint-Sulpice-de-Mareuil runs a local fête on the last Sunday of August.

SAINT-SULPICE-DE-ROUMAGNAC, a pretty commune eight kilometres south-east of Ribérac, on the D43, has a romanesque church with a fine, carved wooden retable of the sixteenth century.

SAINT-VINCENT-DE-COSSE is a village beautifully situated where the river Dordogne winds between Saint-Cyprien and Beynac-et-Cazenac, set among renaissance châteaux of which the finest is Château de Panassou, with its flamboyantly decorated pediment.

SAINT-VINCENT-LE-PALUEL, due east of Sarlat and two kilometres south of Sainte-Nathalène, lies to the east of a hamlet (known as La Salvie) comprising little stone huts.

In June 1944 the Nazis executed a partisan outside the Church of Saint-Vincent-le-Paluel and set fire to the neighbouring château. Happily this lovely renaissance building, with its mullioned windows, 'Rapunzel' turret and round towers, is being restored. Together with the romanesque church and fifteenth-century manor house, it enhances a charming village. The church was slightly elaborated in the sixteenth century. It seems not to have been touched since, and is in sorry condition. So is its fine rustic reredos, with a carving of Jesus worshipped in the manger. There are two good fonts. See in the index to this book Saint-Vincent-le-Paluel.

SAINTE-COLOMBE, with its domed twelfth-century church and its château (fifteenth and eighteenth centuries), lies five kilometres north of Lalinde.

SAINTE-CROIX-DE-BEAUMONT, south of the river Couze and south-east of Beaumont itself, has a restored romanesque church next to the ruins of an old priory. You can still see the priory's mullioned windows of the fifteenth and sixteenth centuries, and the eighteenth-century bays. Near by, too, is a big seventeenth-century château. See MONTFERRAND-DU-PÉRIGORD.

SAINTE-MARIE-DE-CHIGNAC, twelve kilometres east of Périgueux on the N89, has a romanesque church with a seventeenth-century porch.

SAINTE-MONDANE, see FÉNELON.

SAINTE-NATHALÈNE, on the D47 east of Sarlat, possesses a bare twelfth-century church. North of the village is a fifteenth-century manor with a tower and a gothic chapel. See SAINT-VINCENT-LE-PALUEL.

SAINTE-TRIE: Although the Church of Sainte-Trie, on the D72 north-east of Hautefort, is an attractive romanesque building, what makes the commune eminently worth visiting are the ruins of the Cistercian abbey of Dalon, founded in the twelfth century and once the home of the troubadour Bertrand de Born and his brother. Today four gothic chapels from the west side of the transept and part of the abbot's lodging are all that remain. In the Church of Sainte-Trie is a stone tomb-statue of a nun, dating from the fourteenth century and rescued from Dalon. See in the index to this book Bertrand de Born and Dalon.

SALAGNAC-CLAIRVIVRE is a fascinating spot situated on the D5 north-east of Cherveix-Cubas. On a natural amphitheatre facing due south has been built a delightful little town devoted to the reintegration of handicapped people into society. Constructed between 1931 and 1933 according to the plans of the architect Pierre Forestier, the town possesses a splendid modern medical centre, as imposing as a renaissance château and with grounds that would grace such a building. In addition, Salagnac-Clairvivre provides occupation for those whose physical handicaps make it difficult for them to work save in specially designed conditions. The area attracts tourists because of the forest and lake that once

belonged to the famous Born family. See in the index to this book
Bertrand de Born.

SALIGNAC-EYVIGNES, on the D60 twenty kilometres north of
Sarlat, is a town of narrow streets and lovely houses dominated by
its splendid château. The terraces leading up to the château are
virtually intact, as are its twelfth-century ramparts. Built between
the twelfth and the seventeenth centuries, the château is guarded by
two round towers with pointed caps and, at the other end, by a
great square tower. Everything is impressively covered in stone
lauzes. In the thirteenth century, the Salignac family, who built it,
constructed a chapel inside; the great hall has a magnificent fifteenth-
century fireplace.

In the town of Salignac-Eyvigues are the remains of a thirteenth-
century Abbey Sainte-Croix and a thirteenth-century convent.
Markets are held on the second Thursday and the last Friday of
each month. The road curves around the château and then travels
north away from Sarlat. To the left of the D60 is the village of
Jayac, site of a square twelfth-century keep and a church (restored
in the nineteenth century) that contains a late seventeenth-century
pietà.

SARLAT: Alas, the way into Sarlat – undoubtedly one of the most
picturesque towns in the whole of the Dordogne – is not attractive.
The visitor must pass through banal suburbs and then almost certainly along what the historian Jean Maubourget described as 'the
one street without any history at all – the *Traverse*'.

The *Traverse* (officially, the Rue de la République) was cut through
the medieval town in 1827, to relieve the pressure of traffic going
from north to south. At its opening, church bells and cannons, as
well as speeches from the mayor and *sous-préfêt*, proclaimed a
revolution in traffic-control. Today the visitor should pass through
the *Traverse* as quickly as possible and park in the Place de la
Grande Rigaudie at its southern end.

The Place de la Grand Rigaudie is notable, first for its crumbling
statue of Étienne de La Bóetie, Sarlat's most renowned citizen, and
secondly for the fine Palais de Justice, built in 1866 at its eastern
end. Above the Palais de Justice is by far the best viewpoint for a
first look at Sarlat, the *jardin publique*. Once the private garden of
the bishops of Sarlat, it was set out in the seventeenth century, at

the request of Bishop François de Salignac and his nephew Fénelon, by the famous Le Nôtre, gardener to King Louis XIV. Le Nôtre never personally visited Sarlat; but he produced the design for the bishop's garden, and sent his best pupil, Porchier, to supervise the work.

Today the garden has been much savaged, by neglect in the past as well as by the cyclone of 1911, yet Le Nôtre's grandeur, simplicity of viewpoints and skill in design can still arrest the visitor, making this *jardin publique* one of the most beautiful in the Midi. On the right, as you look down over the town, the young and not-so-young play tennis and children rock on swings. Looking across the town to the heights opposite, it is possible to imagine that moment on 26 November 1587 when the Vicomte de Turenne appeared with 6,000 Protestant soldiers to lay siege to Sarlat. (The citizens put up such spirited resistance that after three weeks Turenne was obliged to lift the siege and retire, leaving behind 500 dead soldiers.)

On either side of the *Traverse*, Sarlat is filled with so many fine medieval and renaissance buildings that the visitor's eyes continually pick out a renaissance doorway here, a couple of finely wrought door-handles there, a broken pediment in a wall which still shows the beams of its medieval construction. Everywhere are romantic traces of doorways long since blocked up and of fine embellished gothic windows. Many houses are dated on the outside. Very many bear the steep ancient roofs made of stones instead of tiles. On odd corners, gargoyles or religious carvings stare back to the tourist.

But any visit to Sarlat must include a number of very fine sights, as well as these countless delights. Returning from the *jardin publique* to the Place de la Grande Rigaudie, the visitor should turn right not along the *Traverse* but the street immediately before it (the Rue Tourny). By taking the first little street right, off the Rue Tourny, the visitor comes upon an old, still functioning fountain. Here, sometimes between the sixth and the eighth century A.D., Benedictine monks founded the abbey of Sarlat, beside the river Cuze (which now flows underground through the town). The monastery flourished, and the great church with its flying buttresses which can be seen from the little square with its fountain, is its successor. By the end of the twelfth century, the abbey of Sarlat ruled eighty-five daughter churches or chapels, stretching to Toulouse.

The monks became the temporal lords of Sarlat – a lordship bitterly contested by the rising lay bourgeoisie, who at the end of the thirteenth century won the right to elect their own consuls and representatives. No doubt to raise the prestige of the monastery after this rebuff, Pope John XXII (who came from Cahors) made Sarlat into a bishopric in 1317. (Thirty-seven bishops served it thenceforth until the bishopric was abolished during the Revolution.)

The visitor should press on through archways to reach the tiny graveyard of the monastery, from which appear not only yet more splendid views of the great church but also access to Sarlat's most bizarre sight – the mysterious 'Lantern of the Dead'. Atur is one of the few other places with any building comparable to this strange, stone-built tower, domed inside, the outside resembling a kind of pyramid with an ovoid rather than conical top. The 'Lantern of the Dead' was erected in the last quarter of the twelfth century to commemorate a miracle performed by St Bernard when he preached in Sarlat in August 1147. Many presented bread to the saint, which he blessed, adding that (as a sign that he spoke the truth and that the heretics against whom he preached were in error) any sick person who ate the blessed bread would begin to recover. The Bishop of Chartres, Geoffroy de Lèves, who was present, added, 'If they eat in perfect faith.' St Bernard replied, 'I didn't say that.' Apparently the miracle happened, and so 'St Bernard's tower', later the 'Lantern of the Dead', was built.

In spite of its name, no one is sure what its purpose was. Under the tower was once an ossuary, and above it a chapel. From this chapel there is now no access to the first floor, which must be reached by a ladder placed outside. Even then, a man cannot squeeze in through the narrow windows. Could lights once have been placed there as a corpse lay in state? We have no record, though we know that in the seventeenth century the bourgeoisie of Sarlat elected their consuls in the tower.

The great church can be entered either through a side door from the monks' graveyard or by retracing one's steps to the Rue Tourny and turning right. Founded in the twelfth century, it was dedicated to St Sacerdos, who was born in Calviac and become Bishop of Sarlat around the year A.D. 515. A monk and later abbot of the monastery at Calviac, St Sacerdos could cure lepers and is reputed to have raised his own father from the dead. He himself died at Argentat on 5 May 520, and his body was brought back down the river Dordogne to his old monastery. From here it was transferred to the church in Sarlat. Even now he did not rest for ever. In the sixteenth century the famous Protestant Chevalier Geoffroi de Vivans, during the Wars of Religion, had the saint's body burned and his ashes thrown to the winds. Only a few bones were left, to be carried in procession by the Catholics twice a year round the town.

The church nevertheless remains dedicated to St Sacerdos. Its early history was not without strife, even before the Wars of Religion. In 1273 the building had to be reconsecrated after Abbot Arnaud de Stapone died in the choir, killed by an arrow fired by one of his own monks! The Hundred Years War led to neglect, so that at the beginning of the sixteenth century it was decided to demolish almost the whole of the old twelfth-century structure and rebuild. Today the romanesque elements of the church that remain are chiefly found in the belfry, which is itself topped by a bulbous tower added in the second quarter of the eighteenth century by Bishop Alexandre le Blanc. On the west façade are statues so worn and defaced that today nobody knows what they were meant to represent.

The new building began on 6 February 1505, when the first stones were laid by the vicar-general, Jean de Magnanat, and the provost of the chapter, Guillaume de Plamon. The new architect was Pierre Esclache, and the whole building took 150 years to complete. The right aisle is probably original. The sacristy on the right is the one built in 1320 by the first Bishop of Sarlat, its two round columns, without capitals, supporting the roof. The choir and its chapels were rebuilt between 1515 and 1519. The rest was restored in the next 200 years. The pillars are enormous, impressive, very slightly decorated. The roof of the nave was vaulted in 1683. The stalls of the cathedral canons, complete with misericords carved under their seats, remain. On the west wall is an impressive organ case, designed and executed by Cliquot in 1770.

On the left and right of the square at the west end of the Church of Saint-Sacerdos (the Place du Peyrou) are two remarkable buildings.

Abutting on to the south side of the cathedral itself is the former bishop's palace, now the theatre. This renaissance building was created for the Italian Cardinal Niccolò Gaddi, who was appointed Bishop of Sarlat in 1533.

Gaddi took four years to arrive in Sarlat for his enthronement. But his coming enhanced the town in ways that we can see today. A passionate humanist, he had lived at the court of the Medicis in Florence and he brought with him Italian workmen and artists to embellish his palace. Bishop François de Salignac added to it in the next century. But the Italian influence is plain to see. Two storeys built in stone are topped by one in delicate brick. The details of the ornament and the polygonal tower on the corner have been beautifully restored.

On the opposite corner is the house where, on All Saints' Day 1530, Montaigne's friend Étienne de La Boétie was born. This is one of the many great secular houses (or 'hôtels', as they are called) built by the prosperous civic leaders of Sarlat. Today its façade, with delicate columns and spiralling tracery, is perfectly restored. The house was built by Étienne's father, Antoine de La Boétie, between 1520 and 1525.

A passageway on the left of the Hôtel de La Boétie, the passage Henry de Secogne, leads to a charmingly restored cluster of ancient and renaissance buildings, with balconies and narrow archways. On the wall is a tribute to General de Gaulle's minister of culture, André Malraux, who enabled much of the fine restoration of Sarlat to be accomplished. In promulgating the law allowing parts of historic towns to be designated areas particularly suited for careful preservation, Malraux specifically instanced the whole of Sarlat.

Turning right through this enchanting complex of buildings, you join the Rue de la Liberté and – passing left along it – reach the Place de la Liberté. On the left is another sixteenth-century hôtel, formerly known as the Hôtel de Vienne, now the Hôtel de Maleville, and today housing the Sarlat tourist office. Jean Vienne was born in Sarlat in June 1557, of humble stock, and rose to high office in the court of Henri IV, partly through the good favour of the king's favourite, Gabrielle d'Estrées. When she fell from power, he managed to secure the goodwill of the next favourite, Catherine de Balzac d'Entraygues. Nevetheless, two medallions on either side of the main door of his Hôtel in Sarlat, depicting Henri IV and Gabrielle d'Estrées, acknowledge his first patroness. The building is yet more remarkable in that the side facing the Place de la Liberté is decorated in the style of the French renaissance, whereas the other façade is in that of the Italian renaissance.

Opposite is the imposing Hôtel de Ville, restored, but in its original style, built between 1618 and 1625 by Henri Bouysson, an architect from Monpazier, in place of the old communal house erected in 1330. A delightful touch is that the list of consuls of Sarlat (till the Revolution), put up inside the Hôtel de Ville, is filled with errors.

Up the Rue de la Salamandre (on the right of the Hôtel de Ville), and then left along the Rue du Présidial, leads to the Présidial itself, the old seat of royal justice – with its polygonal lantern, its two bays, its fine ironwork and its spacious garden. Henri II set up the Présidial in 1552, in face of great opposition from the justices of Périgueux. Its jurisdiction was suppressed in 1560, but re-established in 1641. Today the Présidial is a private house. Apart from its own charm, the brief diversion to see it takes the visitor through a good number of delightful buildings, all dating from Sarlat's medieval and renaissance prosperity.

To return to the Place de la Liberté is to re-enter a square surrounded by noble houses, with fascinatingly different styles of roofs. But the square is also overlooked by one of Sarlat's saddest sights – the ruined Parish Church of St Mary.

In 1365 the citizens of Sarlat decided to built a new parish church, under the architect Jacques Cavaille. War interrupted the work in 1370. By 1431 only the choir and its span had been completed. The church was finally completed, under the supervision of the architect Pierre Esclache, in 1507. It remained the parish church of Sarlat until the Revolution. Then began its sad decline. St Mary's was used for storing arms and for making saltpetre. The building was sold for 600 francs in 1815. In 1821 the span of the choir was destroyed. A baker and a coalman used the nave for their trades and shops occupied the chapels on the south side. Then the church became the main post office. After the First World War an attempt was made at a restoration of part of the building. Today discreet offices occupy the interior. But the great belltower, 25 metres high, looks forlornly down on the city. Its bells have gone, as have the pulpit from which St Bernard preached, the medieval carving depicting his miracle with the loaves, and the consuls' pews, with their finely carved coats of arms.

The Place de la Liberté runs into the Place du Marché, which is overlooked by a fine sixteenth-century hôtel, with a hexagonal stair-tower and high, pointed stone roofs. This, the Hôtel de Gisson, is also known as the 'Maison Chassaing', since it was the house of Jean Chassaing, one of the leaders of Sarlat's resistance against Turenne in 1587. Chassaing later took part in the conspiracy of the Duc de Bouillon against Henri IV, for which he was beheaded on 15 December 1605.

The Place du Marché leads through the Place du Marché aux Oies into the Rue des Consuls. The visitor, turning right, will find on his left the beautiful Hôtel Plamon. Guillaume Plamon was a member of an important family of cloth merchants. He became a consul of Sarlat in 1330. He sold to the town the land on which the present Hôtel de Ville is built. The Hôtel Plamon was built in his time, though the great vaulted door was added three centuries later. The ground floor, which is a kind of courtyard, probably at one time served for the dyeing of cloth. The first floor, reached by an ornamental staircase, is lit by gothic windows with slender columns. And the next floor is an impressive stone room with fifteenth-century mullioned windows.

Cloth merchants have always needed water for their trade. In the time of the Plamons, the river Cuze supplied this, and now passes under their great hôtel. On the other side of the Rue des Consuls is the fifteenth-century fountain of St Mary – only the second to be created in the town. (Till then, everyone was obliged to rely either on the fountain of the monks or on the pestilent waters of the Cuze.)

The Cuze itself makes its one modern appearance overground between the corner of the Rue des Consuls and the *Traverse*. At many points along the *Traverse* it is easy to see how the new road of 1827 sliced through medieval streets. The Rue des Consuls crosses to the west side of the *Traverse* at such a point. The visitor enters an astonishing cluster of tiny medieval streets. The first road on the left leads to the Rue Jean-Jacques Rousseau, which climbs steeply, passing on the right the Chapel of the Blue Penitents – looking quite huge amidst such narrow streets and domestic buildings. The Blue Penitents were an order designed for those members of the nobility drawn to the religious life. (The White Penitents, an order designed for lesser folk, were housed in a twelfth-century chapel near the monks of Saint-Sacerdos.) Today the Chapel of the Blue Penitents, with its impressive doorway – incorporating a renaissance broken pediment and two great Doric columns – houses a museum of religious art of much interest (especially if the visitor likes to look at bones and relics).

The west side of the *Traverse* is remarkable for its curious towers – especially the fine Tour du Guet, with its fifteenth-century machicolations, on the Rue Rousset, and the Tower of the Executioner, built into the ramparts north of the Rue Jean-Jacques Rousseau. Close by is one of the many fine houses of the west quarter, the Hôtel de Cerval, built in the early sixteenth century and containing a splendid walnut staircase.

But what this part of Sarlat offers above all is a glimpse of a virtually unspoiled medieval town plan – if plan is the word – with small, twisting streets, steep ascents, bounded by the ancient city wall, with the one gate (of four) that still remains. Even here, homes are let into the wall. Small wonder that in the days before modern sanitation, plague regularly attacked townsfolk living in such picturesque, unsanitary conditions.

Life in Sarlat changed only slowly. In 1750 the ditches outside the city wall were filled in to make what are now the ring roads (or *boulevards*). An abattoir was constructed in 1864, and beasts ceased to be killed in the streets on market days. In the early 1880s, the Sarlat–Siorac railway – including the remarkable viaduct of Pontet on the outskirts of the city – was built, using chiefly Spanish labour.

Sarlat copes splendidly with its dual role as a country town and an important centre of tourism. Every Saturday the picturesque market, occupying the whole of the *Traverse* and many streets and squares to the east, draws in both tourists and those who live their lives in the area. No longer can one buy cattle at this market (as is still possible at the Tuesday markets in Gourdon, only twenty-four kilometres away); but chickens, geese and all manner of livestock are on display alongside fruit, vegetables, cheese and fish. And there are stalls aimed directly at the holiday visitor.

The suburbs of Sarlat offer tennis and open-air swimming. Hotels and restaurants are splendid. (Good food at the Hôtel-Restaurant Saint-Albert, Place Pasteur. Look out on the menu for the scrumptious *gâteau au Monbazillac*.) The *Traverse* itself brims with charcuteries, cafés, dress- and shoe-shops. The town possesses fine bookshops and a splendid public library. In summer art and photography exhibitions, concerts and a theatre festival are set up under the auspices of the local *Syndicat d'Initiative*.

Yet it remains a charming, almost wholly unspoilt, medieval and renaissance town. Market day at Sarlat is Wednesday as well as Saturday. Open to the general public in July and August is the former Abbey of Sainte-Claire, on the west side of the *Traverse* (Côte de Toulouse/Rue Jean-Jacques Rousseau), occupied by the sisters of the order from 1621 until the Revolution. Much of the sixteenth- and seventeenth-century abbey is still intact, including fine vaulting, lovely windows and splendid carved chimneys. See TEMNIAC and, in the index to this book, Étienne de la Boétie, André Malraux, Michel de Montaigne and Sarlat.

SARLIAC-SUR-L'ISLE, where the N21 meets the D705 north-east of Périgueux, boasts a romanesque church with a sixteenth-century belltower and (on the outskirts of the village) the fifteenth- and seventeenth-century manor de Grézignac. At Sarliac-sur-l'Isle you eat well at the Restaurant les Palmiers.

SAUSSIGNAC, situated on the D4 in the south-west corner of the Dordogne, is a village clustered around an enormous château, lying amid vineyards producing sweet white wine (often 'liquoreux'). Enormous though it is, the château, begun in the sixteenth century and continued in the seventeenth, was never finished. One of its builders, le Capitaine de Boisse, was assassinated in 1621. Nevertheless, its great pavilions and dormer windows and the classical regularity of its façade remain impressive. Rabelais spent some months here. Pierre de Bourdeille paid court to a 'beautiful and virtuous' lady who lived here in the sixteenth century. She was Louise de la Béraudière, wife of Louis d'Estissac; she also captivated Michel de Montaigne, who devoted one of his essays to her praise.

In Saussignac are the ruins of the fourteenth-century Tour de

Lonvège. Two kilometres to the east is the village of Gageac-et-Rouillac, filled with delightful houses and guarded by the fourteenth-century château which belonged to Geoffroi de Vivans, the great Protestant leader during the Wars of Religion. See in the index to this book Pierre de Bourdeilles, Michel de Montaigne, Geoffroi de Vivans and Soussignac.

SAVIGNAC-LÉDRIER, south-east of Lanquaille, has a fine château, a typical Dordogne mixture of medieval and renaissance styles, and a romanesque church.

SEGONZAC, a village hidden away south-east of Ribérac, boasts not only its own fifteenth-century château (to the west of the village) and an older church beautified in the sixteenth century, but also the rather impressive medieval/renaissance Château de la Martinie.

SERGEAC, on the D65 between Les Eyzies and Montignac, is a typical old Périgord village, with stone-roofed houses, a twelfth-century fortified church (with a lovely porch), and the ruins of a thirteenth-century bastion of the Knights Templars. But, lying as it does in the valley of the river Vézère, it has a particular importance for prehistory. No less than five prehistoric shelters have been discovered near Sergeac, and 500 metres downstream from the village, at Castel-Merle, where you have an astonishing view of the valley, is a fascinating little museum of prehistory. See SHELTERS.

SHELTERS (ABRIS): Our prehistoric ancestors sheltered not only in caves but, more frequently, underneath the many overhanging rocks of the Dordogne, especially in the rich valley of the river Vézère. These silted up over the centuries. Excavations have brought to light tools, skeletons and – most fascinating of all – carvings and bas-reliefs done 30,000 years or so ago on the walls of these shelters. Many of these prehistoric shelters are open to the public and are scarcely less exciting than the prehistoric caves of the Dordogne.

Bayac lies south of Lalinde on the river Couze. Prehistoric remains have been discovered in the Abri de la Gravette.

Cap-Blanc: East of Les Eyzies along the D48, a signpost directs you left along the winding road up into the forest and then down a little path to where, in the early years of this century, archaeologists discovered under an overhanging rock the skeleton of a prehistoric woman and, on the wall near where she had been buried, a huge frieze of horses, a couple of bison and other sculptures of the 'Magdalenian' Age (10,000 to 20,000 years ago). The skeleton is now in a museum in the U.S.A. The shelter is protected by a stone wall, and a model skeleton has been put in the place of the original. See in the index of this book Cap-Blanc.

Chancelade: Not far from the former Abbey of Chancelade was discovered the prehistoric Abri de Raymonden. The skeleton of 'Chancelade man' and his goods are now in the Museum of Périgord, Périgueux.

Domme: In the Abri de Combe-Grenal, at the foot of the great rock on which Domme is built, prehistoric families lived over many centuries, revealed by the excavation of successive layers of their goods and remains.

Enfer: Almost in Les Eyzies itself is the Gorge d'Enfer. Here in 1912 the Abri du Poisson was discovered, where prehistoric man had engraved a salmon, 1.10 metres long. You can see it in conjunction with the museum of Laugérie Haute (see below). Here, too, is a park of allegedly prehistoric animals.

Laugérie Basse and *Laugérie Haute* are prehistoric shelters two kilometres from Les Eyzies where our ancestors lived for over 20,000 years. You can see how they incised the walls to stop water trickling into their living quarters. These *abris* have been excavated at various times for over 120 years. Two skeletons were discovered in Laugérie Haute, where a museum displays the pottery, stone lamps, needles, carved bones and so on once used by our prehistoric ancestors. The successive stages of inhabitation in these shelters are very well exposed today.

La Madeleine: In this shelter near Tursac (on the D706 north of Les Eyzies) was discovered such a wealth of prehistoric remains – weapons, tools and instruments made out of ivory, stone, reindeer bone, engraved and decorated, over 600 pieces altogether – that the name of the shelter (or 'Magdalenian') is now used to describe the last great period of prehistory. Many of the objects found there can been seen in the museum of prehistory at Les Eyzies.

Peyzac-le-Moustier: In 1908 German archaeologists discovered here in a prehistoric shelter a skeleton which they considered closely resembled their own prehistoric Neanderthal man. Kaiser Wilhelm II bought it for D M 120,000 and the skeleton was placed in the Berlin museum, where it perished during the bombardments of the Second World War. So much else of value was found at Le Moustier that the term 'Mousterian' was coined to describe the middle-palaeolithic era (roughly, the 20,000 years leading to 40,000 B.C.). The *abri*, at the foot of the rocks of Le Moustier in the Vézère valley, is still well worth a visit, and the successive layers of prehistoric deposit are clearly visible. See (index) Peyzac-le-Moustier.

Poisson: For the famous Abri du Poisson see *Enfer* above and, in the index to this book, Poisson.

Regourdou: In 1957 the owner of this *abri* at Montignac discovered in it the jaw of a Neanderthal man. You can visit both the shelter and the little museum near by.

Saint-Avit-Sénieur: Here in the valley of the river Couze prehistoric shelters have been discovered, one containing the remains of so-called 'Combe-Carelle' man.

Sergeac: Near the belvedere of Castel-Merl is the Abri Reverdit, where you can see vestiges of a sculptured frieze, as well as visit an interesting small museum of prehistory.

Tursac: See *La Madeleine* (above).

See also BOURDEILLES. The noted bas-relief of oxen from Bourdeilles is now in the museum at Les Eyzies.

SIGOULÈS: Fine wine-tasting country (with a *cave coopérative*) south of Monbazillac. Sigoulès offers good food. Try La Closerie Saint-Jacques for its *fricassée de pigeons au Monbazillac*; the Traiteur au Château de Monbazillac for the *caille rôtie de nos vignes*; or the Relais de la Diligence, for its *steaks de canard au Pécharmant*. See Chapter 3 of this book. See MONBOS.

SIMEYROLS, four kilometres north of Carlux, is a small village with a romanesque church and some lovely views of Périgord Noir.

SIORAC-EN-PÉRIGORD, where the D25 and the D710 meet on the south bank of the river, boasts a fine seventeenth-century château, once dominating the river traffic, now housing the local *mairie*.

Siorac, today an important tourist centre, holds a market every Wednesday. Near by is the dolmen of Cayrelevat.

SIREUIL, four kilometres east of Les Eyzies, has a domed romanesque church. See COMMARQUE.

SORGES, on the N21 seventeen kilometres north of Périgueux, has a château open to the public, as well as a delightful museum of the ecology of the truffle. Château de Jaillac, built in the thirteenth century and much reconstructed, is pierced with no fewer than seventy-five loopholes for firing arrows at the enemy. Huge rooms, a fine stone staircase, splendid chimneys and furniture from various eras of French history are on display. Sorges also boasts a domed romanesque church, partly rebuilt in the sixteenth century, with a renaissance doorway.

Visitors to the museum of the truffle are also taken on a short truffle-hunt. Friday is market day in Sorges. The town offers excellent swimming facilities. See in the index to this book Truffles.

SOURZAC, on the N89 north-east of Mussidan, has a fine gothic church (with ogive vaulting) and a great keep of a belltower. You can see next to the church bits of the ruined priory it once served. See, under CAVES, *Gabillou*.

TAMNIÈS, perched on a rock above the river Beaune, has collected together many troglodyte remains to entrance the visiting tourist. Fishing, camping and *gîtes* abound. The twelfth-century church contains seventeenth-century polychrome statues.

TEMNIAC, two kilometres north of Sarlat, is a splendid site where the bishops of Sarlat decided to transform an old fortification (put there by Pepin the Short) into a palace. Much of the building of the thirteenth and fifteenth centuries is now in ruins; but the crypt of the chapel, the fine cellars, and round tower are open to the public and worth seeing. Even finer is the restored Chapel of Notre-Dame. A miraculous survivor, this chapel, built by the first Bishop of Sarlat, was destroyed in 1397 by the soldiers of Jean Harpedane, Seneschal of Périgord. Rebuilt, it survived until 1562, when the Huguenots set fire to it. Rebuilt a second time, it passed to the State during the Revolution and was for many years used as a barn. Yet the much-pillaged and restored church retains the romanesque domes, fine vaulting and great 'blind' arches on its exterior walls. The site alone is marvellously romantic.

TERRASSON, on the N89 where the river Vézère flows into the *département* of the Dordogne, is divided into an old and new city by the river, which is here crossed by a modern bridge and a twelfth-century medieval one. At Terrasson St Sour founded an abbey in the sixth century. The church still dominates the old town (it was built in the fifteenth century and the Place de l'Église is known as '*le Fort*'). Splendid houses gather higgledy-piggledy around it. The remains of the fourteenth-century château are still impressive, and its ramparts have now been terraced. Just outside the city is Château de la Fraysse (fifteenth and eighteenth centuries), and two kilometres south is Château de Montmège (thirteenth and seventeenth centuries). There is a busy market at Terrasson every Thursday. See CHAVAGNAC.

TEYJAT, see under CAVES, *La Mairie*.

THENON, situated where the D67 crosses the N89, was once little more than a fortified camp on a hill, and its old town is still ringed with ditches (long filled in). The English burned down its château, and you can still see traces of fire on the one remaining tower. All that remains of the once great Château de la Mouthe at Thenon is the moat. Tuesday is market day.

THIVIERS, a thriving town on the N21 in Perigord Vert, has a lovely church, domed in the twelfth century, vaulted in the sixteenth, with a good porch built in 1515. Its belltower was added in the nineteenth century. Inside, its romanesque carvings are very fine (see in the index to this book Thiviers). Next to this church is a fortified presbytery. The town retains a surprising number of interesting old houses, including the (much-restored) Château de Vaucocour. There is a market every Saturday (try the sausages there). Good swimming pools.

THONAC, six kilometres south of Montignac on the D706, offers two tempting prizes to the tourist. First, the exquisite Château de Losse (one kilometre north) is open to the general public from mid July to mid September. Built in the late sixteenth century by Jean de Losse, governor of Périgord, after his thirteenth-century château had been partially destroyed by the Huguenots, Château de Losse is beautifully placed on the river Vézère, a dry moat protecting the other three sides. Inside are tapestries and furniture dating from the sixteenth and seventeenth centuries. You can see carved inside Jean de Losse's Churchillian motto: 'Cum sudore, sanguine et carcere'.

The second treat, two kilometres out of Thonac, is to visit the excellent centre of prehistoric art at Le Thot. And Thonac itself has a small romanesque church containing a twelfth-century wooden statue of the Virgin.

TOCANE-SAINT-APRE, on the D710 west of Périgueux, is the agricultural centre of the valley of the river Dronne and holds an important market on Mondays. Excavations have revealed that this was a great Gallo-Roman centre: a mosaic pavement, a little aqueduct, a bakery and baths have all been uncovered. Near by, too, are ancient dolmens (the finest is called 'Pierre-Levée', at the *lieu dit* bearing that name). Six kilometres south on the D103 is the classical Château de la Fayolle, built in the eighteenth century. The centre of Tocane-Saint-Apre is charming.

LA TOUR BLANCHE, due south of Mareuil by way of the D99, is a village with picturesque renaissance houses and at its peak a fascinating ruined château, now open to the general public. Built in the tenth century on the site of a Gaulish hill-fort, it had passed into the hands of the French king by the fourteenth century. The English took it and were expelled by Du Guesclin on 9 March 1356. In 1544 Henri de Navarre and his wife Marguerite stayed there for several weeks. It stands today, a gaunt memorial to its past glories.

The romanesque church of La Tour Blanche, much enlarged in our own century, possesses an eighteenth-century picture by Lorenzo di Credi. In the forest of Jovelle west of La Tour Blanche are the ruins of another château. See CERCLES.

TOURTOIRAC, lying on the river Vézère (and on the D5 due west of Hautefort), was chosen by Richard, Abbot of Uzerche, as the site of a Benedictine abbey in the eleventh-century. Thirty-five monks inhabited the abbey 200 years later, but soon Tourtoirac Abbey went into decline. You can explore its romantic ruins between the present (romanesque/gothicized) church and the river. There is a fair here on the third Tuesday of each month. At Saint-Pantaly-d'Ans, further south and across the river, are the melancholy ruins of three châteaux, one of which contained a fine forge.

TRAPPE DE BONNE-ESPÉRANCE: A Trappist monastery near the D708 in the Double forest, producing a locally renowned cheese.

TRÉLISSAC, near the river Isle west of Périgueux, has two châteaux near by: the pretty fifteenth-century Château de Caussade and the late eighteenth-century Château de Septfonds, both in the neighbourhood of camp sites and fine walks.

TRÉMOLAT: André Maurois described the view of the great loop (or *cingle*) made by the river Dordogne halfway between Sarlat and Bergerac as 'one of the wonders of the world'. The village itself consists of twisting streets and delightful Périgord houses, surrounding a massive fortress of a church, built in the twelfth century. The newly restored romanesque Chapel of St Hilary contains glass by Paul Becker.

Charlemagne is said to have founded a priory here and given to it the shirt of the infant Jesus. Certainly, architectural historians have found traces of older building in the walls of the parish church. Claude Chabrol used this village as a setting for his noted film *Le Boucher*. You can eat well at Le Vieux Logis.

TURSAC, a village in the Vézère valley north of Les Eyzies, is dominated by the fortified, domed romanesque parish church and the sixteenth-century Château de Marzac. See under SHELTERS, *La Madeleine*.

URVAL: The twelfth-century church of Urval, just south of the river Dordogne and the D25, was fortified by the English during the Hundred Years War. The old presbytery retains a rare medieval bread-oven.

VALEUIL, on the river Dronne between Brantôme and Bourdeilles, has a domed romanesque church (later gothicized) and is surrounded by the dolmen of Laprouges and the megalith of Coutoux. Just outside the village you pass the fifteenth-century Château de Ramefort.

VANXAINS is on the D708 south-west of Ribérac, its romanesque Church of Our Lady much refined in later ages (with fifteenth-century ogive vaulting in parts of the church and a seventeenth-century belltower) without losing its charm. Inside are fine capitals over the choir, where you can also find a twelfth-century inscription. Two kilometres to the west you can see at Festalemps a domed romanesque church, with an 'over-vaulted' apse, set in a lovely village.

VARAIGNES, north of Javerlhac-et-la-Chapelle-Saint-Robert (on the road from Nontron to Angoulême), has a well-preserved fifteenth-century château used as a museum of local folk art. Market day is the 5th of each month. The annual fair (on the first Sunday in August) is a very jolly affair, with a five o'clock feast in the court-yard of the fifteenth-century château. (The polygonal staircase-tower of the château and its imposing square tower are perfectly preserved.) Equally jolly is the turkey fête, which takes place on 11 November each year. Local culinary specialities are turkey, *champignons*, meringues and macaroons. See under CAVES, *La Mairie*.

VAUCLAIRE: For the thirteenth-century Carthusian priory, see MONTPON-MÉNESTEROL.

VÉLINES, beautifully situated for the wine-connoisseur between the vineyards of Montravel and Bergerac (almost on the D936), has a romanesque, domed church, enlarged at the Renaissance. If you follow the minor road east from Vélines through Fougueyrolles, you reach after fifteen kilometres the lovely village of Le Fleix. Set on a Gallo-Roman site (from which many tools and arrow heads have been recovered), Le Fleix is today a cluster of ancient houses, some overhanging the road, with artisans specializing in making replicas of old tiles. Once there was an important monastery here. All traces of it have disappeared – though a fragment of the tombstone of Bishop Safarius of Périgueux (who died at the end of the sixth century), and the local place-names (Champs de Moines, Trou de Moines, Moulins de Moines) betray its former existence. Wednesday is market day at Vélines. See FOUGUEYROLLES.

VENDOIRE, a village on the D102 on the border of Charente, has a twelfth-century church betraying far more characteristics of the Charente style than of the Dordogne. Its façade is decorated with sculptures, and near by is a seventeenth-century château.

VERDON: The long, low, unaggressive Château de Montbrun (open if you ask the owner) in this village south-west of Lanquais is refreshing after so many stern forbidding fortresses. It was built in the eighteenth century.

VERGT, on the D8 twenty kilometres south of Périgueux, is the geographical centre of the Dordogne and also chief town of a canton 3,336 hectares in size. Recently Vergt has taken great steps to make itself the major strawberry market of France, and during the strawberry season (mid April to mid November) selling the fruit is the chief purpose of its Friday market. (The market sells mostly fowl for the rest of the year; and the annual fairs are held on the Friday after 4 August and the third Friday in September.) In the parish church is modern stained glass by the Périgourdin artist Raymond Biaussat. Tourism, in the form of camping, fishing and some flying, is catered for mostly in neighbouring Saint-Amand-de-Vergt.

VERTEILLAC, between Mareuil and Ribérac, has a church rebuilt in the nineteenth century, save for the twelfth-century choir. Near the town is a Gaulish tumulus known as *La Calotte*. Verteillac is a centre of tourism with a market every Saturday afternoon.

VEYRIGNAC: The D50 from Grolejac (on the D704 between Sarlat and Gourdon) winds along the river Dordogne at its most beautiful and peaceful towards this tiny village. You must turn left off the road into the village to see its massive church (which I have known to be open only for the eucharist at the fête de Veyrignac). Near by, and open to the general public in July and August, is the classical Château de Veyrignac – founded as a feudal château in the Middle Ages, converted into a monastery and then bought back for secular use by the Marquis de Therme (one of Louis XIV's marshals), much rebuilt in the eighteenth century, set on fire by retreating Nazis in June 1944, and now beautifully restored.

VÉZAC, between Beynac-et-Cazenac and La Roque-Gageac on the D705, boasts the seventeenth-century Château de Marqueyssac (with its beautiful gardens), set high up over the river Dordogne, commanding a breathtaking view of its valley and the restored Château de Castelnaud. The English burned down the medieval Château de Marqueyssac (hence the classical form of its successor) during the Hundred Years War. Vézac boasts a thirteenth-century church (restored 400 years later) and a thirteenth-century cemetery.

VÉZÈRE: The valley of the river Vézère proved to be the most hospitable region ever discovered by prehistoric man. Sixty or so caves and over 150 shelters have been discovered with prehistoric carvings, remains, engravings or paintings. See CAVES and SHELTERS.

VIEUX-MAREUIL. Try the Auberge de l'Étang Bleu. See MAREUIL.

LE VIGAN, a town almost in the Lot, on the D673 east of Gourdon, has a fourteenth-century church with a massive belltower.

VILLAMBLARD lies due east of Mussidan. The fifteenth-century Château Barrière was burned down by accident, not by warfare. Some fine bits remain. Monday is market day.

VILLARS, a village on the D3 north-east of Brantôme, consists of pretty Périgord houses around a sixteenth-century church (with a fine porch). Near by are a splendid cave and an equally splendid château. (See CAV.ES and PUYGUILHEM.) There are pottery classes at Villars during the holiday season. To the north-west lies the village of Quinsac, guarded by the eighteenth-century Château de Vaugoubert.

VILLEFRANCHE-DE-LONCHAT, on the D9, eight kilometres north of Saint-Michel-de-Montaigne, and just inside the western boundary of the Dordogne, was built as an English *bastide* for Edward III. Today it lies peacefully dominating its vineyards from the crest of a rock, ready to welcome to its *cave coopérative* those who would like to taste the vintages. From the rock you can see two châteaux: de Gurson and the château where Montaigne wrote his essays. The romanesque church of Villefranche-de-Lonchat lies outside the *bastide* itself. See CARSAC-DE-GURSON, SAINT-MICHEL-DE-MONTAIGNE and, in the index to this book, *bastides* and Michel de Montaigne.

VILLEFRANCHE-DU-PÉRIGORD, on the D660, lying at one of the southernmost points of the Dordogne, was built as a *bastide* in the late thirteenth century by Alphonse de Poitiers, brother of King Louis VII, to guard the way to the ancient provinces of Quercy and Guyenne. Attacked, captured and recaptured, pillaged and rebuilt over the centuries, Villefranche-du-Périgord has nevertheless managed to retain the grid pattern of the old *bastide*, as well as its market hall, raised on pillars. The old stone arcades in front of the houses near to the church are also typical of Dordogne *bastides*. One of these dwellings became a religious house of the Pénitents Blancs in the Middle Ages. Over the lintel (between statues mutilated during the Revolution) you can read the inscription, '*Si Deus pro nobis quis contra nos*' – 'If God be for us, who can be against us?' Villefranche-du-Périgord also preserves some old towers (one known as the Tour des Consuls) and a fountain which almost certainly served the *bastide* from its foundation. Annual fairs are held here on 24 July, 16 August and 28 September.

South of Villefranche-du-Périgord lies Loubejac, with a thirteenth-century church, the choir romanesque, the nave ogive-vaulted. Five kilometres north of the *bastide* is Besse, with its fortified romanesque church. Besse church was elaborated in the fifteenth and sixteenth centuries, but it retains an amazingly daring group of sculptures on its porch, dating from the late eleventh century and interpreting the redemption. See PRATS-DU-PÉRIGORD and, in the index to this book, *bastides*.

VILLETOUREIX, see RIBÉRAC.

VITRAC seems to have divided itself into two parts. One lies at a crossroads on the D46 between Sarlat and Cénac-et-Saint-Julien. Here you can enjoy good fishing, swimming in the river Dordogne, camping, and some fine hotels. But Vitrac-Bourg (as it is called) is signposted off the main road, on the Sarlat side of the crossroads. A winding road leads past a mill up to the village square, with its massive romanesque church. I can recognize the stone *pietà*, but the carvings over the porch are to me now indecipherable. Once Vitrac possessed its own château, known as *Le Fort*. It was damaged during the Hundred Years War and the people of Sarlat preferred to dismantle it in 1379 rather than take the trouble of repairing it. Close by is the Château de Mas-Robert, set on fire by the Huguenots in the sixteenth century and well restored. Vitrac also boasts, next to the church, a château built in the nineteenth century in the renaissance style. The road winds on to Château Montfort and to Carsac-Aillac, offering stupendous views of the river Dordogne.

The Hôtel Plaisance offers a very welcoming smile as well as good food.

❖ 9 ❖

Recipes from the Dordogne

❖ AUBERGINES AU FOUR ❖
(for 6 people)

3 onions; 4 cloves of garlic; 12 oz back bacon; 6 large aubergines; 2 lb ripe tomatoes; ½ pint oil; ¼ lb flour; 1 bay leaf, finely ground; 6 teaspoons chopped parsley; thyme; salt and pepper

1. Finely chop the onions and the cloves of garlic. Cut the bacon into *lardons* (i.e. thin strips). Wash and dry the aubergines. Cut them in half lengthways and sprinkle them with salt. Leave to stand for 30 minutes.

2. Cut the tomatoes in half crosswise, not through the stem. Squeeze each half gently to extract (and discard) the seeds and juices from the centre of the tomato. Chop them.

3. Gently cook the *lardons* in oil until brown and set them to one side. In the same oil gently cook the onions – do not brown.

4. Dry the aubergines, flour them and fry them in oil. Rub the garlic on to a hollow dish and then coat the dish with oil. Put the ground bay leaf on the base, and on top place the aubergines. Cover with a layer of tomatoes, then the *lardons*, a little onion, garlic, parsley and thyme. Then make another layer of aubergines, tomatoes, etc. Finally, sprinkle with the rest of the oil, add salt and pepper and cook in a moderate oven for 30 minutes.

❧ POMMES DE TERRE SAUTÉES À LA SARLADAISE ☙
(for 4 people)

2 lb potatoes; ½ glass goose fat; salt and pepper; 1 tablespoon finely sliced truffles

1. Peel the potatoes and cut into slices. Wash them carefully and dry them.
2. Heat the goose fat in a deep frying pan. When it is hot, put in the potatoes, and season with salt and pepper. Fry them quickly at first, and then reduce the heat.
3. Half-cook the potatoes, add the truffles and continue cooking. Warm a serving dish.
4. When the potatoes are cooked, put them in the serving dish. Serve immediately.

❧ FILET DE BŒUF À LA PÉRIGOURDINE ☙
(for 4 people)

4 oz foie gras; 4 slices thick bread; 2 tablespoons oil; 4 oz butter; 4 pieces beef fillet (each weighing 6–7 oz); salt and pepper; ¼ litre Madeira; 1 tablespoon sliced truffles

1. Cut the foie gras into little cubes. Remove the crusts from the bread and cut the bread into small cubes. Heat up 1 tablespoon of the oil and 1 oz of the butter in a frying pan. When it is hot, fry the bread cubes until they are golden brown. Put them to one side.
2. Heat 1 tablespoon of oil and 1 oz of butter in a frying pan. Cook the beef fillets until they are as you like them. Season with salt and pepper. Remove the fillets and put them on to a warm serving dish.
3. Discard the fat from the frying pan and pour in the Madeira with the chopped truffles. Cook quickly, reducing to half the quantity. Add the cubes of foie gras and cook for a further 2 minutes. Remove the frying pan from the heat. With a wooden spoon mix in the rest of the butter a little at a time. Add salt and pepper.
4. Put the canapés on a hot serving dish, put the fillets on top and cover with the sauce. (Delicious served with a Pécharmant wine.)

❧ COU DE MOUTON GRILLÉ ❧
(for 4 people)

2 or 3 carrots; 1 onion; 1 stick of celery; 1 neck of mutton weighing about 2 lb (ask the butcher to chop each cutlet bone into quarters); 1 clove; 3 or 4 cloves of garlic; bouquet garni (parsley, tarragon, thyme and bay leaf); salt and pepper; 2 glasses dry white wine; 2 tablespoons oil; 1 cup breadcrumbs; *Sauce:* 1 tablespoon mustard; 1 glass walnut-oil; salt and pepper

1. Peel the vegetables and wash them. Cut the carrots into sizeable pieces and put them into a casserole along with the pieces of mutton, the onion with the clove pierced in it, the garlic, chopped celery, bouquet garni and seasoning. Add enough water to cover them and add the white wine. Cook the dish slowly either in a covered dish on top of the cooker, or in a casserole in a low oven, for about 2½ hours.
2. Remove the pieces of mutton from the casserole and dry them well in a cloth (the stock is not required). Baste the mutton with oil and cover with the breadcrumbs. Cook them under a hot grill for 20 minutes, turning them so that they cook on all sides.
3. Mix together the mustard and oil. Sieve the mixture into a bowl and add salt and pepper.
4. Put the cooked mutton on to a heated plate, put the sauce in a bowl and serve immediately. (Any good red Bergerac wine complements this dish.)

❧ FILETS DE LIMANDE À L'ORANGE ❧
(for 6 people)

6 average-sized soles; 4 tablespoons flour; 1½ oz butter plus 1 tablespoon oil (for the sole); 4 oranges; 2 lemons; 1½ oz butter (for the oranges); 6 tablespoons fresh cream; salt and pepper

1. Dust the sole fillets with the flour. Melt the butter and oil for the sole in a frying pan, and when it is melted but not foaming, fry the fish gently until browned on both sides. In the meantime peel and thinly slice two oranges. Squeeze and strain the juice from the remaining oranges and lemons.
2. In a small saucepan melt the butter that is left and add the orange

slices (leaving a few slices for garnishing the dish), and the juice from the oranges and lemons. Cook them over a gentle heat.

3. When the soles are cooked, put them on to a warm serving dish. Remove any fat from the top of the sauce and add the cream, salt and pepper. Stir the sauce and pour it over the soles. Garnish the dish with the remaining slices of oranges.

❧ LES ŒUFS À LA PÉRIGOURDINE ❧
(for 4 people)

6 or 8 hard boiled eggs; 6 oz foie gras truffé; a little chervil and some chopped parsley; salt and pepper

Cut the hard boiled eggs in half lengthways and carefully remove the yolks. Mash the yolks with the foie gras truffé, chervil and parsley, salt and pepper. Press the mixture back into the whites.

❧ CÔTES DE PORC À LA GASCONNE ❧
(for 4 people)

4 pork chops, each weighing 8 oz; 4 small cloves of garlic; salt and pepper; ground thyme and bay leaf; enough vinegar to cover the chops; olive-oil; 4 tablespoons goose fat; 2 oz butter; 32 green olives; 1 glass white wine; 1 glass stock; 1 oz flour; 1 tablespoon chopped parsley

1. Prepare the marinade. Pierce each chop, placing into the hole a clove of garlic. Season the chops with salt and pepper and sprinkle over them the ground thyme and bay leaf. Put the chops into a baking dish, cover with the vinegar, add the oil and leave to marinate until the following day.

2. The next day, drain the chops. In a frying pan heat the goose fat, and when it is quite hot put in the pork chops and leave them to cook until they are just browned. Put them to one side.

3. Warm the butter in a casserole. Put in the chops and cover the casserole. Leave to cook gently for 30 minutes.

4. Put some water to boil in a pan. Put in the olives and cook for 3 minutes. Remove the olives, drain and wash in cold water. Add them to the pork chops and cook for a further 15 minutes. During this time warm a serving dish.

5. Remove the chops from the casserole and turn on to the serving dish. Keep warm. Pour into the casserole the white wine and stock, and boil for a few minutes. In the meantime mix the flour with a little cold water and add to the sauce. Leave to cook for 5 minutes on a low heat. Season to taste.

6. Pour the sauce over the pork and garnish with the chopped parsley. Serve immediately.

CONFIT D'OIE AUX POMMES SARLADAISES
(for 4 people)

2 lb potatoes; 1 tablespoon finely sliced truffles; salt and pepper; 3 lb goose fat; 4 pieces of preserved goose (2 thighs, 2 wings); garlic and parsley

1. Make the pommes sarladaises, as described previously (see page 227).

2. While they are cooking, remove the grease from the preserved goose. Brown the pieces in the fat. They should be golden and crusty.

3. Place them around the plate of pommes sarladaises and sprinkle the chopped garlic and parsley over them.

OMELETTE PÉRIGOURDINE
(for 4 people)

2 lb goose fat; 2 medium truffles (either tinned or fresh); 9 eggs; salt and pepper

1. Heat 1 lb of the goose fat and gently cook the peeled and chopped truffles.

2. Beat the eggs and season with salt and pepper. Put to one side 5 or 6 slices of truffle and pour the rest, with the fat, into the eggs, along with the chopped-up peelings of the truffles, and stir them together.

3. Heat 1 lb of goose fat in an omelette pan. Pour the mixture into the pan and cook, stirring with a fork to make sure that all the eggs come in contact with the heat.

4. When the mixture is a light, broken custard (the centre of the omelette should remain soft and creamy) turn the omelette on to a

plate and decorate with the reserved pieces of truffles. (This omelette tastes even more delicious if, just before serving, a tablespoon of Madeira is sprinkled over the top.)

❧ LA TRUITE BRAISÉE AU BERGERAC SEC ❧
(for 6 people)

6 trout; salt and pepper; 2 tablespoons finely chopped shallots; 1 dessertspoon thyme; 2 tablespoons parsley; ½ litre Bergerac blanc sec; 6 fluid oz cream; 2 oz butter

1. Clean the trout and season with salt and pepper.
2. Butter a 2-inch-deep fireproof baking dish. Sprinkle half the shallots on the bottom of the dish, along with some of the thyme and parsley. Arrange the trout on top and cover with lightly buttered greaseproof paper. Pour the Bergerac blanc over them. Cook gently in a moderate oven for about 20 minutes or until they are cooked.
3. Place the cooked trout on a serving dish and keep warm.
4. Heat the remaining juices in the fireproof dish and reduce to two-thirds. Add the cream and reduce a little more. Add the butter and stir. Check the seasoning, and then pass the sauce through a sieve and pour around the trout.

❧ CANARD AUX OIGNONS ❧
(for 4 people)

1 duckling (3 lb); 20 small onions; salt and pepper; 2 cloves of garlic; 1 slice bread; a sprig of sage; thyme; 2 tablespoons oil; 2½ oz bacon rind; 1 glass stock

1. Clean the duckling, and put the livers and the gizzard to one side.
2. Peel the onions.
3. Season the inside of the duckling. Rub the cloves of garlic on to the bread; break it into pieces and put it inside the duck, along with the liver, the gizzard, 4 or 5 leaves of sage (which have been scalded and then dried) and the thyme. Truss the bird with string.
4. Warm the oil in a deep casserole and put in the duckling. Cook it gently until it is a light brown colour.

5. Line the casserole with the rinds which have been cut into 2-inch lengths. Place the duckling in the casserole, along with the onions. Season. Add a twig of thyme and sage to the onions. Pour over the glass of stock.

6. Put a lid on the casserole and place in a medium oven for 1½ hours.

7. Cut up the duck for serving and place on a serving dish. Surround the pieces with onions.

8. Remove the grease from the sauce and pour the sauce over the duckling.

❧ LES FRUITS D'HIVER AU BERGERAC ☙
(for 4 people)

2 pears; 8 prunes; 24 walnuts; a drop of vanilla essence; 1 bay leaf; 1 small stick of cinnamon; 1 clove; 2½ oz sugar; 1 orange; ½ litre Bergerac rouge

1. Peel the pears and arrange them in a casserole with the prunes, nuts, vanilla essence, bay leaf, small stick of cinnamon, clove and the sugar. Slice the unpeeled orange into rounds about ¼ inch thick and place in the casserole.

2. Cover with the Bergerac rouge.

3. Cook in a moderate oven for 30 minutes.

❧ TARTE AUX ABRICOTS ☙
(for 6 people)

pâte sucrée (4 oz plain flour, pinch of salt), 2 oz butter, 1 egg yolk, 1 oz caster sugar); ½ pint crème pâtissière (2 eggs, 2 oz vanilla sugar, 2 tablespoons flour, ½ pint milk, 1 oz unsalted butter); 1½ lb fresh apricots; 4 oz sugar; ½ pint water; 2 teaspoons arrowroot

1. Make the pâte sucrée: sift flour and salt on to a work surface. Cut the butter into small cubes. Make a well in the middle of the flour and put in butter, egg yolk and sugar. Work the butter, sugar and egg yolk together until it is all blended and the work surface clean. Knead the dough for about 2–3 minutes until it forms a smooth ball. Put it in a polythene bag and place in a refrigerator for at least 30 minutes before using.

2. Roll out the pâte sucrée and line a 9-inch flan ring. Fill the centre

with greaseproof paper and dried beans and bake in a moderately hot oven for about 20 minutes. Remove the paper and beans, and cook for a further 5 minutes. Remove from the oven and leave to cool.

3. Make the crème pâtissière: blend together eggs, sugar and flour. Bring milk to the boil and pour on to the egg mixture, stirring continuously. Bring mixture back to the boil, stirring all the time. Remove from the heat and stir in the butter. Cover with a circle of damp greaseproof paper, and leave to cool.

4. Halve the apricots and remove the stones. Dissolve the sugar in the water over a gentle heat. Add the apricots to the pan and poach them gently until they are tender. Allow them to cool.

5. Drain the apricots and dry them.

6. Spread the crème pâtissière over the base of the flan and arrange the apricot halves on top.

7. Blend ¼ pint of the apricot syrup with the arrowroot. Put into a small saucepan and bring to the boil, stirring it all the time until it thickens and becomes clear. Leave it to cool, and then spoon it over the fruit. Leave to set.

Further Reading

IN ENGLISH

Lawrence Adler, *Down the Dordogne*. Nuffield Green, New York, 1932.

Joséphine Baker and Jo Bouillon, *Joséphine*. W. H. Allen, 1978.

Michael de la Bedoyere, *The Archbishop and the Lady: The Story of Fénelon and Madame Guyon*. Collins, 1956.

R. Cameron, *Montaigne and His Age*. Oxford University Press, 1981.

Alexandre Dumas, *Dumas on Food: Selections from 'Le Grand Dictionnaire de Cuisine'*, trans. A. and J. Davidson. Michael Joseph, 1979.

H. R. Kedward, *Resistance in Vichy France*. Oxford University Press, 1978.

André Leroi-Gourhan, *The Dawn of European Art: An Introduction to Palaeolithic Cave Paintings*. Cambridge University Press, 1982.

Emmanuel Le Roy Ladurie, *The Peasants of Languedoc*, trans. John Day. University of Illinois Press, Chicago, 1974.

Philip Oyler, *The Generous Earth*. Penguin Books, 1950.

Ann Sieveking, *The Cave Artists*. Thames and Hudson, 1979.

Freda White, *Three Rivers of France: Dordogne, Lot, Tarn*. Faber and Faber, 1952.

IN FRENCH

Alain Armagnac, *Le Sarladais, La Boétie et son discours de la servitude volontaire*. Périgord Culture, Sarlat, 1982.

Pierre Barrière, *La Vie Intellectuelle en Périgord (1556–1880)*. Delmas, Bordeaux, 1956.

Yves-Marie Bercé, *Croquants et nu-pieds*. Gallimard, Paris, 1974.

Marc Blancpain, *Histoires du Périgord*. Fernand Nathan, Paris, 1982.

M. Bouyou and A.-M. Badoures, *La Paysannerie en Périgord 1940–1950*. Le Mascaret, Bordeaux, 1983.

H. Breuil, *Quatre cents siècles d'art pariétal*. Centre d'études et de documentation préhistorique, Montignac, 1952.

Albéric Cahuet, *Pontcarrel*. Pierre Fanlac, Périgueux, 1978.

Curnonsky, *Cuisine et vins en France*, ed. Robert J. Courtine. Larousse, Paris, 1974.

René Dechère, *Les Huttes du Périgord*. Mallemonche, Le Bugue, 1981.

Jean Delpech-Laborie, *Le Général Fournier-Sarlovèse: 'Le plus mauvais sujet' de Napoléon*. Productions de Paris, Paris, 1969.

J.-J. Escande, *Histoire du Périgord*. Laffitte Reprints, Marseille, 1980.

Pierre Fanlac, *La merveilleuse découverte de Lascaux*. Pierre Fanlac, Périgueux, 1968.

Périgord, terre de poésie. Pierre Fanlac, Périgueux, 1974.

Contes et légendes du Périgord. Pierre Fanlac, Périgueux, 1982.

Gérard Fayolle, *La Vie Quotidienne en Périgord au temps de Jacquou le Croquant*. Hachette, Paris, 1978.

Histoire du Périgord, vol. I: de la préhistoire à la révolution. Pierre Fanlac, Périgueux, 1983.

Capitaine Fred (i.e. Alfred Dutheillet de Lamothe), *La Brigade Rac: Armée Secrète Dordogne-Nord*. Imprimerie Fabrègue, Saint-Yreix, Limoges, 1977.

J. L. Galet, *Périgueux et ses châteaux*. Pierre Fanlac, Périgueux, 1966.

H. Gouhier, *Maine de Biran par lui-méme*. Le Seuil, Paris, 1970.

Arlette Higounet (ed.), *Histoire du Périgord*. Privat, Paris, 1983.

René Lavaud, *Les Trois Troubadours de Sarlat*. Imprimerie Ribes, Périgueux, 1912.

Jean Maubourget, *Châteaux de la Renaissance en Périgord noir*. Pierre Fanlac, Périgueux, 1976.

Sarlat et ses Châteaux. Pierre Fanlac, Périgueux, 1978.

André Maurois, *Périgord*. Hachette, Paris, 1955.

Michel de Montaigne, *Essais*. Classiques Garnier, Paris, 1948.

Pauline Newman, *Un romancier périgourdin: Eugène Le Roy et son temps*. Nouvelles Editions Latines, Paris, 1957.

Lucile Oliver, *Le Mobilier Aquitain, Périgourdin et Landais*. Ch. Massin, Paris, n.d.

Henri Philippon, *Cuisine de Quercy et du Périgord*. Denoël, Paris, 1979.

Jean Ribière, *La Truffe du Périgord*. Pierre Fanlac, Périgueux, 1981.

Georges Rocal, *Léon Bloy et le Périgord*. Librairie Fleury, Paris, n.d.

Croquants du Périgord. Pierre Fanlac, Périgueux, 1970.

Le vieux Périgord. Pierre Fanlac, Périgueux, 1980.

Eugène Le Roy, *Les Gens d'Auberoque*. R. Domège, Périgueux, 1934.

'La Belle Coutelière', in *Au Pays des Pierres*. Les éditions du Périgord noir, Périgueux, 1966.

Jacquou le Croquant. Pierre Fanlac, Périgueux, 1966.

Le Moulin de Frau. Pierre Fanlac, Périgueux, 1966.

Jean Secret, *Le Périgord: Châteaux, manoirs et gentilshommières*. Tallandier, Paris, 1966.

L'Art en Périgord. Pierre Fanlac, Périgueux, 1976.

Itinéraires Romans en Périgord. Zodiaque, Paris, 1977.

J. Sigala, *Cadouin en Périgord*. Demas, Bordeaux, 1950.

Alfred de Tarde, *L'Esprit périgourdin et Eugène Le Roy*. Ronteix, Périgueux, 1923.

Andre Toulemon, *Étienne de La Boétie, un enfant de Sarlat*. Librairies Techniques, Paris, 1980.

J. de Verneilh and L. Gaucherel, *Le vieux Périgueux*. Pierre Fanlac, Périgueux, 1967.

Index

Abadie, Paul, 22, 97f., 151, 191f.
Abjat-sur-Bandiat, 139
Abzac, Anne d', 28
Achilles, 125
Agen, 89
Agincourt, 68
Agonac, 140
agriculture, 28f., 38, 51f., 147, 197, 222
Aillac, 140
Ajat, 140
Albigensians, 64f., 148, 199
Ales-sur-Dordogne, 140
Allas-les-Mines, 140
Allemans, 140
Angers, 44
Angoisse, 140
Anjou, 46
Anne, Queen, 53
Annesse-et-Beaulieu, 140f.
Antioch, 63, 89
Antiope, 125
Antonne-et-Trigonant, 141
Archignac, 141
Asterius, St, 29, 198
Atur, 141
Aubas, 141
aubergines au four, 226
Auberoche, 141f.
Aubisson, François d', 27f.
Auden, W. H., 121f.
Audrix, 142
Augignac, 142
Augustinian monks, 174, 198
Auriac-du-Périgord, 142
Auvergne, 90
Auvézère, river, 93, 145, 171
Aymar of Limousin, 63
Avignon, 66
Avitus, St, 199
Azerat, 142

Babinski, Henri, 40f.
Bachellerie, La, 142f.
Badefols d'Ans, 143
Badefols-sur-Dordogne, 143
Baker, Joséphine, 25ff., 143, 180
Balou, 143
Baneuil, 143f.
Bannes, 144
Barade forest, 129, 143f.
Bardonnie, Louis de la, 78
Bardou, 144
Bars, 144
Bassilac, 144f.
Bastide, La, 145
bastides, 61, 69–72, 76f., 88, 104, 145f., 165f., 168, 171, 175f., 180–82, 199, 224f.
Bataille, Georges, 109, 111
Bauzens, 145
Beaulieu-sur-Dordogne, 15, 19
Beaumont, Amiccia de, 65
Beaumont-du-Périgord, 69f., 145f.
Beaupouyet, 146
Beaussac, 146

Bedoyere, Michael de la, 126
Belcayre, Château, 23, 146
Belet, 146
Beleymas, 146f.
Belvedère-de-Sors, 147
Belvès, 87, 147
Benedictines, 86f., 89f., 92, 177
Béraudière, Bishop François de la, 95
Berbiguières, 147
Bergerac, 15, 20f., 32f., 37f., 56, 58f., 61, 67, 89, 94, 127f., 147f.
Bergerac, Cyrano de, 16, 18, 55, 57, 134f.
Bergson, Henri, 128
Bernard, St, 65, 191, 208, 212
Besse, 224f.,
Beynac, Aymery de, 51f.
Beynac-et-Cazenac, 20, 51f., 63, 94, 148f.
Beyssac, 149
Biran, Maine de, 127f.
Biras, 149
Biron, 74, 149f.
Bishop, J. P., 16f.
Black Prince, 61, 66f.
Blanc, Dolmen de, 146
Bloy, Léon, 135
Boeswillwald, Jacques Émile, 97
Boétie, Antoine de La, 122
Boétie, Étienne de La, 16, 122–4, 126, 136, 206, 210
Boisseuilh, 150
Bordeaux, 58, 61, 66, 68, 119, 121, 124
Born, Bertrand de, 63, 113–16
Boschaud abbey, 87, 89, 150
Bossuet, Bishop Jacques Bénigne, 126
Bouillon, Jo, 26f.
Boulazac, 150
Bourdeille, Pierre de, *see* Brantôme
Bourdeilles, 117, 150f.
Bourdeix, Le, 151
Bourg-des-Maisons, 151
Bourg-du-Bost, 151
Brantôme, 21, 38, 86f., 93f., 104, 151f.
Brantôme (Pierre de Bourdeille), 45, 117f., 152, 196, 214
Brétigny, Treaty of, 67, 188
Breuil, 149
Breuil, Abbé Henri E. P., 100, 103, 105, 107, 109f.
Bridoire, 152
Brillat-Savarin, J. A., 42–5
British, the, 61–83 *passim*
Bruyère, de, architect, 97
Bugeaud, General, 66, 167, 193
Bugue, Le, 39, 103, 152f.
Buisson-de-Cadouin, Le, 153
Bussière-Badil, 90–92, 153

Cadouin, 63, 87–9, 94, 146, 153
Caesar, Julius, 84
Cahuet, Albéric, 135f.
Calviac, 86, 154
Calvimont, John de, 27, 143
Campagne, 154
canard aux oignons, 231
Cancon, 154
Cantillac, 154

Carcassonne, 65
Carels, Élias, 113
Carlux, 154
Carsac-Aillac, 87, 98f., 154f.
Carsac-de-Gurson, 155
Cartaillac, Émile, 111
Castelnaud, 20, 25, 65, 155f., 170
Castels, 156
Castile, 67f.
Castillon-la-Bataille, 68, 154, 176
Cathars, see Albigensians
Catherine de' Medici, 24f., 184, 196
Caumont, François de, 25
Causse-de-Clérans, 94
caves
   Bara-Bahau, 103, 156; Bernifals, 156; Carpe-Diem,
   156f.; Les Combarelles, 103, 156; Commarque, 157;
   Cro-Bique, 149; Le Diable, 104; Domme, 104, 157;
   Font-de-Gaume, 103, 109, 157; Gabillou, 157; Grand-
   Roc, 157f.; La Grèze, 158; La Mairie, 103, 158; La
   Mouthe, 102f., 111, 158; Lascaux, 100-102, 105, 110f.,
   158, 184; Proumeyssac, 158; Raymonden, 108; Rouf-
   fignac, 103f., 110, 158f.; Sorcier, 159; Villars, 104-7,
   109, 159
Cazelle, 159
Celles, 159
Cénac-et-Saint-Julien, 57, 88, 92, 159-61
Cendreix, 161
Cercles, 161
Chaleix, 161
Châlus, 64, 161
Champagnac-de-Belair, 129, 161
Champagnac-et-Fontaines, 161f.
Chancelade, 97, 108, 162
Change, Le, 162
Chapelle-Faucher, La, 162
Chapelle-Mouret, La, 163
Charlemagne, 86, 89, 94, 151, 220
Charles V, 70, 188
Charles VII, 68
Charles IX, 184, 195
Charles X, 130
Chassaigne, Françoise de, 119
cheeses, 38, 220
Chenaud, 163
Cherval, 90, 163
Cherveix-Cubas, 163
Churchill, W. S., 76f., 81
Cingria, C. A., 112
Cistercians, 87
Claudel, Paul, 155
Clement V, 160
Clement VI, 66
Clermont-de-Beauregard, 163
Clifford, Rosamund de, 62
Clifford, Walter de, 62
Clotis, Josette, 79
Clovis, 86
Combe-Capelle, 108
Colombier, 163
Coly, 163
Commarque, 163f.
Condat-le-Lardin, 164
Condat-sur-Trincou, 164
confit d'oie aux pommes sarladaises, 230
Corgnac-sur-l'Isle, 164
Cornishie, F., 42
côtes de porc à la gasconne, 229
cou de mouton grillé, 228
Coubjours, 164
Coulanges, Château de, 116
Coulaures, 164
Coulouneix, 164
Coursac, 164
Coux-et-Bigaroque, Le, 164f.
Couze-et-Saint-Front, 165
Crécy, 66
Creighton, Bishop Mandell, 65
Cro-Magnon man, 107-9, 169
croquants, 28, 182
Cunard, Nancy, 61, 81f.
Curnonsky, Prince, 40, 42f., 46-8, 51
Cuze, river, 67

Cybard, St, 89
Cyprien, St, 200

Daglan, 165
Dalon, 87, 89, 205
Daniel, Arnaut, 112, 196
Dante, 112, 114f.
Dardé, Paul, 169
Daumesnil, Yrieux, 32, 189, 193
Deffarges, Henri, 45
Deltreil, Roger, 99
Derby, Earl of, 66f.
Descartes, 128
Deschamps, Eustache, 45
Doissat, 165
Domme, 15, 18, 30f., 33, 61, 65, 67, 69-72, 104, 129,
   133, 165f.
Domme, Gilbert of, 67
Dordogne, river, 15f., 19-22, 47, 136, 142, 147, 175-7,
   223
Douglas, Norman, 105
Douzillac, 166
Dronne, river, 20f., 151, 185
Duhamel, Georges, 60
Dumas, Alexandre the Elder, 40f., 42, 48-50, 52f.
Dussac, 167

Edward I, 70f.
Edward III, 66f.
Eleanor of Aquitaine, 61-4, 200
Élie of Périgord, 63
Essendiéras, 75, 137, 168
Excideuil, 167f.
Eymet, 138, 168
Eyzies-de-Tayac, Les, 91, 102, 106f., 138, 168f.

Fanlac, 169
Faye, 91
Fénelon, Archibishop, 124-7, 170, 207
filet de bœuf à la périgourdine, 227
forests, 36, 129, 143f., 177
Foucauld, Charles de, 152
Fournier, Louise, 128
Fournier-Sarlovèze, Baron, 32
François I, 188f.
François de Sales, St, 147
Froidevaux, Yves, 99
Fronde, 29, 95, 199
Front, St, 85f., 186f., 191
furniture, 35f., 178

Gaddi, Niccoló, 210
Gaulle, Charles de, 25, 61, 76-8, 80f.
Gauls, 84, 149, 172, 186f., 196, 201, 220, 223
geese, 38, 47f., 51-3
Genis, 171
gîtes, 19f.
Gontaut, Pierre de, 71
Gourdon, 64, 82f.
Grand-Brassac, 171
Grolejac, 20, 50, 172
Guesclin, Bertrand Du, 67, 167, 203, 220
Guinevere, 16
Guyon, Mme, 125f.

Hautefort, 23f., 90, 92, 114, 129, 143, 172f.
Henri IV, 145, 170, 183, 185, 211f.
Henry II, 62f., 114
Henry III, 69, 76
Henry V, 68
Henry VI, 68
Hercules, 125
Herm, Château de l', 27f., 143
Herod, King, 21, 93, 151
Hitler, Adolf, 61, 76, 78
Holleaux, André, 80
Huguenots, 23, 95, 120f., 125, 148, 161, 165, 167, 170f.,
   173, 175, 184, 187, 195, 198, 203, 218f., 225

Innocent III, 64f.
Innocent VI, 66
Isle, river, 21, 144
Issac, 173

Issigeac, 91, 173f.

Jacquou le Croquant, 27f., 34–6, 96, 129–34, 143f., 169
Jarry, Alfred, 20
Javerlhac-et-la Chapelle-Saint-Robert, 174
Jesus, 21, 54, 85f., 89, 91–4, 151, 152, 199, 221
Joan of Arc, 68
John the Baptist, St, 94
John of Gaunt, 67
John, St, 93f., 141, 151
John XXII, 208
Jumilhac-le-Grand, 129, 174f.
Jumilhac-le-Petit, 175

Kennedy, J. F., 143
Kipling, John, 72f.
Kipling, Rudyard, 72–4

Labrousse, Suzette, 30
Lacrousille, A. de, 50
Ladouze, 72, 175
Ladurie, E. Le Roy, 28, 132f.
Lafayette, 32
Laforce, 175
Lalinde, 68, 76, 107, 175f.
Lamonzie-Montastruc, 176
Lamothe-Montravel, 176
Lancelot, 16
Lanquais, 176f.
Laussel Venus, 107
lauzes, 35, 91, 140, 148, 155, 172
Leakey, Richard E., 100f.
Leroi-Gourhan, André, 110
Liborne, 21, 68
Ligueux, 177
Limeuil, 21, 140, 177
Limeyrat, 177
Liorac-sur-Louyre, 177
Limousin, 21, 63, 139f.
Loire, river, 22
Longspee, William, 12
Losse, Château de, 23, 219
Lot, 16, 40, 80, 83
Louis VII, 61f., 69, 168, 200, 224
Louis XII, 118
Louis XIII, 24, 35f.
Louis XIV, 24, 126f., 207
Louis XVI, 130
Louis-Napoleon, 33
Louis-Philippe, 33

Magdalenian man, 216
Maintenon, Mme de, 127
Maleville, Jacques de, 18, 30f.
Malraux, André, 79–81, 111, 210
Manaurie, 178
Mareuil, 24f., 27, 113, 178f.
Mareuil, Arnaut de, 113, 115
Marquay, 179
Mary, Queen of Scots, 117
Mary, Virgin, 26, 89, 93f., 96, 141, 146, 151, 177
Maurois, André, 40f., 72, 74–6, 137, 168, 221
Merlande Priory, 179f.
Meyrals, 180
Michelet, Jules, 62, 125
Milandes, Les, 25–7, 180
Miller, Henry, 15–17, 107, 112, 137
Mirabeau, 19
Molière, 23
Molières, 180
Monbazillac, 56–8, 181
Monbos, 181
Monpazier, 18, 28, 30, 61, 69–71, 107, 146, 181f.
Montagrier, 182
Montaigne, Michel de, 41, 54–6, 59, 102, 119–25, 202, 214
Montcaret, 85, 119, 182
Montfort, Château, 22f., 65, 183, 225
Montfort, Guy de, 65f.
Montfort, John de, 67
Montfort, Simon de, 22, 61, 65f., 148f., 183
Montignac, 38, 61, 67, 100, 102, 111, 129, 134, 183f.
Montpon-Menestérol, 184

Musset, Alfred de, 43
Mussidan, 184

Napoleon, 18, 32f., 128, 130
Nazis, 61, 76, 143, 184, 204, 223
Neuvic-sur-l'Isle, 185
Noah, 96
Nontron, 185

Oliver, Raymond, 50
omelette périgourdine, 230f.
Oyler, Philip, 37

Palinurus (Cyril Connolly), 16, 61
Paris, 44, 47, 66, 82, 121, 125, 128, 135
pâté de foie gras, 38, 43
Paternus, Bishop of Périgueux, 85
patois, 29, 41, 50, 133
Paul, St, 54, 92, 175
Perera, Emmanuel, 198
Périgord Blanc, 36
Périgord Noir, 15, 36f., 136, 141
Périgord Vert, 36, 91, 103, 129
Périgueux, 18, 21, 30, 32f., 39, 47, 58, 61, 77, 80, 84–7, 89–91, 95–8, 127, 135, 139f., 186–94
Perusin, Mario, 79
Pétain, Marshal, 77
Peter, St, 85, 92f.
Petrarch, 66
Peyronnet, Marie, 129, 134
Peyrony, Denis, 103, 107
Peyrouse, 87
Peyzac-le-Moustier, 194
phylloxera, 34
Piégut-Pluviers, 194
Pierre-Levée, dolmen, 194
Pinet, Jacques, 32
Pius VI, 30
Pius XII, 26
Poitiers, 66, 86
Poitiers, Alphonse de, 69, 224
Poitou, 46
pommes de terre sautées à la sarladaise, 47, 227
Pound, Ezra, 81, 116
Prats-de-Carlux, 195
Prats-du-Périgord, 91, 195
Protestants, *see* Huguenots
Puy de Sancy, 20
Puyguilhem, 195
Puymartin, 195
Puy-Saint-Front, 63

quails, 49
Quercy, 16, 38, 46

Rabelais, 46, 214
relics of saints, 21f., 29, 63, 85f., 89, 95, 142, 151, 153, 163, 183, 192f., 209, 213, 221
Resistance, the, 76–80, 198, 204
Ribérac, 30, 38f., 195f.
Richard Cœur de Lion, 62f., 114f., 148, 167, 194
Richemont, 196
Rocal, Georges, 135
Rochebeaucourt-et-Argentine, La, 179
Romans, 84f., 182, 186f., 196, 201, 220
Rome, 30, 118f.
Rostand, Edmond, 16, 134f.
Roquebrune, 79
Roque-Gageac, La, 196f.
Roque-Saint-Christophe, La, 197
Rouerque, 46
Rouffignac, 39
Roux-Fazillac, 32
Roy, Eugène Le, 27f., 34, 41, 96, 128–34, 136f., 142–4, 175

Sacerdos, St, 86, 208f.
Sadillac, 138, 197
Sailland, Maurice Edmund, *see* Curnonsky
Saint-Amand-de-Coly, 87–9, 93, 197f.
Saint-André-Allas, 198
Saint-Antoine-Cumond, 198
Saint-Astier, 29f., 198f.

Saint-Aulaye, 199
Saint-Avit-Sénieur, 87, 90, 199f., 217
Saint-Capraise-d'Eymet, 200
Saint-Cyprien, 87, 200
Saint-Geniès, 200
Saint-Georges-de-Montclard, 200
Saint-Jean-de-Côle, 87, 200f.
Saint-Julien-de-Lampon, 125, 201
Saint-Léon-sur-Vézère, 201f.
Saint-Martial-Viveyrol, 202
Saint-Martin-l'Astier, 202
Saint-Martin-le-Pin, 90–92, 202
Saint-Michel-de-Montaigne, 119f., 202
Saint-Pardoux-la-Rivière, 94, 202f.
Saint-Pierre-de-Côle, 203
Saint-Pompont, 203
Saint-Privat-des-Prés, 90, 203
Saint-Raphaël, 203
Saint-Rémy-sur-Lidoire, 203f.
Saint-Sauveur, 127, 204
Saint-Sulpice-de-Mareuil, 92, 204
Saint-Sulpice-de-Roumagnac, 204
Saint-Vincent-de-Cosse, 204
Saint-Vincent-le-Paluel, 79, 204
Sainte-Colombe, 205
Sainte-Croix-de-Beaumont, 205
Sainte-Foy-la-Grande, 77f.
Sainte-Mondane, 125, 170
Sainte-Nathalène, 205
Sainte-Trie, 205
Saintsbury, George, 53–5
Salagnac-Clairvivre, 205f.
Salignac-Évigues, 206
salt tax, 124
Sarlat, 86f., 89, 113, 122f., 125, 136, 206–14
Sarliat-sur-l'Isle, 214
sauce périgourdine, 48, 227
sauce rouilleuse, 48
Saussignac, 214f.
Scott, Sir Gilbert, 22
Secret, Jean, 90, 152, 185
Segonzac, 92, 215
Sergeac, 87, 215
Sévigné, Mme de, 23
shelters
    Bayac, 215; Cap-Blanc, 106, 215f.; Chancelade, 216;
    Domme, 216; Enfer, 216; Laugérie-Basse, 216; Laugér-
    ie-Haute, 216; La Madeleine, 108, 216; Peyzac-le-
    Moustier, 108, 216f.; Poisson, 217; Regourdou, 217;
    La Roche, 107; Saint-Avit-Sénieur, 217; Sergeac, 217;
    Tursac, 216
Sieveking, Ann, 100
Sigala, Jean, 77
Sigoulès, 217
Siorac-en-Périgord, 217f.
Socrates, 120
Solignac, 89
Sorges, 45, 218
Souillac, 15, 19
Sour, St, 219
Sourzac, 218
Spain, 32, 44, 82
strawberries, 38, 197, 222

Talbot, John, 68, 176
Talleyrand family, 27, 51, 86, 185
Tamniès, 218
Tannahill, Reay, 45
Tarn, river, 40

Temniac, 218
Templars, 24, 87, 215
Terrasson, 90, 219
Thenon, 219
Thiviers, 91f., 96, 219
Thonac, 219f.
Thot, Le, 220
tobacco, 143, 148
Tocane-Saint-Apre, 129, 220
Tour Blanche, La, 220
Toulouse, 65f.
Touraine, 46
Tourtoirac, 92f., 220
Trémolat, 87, 89, 140, 147, 176, 221
troglodyte villages, 108, 161, 197
troubadours, 112–16
Troyes, Treaty of, 68
truffles, 37, 43–6, 51f., 74, 218, 227, 229–
    31
la truite braisée au Bergerac sec, 231
Tuchman, Barbara, 69, 72
Turenne family, 22f., 183, 207
Turnac, 98, 183, 207
Turnbull, P., 45
Tursac, 108, 221

Ulysses, 125
Urval, 221

Valeuil, 221
Vanxains, 30, 92, 221
Varaignes, 221f.
Vélines, 222
Verdon, 222
Vergt, 222f.
Verteillac, 223
Veyrignac, 223
Vézac, 223
Vézère, river, 20f., 47, 108f., 136, 142, 177,
    215, 223
Vienna, 51
Vigan, Le, 223
Villamblard, 223
Villars, 104, 224
Villefranche-de-Lonchat, 224
Villefranche-du-Périgord,   38,   69f.,   182,
    224f.
Villetoureix, 196
Viollet-le-Duc, 191
Vitrac, 33, 50, 225
Vivans, Geoffroi de, 72, 160, 165f., 215

walnuts, 38, 51f., 147
wars
    First World War, 72–5, 211; Franco-Prussian War,
    129; Hundred Years War, 22, 61, 66–9, 72, 87f., 95,
    142, 149f., 154f., 162, 166, 183, 197ff., 203; Second
    World War, 15, 61, 76–81, 143, 184, 204, 217, 223;
    Wars of Religion, 22–5, 72, 87, 95, 119–21, 160, 162,
    165, 167, 171, 179–81, 183, 186, 195, 203, 215; War of
    the Spanish Succession, 127
White, Freda, 21–3, 40, 79, 181f.
wine, 32, 34, 53–61, 176, 180, 217, 224,
    227, 231f.

Xenophon, 123

Zack, Léon, 99, 155
Zeldin, T., 41